Praise for *Living a Feminist Life*

"From the moment I received Sara Ahmed's new work, *Living a Feminist Life*, I couldn't put it down. It's such a brilliant, witty, visionary new way to think about feminist theory. Everyone should read this book. It offers amazing new ways of knowing and talking about feminist theory and practice. And, it is also delightful, funny, and as the song says, 'your love has lifted me higher.' Ahmed lifts us higher."
—bell hooks

"Beautifully written and persuasively argued, *Living a Feminist Life* is not just an instant classic, but an essential read for intersectional feminists."—Ann A. Hamilton, *Bitch*

"Anyone at odds with this world—and we all ought to be—owes it to themselves, and to the goal of a better tomorrow, to read this book."
—Mariam Rahmani, *Los Angeles Review of Books*

"*Living a Feminist Life* is perhaps the most accessible and important of Ahmed's works to date. . . . [A] quite dazzlingly lively, angry and urgent call to arms . . . In short, everybody should read Ahmed's book precisely because not everybody will."—Emma Rees, *Times Higher Education*

"Fans of bell hooks and Audre Lorde will find Ahmed's frequent homages and references familiar and assuring in a work that goes far beyond Betty Friedan's *The Feminine Mystique*, capturing the intersection so critical in modern feminism."—Abby Hargreaves, *Library Journal*

"*Living a Feminist Life* offers something halfway between the immediacy and punch of the blog and the multi-layered considerations of a scholarly essay; the result is one of the most politically engaged, complex and personal books on gender politics we have seen in a while."
—Bidisha, *Times Literary Supplement*

"*Living a Feminist Life* hopes we can survive doing feminist theory, and energizes us to do so."—Clare Croft, *Feminist Theory*

"Undeniably, Ahmed's book is a highly crafted work, both scholarly and lyrically, that builds upon itself and delivers concrete, adaptable conclusions; it is a gorgeous argument, crackling with kind wit and an invitation to the community of feminist killjoys."—Theodosia Henney, *Lambda Literary Review*

"Ahmed gifts us words that we may have difficulty finding for ourselves. . . . [R]eading her book provides a tentative vision for a feminist ethics for radical politics that is applicable far beyond what is traditionally considered the domain of feminism."—Mahvish Ahmad, *The New Inquiry*

Praise for *On Being Included*

"Just when you think everything that could possibly be said about diversity in higher education has been said, Sara Ahmed comes along with this startlingly original, deeply engaging ethnography of diversity work. *On Being Included* is an insightful, smart reflection on the embodied, profoundly political phenomenology of doing and performing diversity in predominantly white institutions. As Ahmed queers even the most mundane formulations of diversity, she creates one eureka moment after another. I could not put this book down. It is a must-read for everyone committed to antiracist, feminist work as key to institutional transformation in higher education."—Chandra Talpade Mohanty, author of *Feminism without Borders: Decolonizing Theory, Practicing Solidarity*

"This book offers a grounded and open exploration of what it means to 'do' diversity, to 'be' diverse. It challenges the reader, both in style and in content, to reconsider relations of power that stick to the multiple practices, meanings, and understandings of diversity, and to reconsider how we engage, reproduce, and disrupt these relations."
—Juliane Collard and Carolyn Prouse, *Gender, Place, and Culture*

Praise for *Willful Subjects*

"Like her other works known for their originality, sharpness, and reach, Ahmed offers here a vibrant, surprising, and philosophically rich analysis of cultural politics, drawing on feminist, queer and anti-racist uses of willing and willfulness to explain forms of sustained and adamant social disagreement as a constitutive part of any radical ethics and politics worth its name."—Judith Butler, Maxine Elliot Professor of Comparative Literature, University of California, Berkeley

"Ahmed's insights, as always, are both intellectually fertile and provocative; *Willful Subjects* will not disappoint."—Margrit Shildrick, *Signs*

"There is no one else writing in contemporary cultural theory who is able to take hold of a single concept with such a firm and sure grasp and follow it along an idiosyncratic path in such surprising and illuminating ways."—Gayle Salamon, author of *Assuming a Body: Transgender and Rhetorics of Materiality*

Praise for *The Promise of Happiness*

"Ahmed's language is a joy, and her work on each case study is filled with insight and rigor as she doggedly traces the social networks of dominance concealed and congealed around happiness. . . . *The Promise of Happiness* is an important intervention in affect studies that crucially approaches one of the major assumptions guiding social life: the assumption that we need to be happy."—Sean Grattan, *Social Text*

"*The Promise of Happiness* bridges philosophy and cultural studies, phenomenology and feminist thought—providing a fresh and incisive approach to some of the most urgent contemporary feminist issues. Ahmed navigates this bridge with a voice both clear and warm to convey ideas that are as complex as they are intimate and accessible. Her treatment of affect as a phenomenological project provides feminist theorists a way out of mind-body divides without reverting to essentialisms, enabling Ahmed to attend to intersectional and global power relations with acuity and originality."—Aimee Carrillo Rowe, *Signs*

Praise for *Queer Phenomenology*

"Ahmed's most valuable contribution in *Queer Phenomenology* is her reorienting of the language of queer theory. The phenomenological understanding of orientation and its attendant geometric metaphors usefully reframes queer discourse, showing disorientation as a moment not of desperation but of radical possibility, of getting it twisted in a productive and revolutionary way."—Zachary Lamm, GLQ

"In this dazzling new book, Sara Ahmed has begun a much needed dialogue between queer studies and phenomenology. Focusing on the directionality, spatiality, and inclination of desires in time and space, Ahmed explains the straightness of heterosexuality and the digressions made by those queer desires that incline away from the norm, and, in her chapter on racialization, she puts the orient back into orientation. Ahmed's book has no telos, no moral purpose for queer life, but what it brings to the table instead is an original and inspiring meditation on the necessarily disorienting, disconcerting, and disjointed experience of queerness."—Jack Halberstam, author of *Female Masculinity*

What's
the
Use?

What's the Use?

On the Uses of Use

Sara Ahmed

DUKE UNIVERSITY PRESS *Durham and London* 2019

© 2019 Duke University Press
All rights reserved
Printed in the United States
of America on acid-free paper ∞
Designed by Amy Ruth Buchanan
Typeset in Chaparral Pro and Helvetica Neue
by Westchester Publishing Services

The Cataloging-in-Publication Data is available
at the Library of Congress.
ISBN 978-1-4780-0721-0 (ebook)
ISBN 978-1-4780-0584-1 (hardcover)
ISBN 978-1-4780-0650-3 (paperback)

Cover art: Photo by Sara Ahmed

This book is for my queer family,
Sarah and Poppy.

Contents

....

Acknowledgments

....

I began working on the uses of use while I was a visiting professor in gender studies at Cambridge University in 2013. Being based at Cambridge gave me an opportunity to hang out with many old books in libraries. I would like to thank the Centre for Gender Studies for that opportunity. This book was put on hold while we fought a series of institutional battles against the normalization of sexual harassment at universities. Thanks to those who shared the battle, from whom I have learned so much, especially Leila Whitley and Tiffany Page, as well as to my PhD students, especially Morgane Conti and Chandra Frank, for their patience and support over many years. This book would not have been possible without many intellectual companions who have wandered with me: thanks especially to Sarah Franklin, Rumana Begum, Sirma Bilge, Elaine Swan, Judith Butler, Jonathan Keane, Ulrika Dahl, and Heidi Mirza. Thank you to Duke University Press for providing a nest for my words; to Ken Wissoker, whose guidance and support have been indispensable over many years; to Susan Albury for her editorial care and patience; and to Josh Tranen for working with me closely on collecting images—a task that taught me even more about use! Thanks to Richard Burkhardt, Ludmilla Jordanova, and Jessica Riskin for kindly answering my questions about Lamarck. Thanks also to Dan

Mitchell for helping me to access the SDUK collection and UCL special collection. Finally, I would like to express my appreciation to all those who read my blog, exchanged thoughts with me on Twitter, came to hear talks, and helped me feel part of a killjoy collective as I made the difficult but necessary transition to working as an independent scholar.

Introduction

A Useful Archive

The title of this book is a use expression, one that seems to point to the pointlessness of doing something. This expression often has an intonation of exasperation. What's the use, what's the point? Said in this way, "what's the use?" operates as a rhetorical question. We might ask "what's the use?" when we have reached a conclusion that there is no use. I imagine hands flung in the air expressing the withdrawal of a commitment to some difficult task. I hear a drawn-out sigh, the sound of giving up on something that had previously been pursued. We might be more likely to say "what's the use?" when the uselessness of something had not been apparent right from the beginning, when we have given up on something that we had expected to be useful such that to become exasperated can point not only to *what*, that which is now deemed pointless, but also to *who*, those who had assumed something had a point. It seems appropriate to ask about use, what it means to use something or to find a use for something, with such a moment of exasperation—a moment when we lose it rather than use it.

"What's the use, what's the point of saying that?" This is the question asked by the character Peggy in the last segment of Virginia Woolf's novel *The Years*, first published in 1937. Peggy is having what we might call a feminist killjoy moment; she is interrupting a family gathering with this question, posed sharply, pointedly. Her aunt Eleanor has already suggested to Peggy that she should enjoy herself: "'But we're enjoying ourselves' said Eleanor, 'Come and enjoy yourself too'" ([1937] 2012, 264). Peggy does not obey her command. She seems alienated from happiness by making happiness into a question: "What does she mean by 'happiness,' by 'freedom'? Peggy asked herself, lapsing against the wall again" (265). Happiness for Peggy seems unjust: "How can one be 'happy'? she asked herself, in a world bursting with misery" (266). She is listening to scraps of conversation, to laughter bubbling away at the surface. Perhaps she can hear what is being said because she does not find happiness convincing. It is then that she asks the question, "What's the use, what's the point of saying that?" Once she asks this question, which she addresses to her brother (the discussion is about him), she is overwhelmed by bad feeling: "She looked at her brother. A feeling of animosity possessed her. He was still smiling, but his smile smoothed itself out as she looked at him. 'What's the use?' she said, facing him. 'You'll marry. You'll have children. What'll you do then? Write little books to make money'" (268). Peggy flounders, describing her own words as "wrong," as "personal" when "she had meant to say something impersonal" (268). The question of use becomes a personal question, a question about how a person lives their life. Once Peggy has started on this path, she has to keep going: "'You'll write one book, then another little book,' she said viciously, 'instead of living . . . living differently, differently'" (268).

Her utterance is too sharp; she regrets it. This wrinkle in the smile of the occasion is passed over; the conversation is smoothed out again, which means Peggy's question is passed over, just as she is. The question "what's the use?" is often articulated by Woolf's characters at the moment they seem to be losing it. It is a question posed by sisters, such as Peggy, who are interrupting the flow of a conversation about the lives of men. Or it is a question posed by wives, such as when Mrs. Flushing asks Wilfrid in *The Voyage Out*, "What's the use of talking? What's the use—?" ([1915] 2001, 418). The word talking is replaced by a dash; we might think of the dash as *anything*. The next sentence, "She ceased," implies not only that she stops talking but that she stops being. The wife becomes the one who ceases, for whom the questioning of use is a questioning of being. One thinks here also of Mrs. Dalloway, who also watches herself disappear in becoming wife, becoming mother (Woolf [1925] 1953, 14). Mrs. Thornbury follows Mrs. Flushing by also asking a question to Wilfrid, not to his wife, "because it was useless to speak to his wife" (Woolf [1915] 2001, 418). To become useless: not to be addressed. Perhaps to be defined in relation to men, as sisters, as wives, is to be deemed useful to them but not to others.

When you question the point of something, the point seems to be how quickly you can be removed from the conversation. Maybe she removes herself. The question "what's the use?" allows Woolf to throw life up as a question, to ask about the point of *anything* by asking about the point of *something*. It is a question Woolf poses to herself, a question she poses about her own writing. In a letter to Margaret Llewelyn Davies, Woolf writes, "My dear Margaret what's the use of my writing novels" (cited in Q. Bell 1972, 29). The question of use matters to a woman writer as a question of confidence, a question of whether the books she sends out can enable a way of "living differently," to borrow Peggy's terms. It implies that some things we do, things we are used to, things we are asked to get used to, are in the way of a feminist project of living differently. The woman writer is trying to craft an existence, to write, to make something, in a world in which she is usually cast as sister or wife. It is not surprising that when the world is not used to you, when you appear as unusual, use becomes what you question.

From Words to Things

My task in this introduction is to explain how I arrived at the question of use; how use became, as it were, my task; what I have been *working out* as well as *working on*; as well as to reflect on how my own work has been redirected by taking up that task. In this book, in asking about *use*, I have been following *use* around. *What's the Use?* is the third in a series of books concerned with following words, the first being *The Promise of Happiness* (2010) and the second *Willful Subjects* (2014).[1] In these books, I follow words around, in and out of their intellectual histories.[2] To follow a word is to ask not only how it acquires the status of a concept in philosophy but how that word is exercised, rather like a muscle, in everyday life. Even to reference the exercising of a muscle is to point in the direction of use. To exercise means to put into active use. Use could thus be understood as central to how I have developed my method across all these books even though I have not always described my projects in these terms: in other words, I have been exploring the *uses of happiness*, the *uses of will*, and the *uses of use*. Thinking about the use of words is to ask about *where* they go, *how* they acquire associations, and in *what* or *whom* they are found.

It is a rather daunting task to follow the word *use*; use is a much-used word, a small word with a lot of work to do. It would be impossible to follow use wherever use is used. By thinking about the use of words, I am asking how they are put to work or called upon to do certain kinds of work. And by suggesting words are put to work, I am implying that it is not always clear from the words themselves what they are doing. In *The Promise of Happiness* (2010) and *Willful Subjects* (2014), I became intrigued by how the languages of happiness and will are exercised in speech acts such as "I am happy if you are happy" or "I am willing if you are." These speech acts often work by creating conditions: one person's happiness or will is made conditional upon another's. These conditions might seem to be about reciprocity and care. But they also teach us how happiness and will can become obligatory and even coercive: if someone says they will be happy if you are happy, then you might have to be willing to be happy in order to ensure that person's happiness. And then, if some people come first, their happiness comes first. My exploration showed how happiness and the will, even when they are written in the language of freedom (as free will, as freedom to be happy), can be experienced as the requirement to live your life in a certain way.

Duty can disappear under the guise of freedom. There is often a gap between what words say and what they do. I also find the languages of use intriguing. We could think, for example, of the expression "use it or lose it." This expression itself travels across domains; it is used in personal training as a kind of motivational phrasing as well as in self-help books, especially those concerned with the effects of aging. The expression also appears in academic literatures such as neuroscience. An obituary for the neuroscientist, Marian Diamond, notes that a healthy brain requires "good diet, exercise, challenges and novelty."[3] It summaries Diamond's contributions to theories of neuroplasticity thus: "After more than six decades of studying the human brain, Marion Diamond boiled her findings down to this advice: 'use it or lose it.'" The expression might indeed boil down an even longer history, condensing an idea that has circulated widely: that use keeps something (and something can include one's own body or mind) alive such that not to use something is to lose something, to let it wither away and die. Use it or lose it has also been applied to the example of minority languages. One articles notes: "The phrase 'use it or lose it' applies to few things more forcefully than to obscure languages. A tongue that is not spoken will shrivel into extinction. If it is lucky, it may be preserved in a specialist lexicographer's dictionary in the way that a dried specimen of a vanished butterfly lingers in a museum cabinet. If it is unlucky, it will disappear for ever into the memory hole that is unwritten history."[4] Not using a language, not exercising a spoken tongue, can mean to participate in its extinction. The moral stakes of use are high. A miserable fate follows falling out of use, becoming an item in a museum display, disappearing into "the memory hole that is unwritten history." We can note how quickly use can turn from being a description of an activity to a prescription: in positive terms, use becomes an obligation to keep something alive; or, in more negative terms, use becomes necessary in order to avoid something being lost. Use comes to acquire an association with life, disuse with death. *What's the Use?* tracks the history and significance of these associations.

Following happiness, the will and use does not mean going in the same direction. Happiness and the will seem to reference a subject, one who is happy or not, willing or not, although we can complicate that apparent referencing: things can be happy objects, anticipated to cause happiness; anything can be attributed as willful if it gets in the way of a will. Use seems to point more to objects than subjects or at least to activities in which subjects are occupied in tasks that require they have a hold of things. We might, however, make use of the language of use to describe ourselves: we might feel used, wish to be of use or useful, and so on. These uses of use seem to borrow their point from objects: the word *used* especially, when used to describe ourselves, tends to imply the injustice of being treated as an object, or as a means to someone else's ends. I will return to the implications of *used* in due course.

To follow words is to go where they go: that is the point. By following *use* I ended up following things. In her introduction to a special issue of *New Literary History* on use, Rita Felski attends to the word *use* itself: "The very word is stubby, plain, workmanlike, its monosyllabic bluntness as bare and unadorned as the thing that it names. It radiates overtones of sturdy practicality, bringing to mind images of shapeless overalls and sensible shoes. We tend to equate the useful with what is plodding, rational, and charmless, to oppose the useful to the dance of the imagination, the play of fantasy, the rhythms and rollings of desire" (2013, v). The word *use* radiates with potential even if we tend to associate the useful with the charmless and unadorned.

Use brings *things to mind*. Perhaps the word *use* is workmanlike, with its "monosyllabic bluntness," because of *how* it evokes everyday life. When we think of use, we might think of things that are shaped in order to be useful: those practical sturdy shoes that enable us to walk further or faster; those baggy overalls that allow us to move around comfortably so we can throw ourselves into the task at hand. The bluntness of the word seems to convey an attitude that can be adopted in life. We might organize ourselves and our worlds around the need to accomplish certain tasks the best we can: use as practical; use as efficiency. Being blunt is, of course, not the only point of use. Those overalls are not in fact shapeless: they have a shape that is loose enough to accommodate different shapes. To be practical can also mean to be versatile. And those sensible shoes might be filled by an idea of comfort; they might catch our imagination and desire, longed for at the end of a hard day. As Felski concludes, use is "a more complex and capacious term than we have often held it to be" (2013, vi). The magical and mundane can belong in the same horizon; use can be plodding and capacious at the same time.

To follow something it first needs to catch your attention. Use caught my attention because of a description of an object I found in a text I was reading because I was writing about the will. That text was George Eliot's *Silas Marner* and the object was Silas Marner's brown earthenware pot. The pot is Silas's companion. And the pot has become my writing companion.[5] I consider the following quote as one of my starting points in my journey to and through use.

> It was one of his [Silas's] daily tasks to fetch his water from a well a couple of fields off, and for this purpose, ever since he came to Raveloe, he had had a brown earthenware pot, which he held as his most precious utensil, among the very few conveniences he had granted himself. It has been his companion for twelve years, always standing on the same spot, always lending its handle to him in the early morning, so that its form had an expression for him of willing helpfulness, and the impress of its handle on his palm gave a satisfaction mingled with that of having fresh clear water. (Eliot [1861] 1994, 17)

A relation of use could be thought of as an instrumental relation; the pot is described as a utensil, a precious utensil. Something is a utensil when it is used in order to do something. Silas is certainly using his pot to do something: to get the water from the well to the house. Use is also represented here as companionship; the pot is reliable, kind even, standing there, ready for him. A relation of use can be one of affection. In this book, I take up *forness* as key to why use matters, forness as not only the point of an action (I know what a pot *is* by what it is *for*; the pot is a pot because I can use it for carrying) but also as an affecting or an affection. To be *for* something is to endow it with positive value. The pot thus acquires an expression: willing helpfulness. If Silas and the pot are in agreement with each other, the form of the pot gives expression to that agreement. To be in a relation of use is to acquire an expression. Use also leaves an impression: Silas feels the handle of the pot as an "impress" on his hand. I will return to the warmth of such impressions in chapter 1.

Silas's pot has become, for me, a pedagogic tool. It teaches me how affection and instrumentality can be different threads woven together in the same story about use. And the story is a useful tool because of how it complicates the relation of use. It might seem like a simple albeit meaningful relation, a body and a pot—a one-to-one connection, even. But there is much more, many more, involved in the story. To be in a relation of use is to be in an environment with other things: the fresh, clear water; the well from which Silas draws the water; a well that would have been built by hands and tools; the path taken in carrying the pot from the well to the house. Use is thus an intimate as well as a social sphere. Use is *distributed* between persons and things. From this short description of a relation between a person and a pot in a fictional text, we can begin to complicate our understanding of use. Who gets to use what? How does something become available to use? Can something be available as a public facility—like a well from which we can draw water—without it being usable by everyone? One use question leads to others.

In following leads, we can value how we arrive somewhere. It is important that it was an object that brought me to use. My interest in the word came from an interest in a thing. I realized very quickly that if use brings things to mind, use provides another way of telling stories about things. In the first chapter of the book, I assemble things in accordance with what I call simply their *use status*, including a well-used and unused path, a used book and a used bag, a used-up tube of toothpaste, an out-of-use postbox, an overused exclamation point, and usable and unusable doors. I began to think of use biographically, as traveling through things. My useful archive thus includes many things, old and worn things, for which I acquired so much affection.

A History of an Idea

If following use led me to travel through things, how have I followed use as an idea? I understand this book to be an exploration of *the uses of use*. By using *use* twice, first in the plural and second in the singular, I am making a commitment: there are different uses of use, and these differences matter. In some instances, then, by "uses of use," I am referring to how scholars have made use of use in developing their arguments. In reading for use, we are making connections that might not otherwise have been made across domains that might otherwise have remained distinct, such as biology, psychology, architecture, and design, which all make use of use to explain the acquisition of form. In some of these domains, we might expect use to be central; in others, perhaps less so.[6] What has been striking to me is just how central use has been to many scholarly traditions, that is, how often use has been given the status of an organizing concept; use is used to explain different kinds of phenomena from the number of tines in a fork to the long neck of a giraffe.

It is always possible, however, to overlook what is central. I think the centrality of use has not always been clear. Scholars from the past who have made use of use as a concept have not always been understood as having done so. An example from political science would be John Locke's *Second Treatise*, which is generally interpreted and taught as providing a labor theory of property. Locke did, in fact, make significant use of the categories of used and unused by defining the proper use of the land as agriculture. This is significant given how the category of "unused" was used to justify the colonial appropriation of land (see chapter 1). An example from biology would be Jean-Baptiste Lamarck, whose primary law is articulated as a law of use and disuse. Many contemporary discussions of Lamarck focus not so much on his use of use to explain how characteristics are acquired but rather on the thesis of the inheritance of acquired characteristics. Reading Lamarck on use, habit, and habitat has had a lasting impression on my own thinking. I was particularly struck by the implied relation between the acquisition of form and the lessening of effort (see chapter 2). Tracking the movement between biological and social models of use allowed me to make connections I had not made before, and I do not think I would have otherwise made, between inheritance, fitting, and the lessening of effort (see chapter 4). Pulling use out as a thread is to pull together different kinds of intellectual work.[7] We learn from the connections.

There is one school of thought that has been defined in relation to its use of use: utilitarianism. Utility is a use word albeit one that is given a narrow philosophical pedigree.[8] Utilitarianism has tended to be understood primarily as a branch of moral philosophy or normative ethics with a distinct canon founded upon the work of Henry Sidgwick, Jeremy Bentham, and John Stuart Mill, who are usually described as *classical utilitarians*. Mill defines utilitarianism as "the creed which accepts as the foundation of morals 'utility' or 'the greatest happiness principle' holds that actions are right in proportion as they tend to promote happiness; wrong as they tend to produce the reverse of happiness" (Mill [1863] 2001, 7).[9] Utilitarianism focuses on consequences; something is right to the extent that it promotes happiness and wrong to the extent that it does not.

The tendency to approach utilitarianism purely as a branch of moral philosophy has had consequences for the history of ideas. Utility and use have been treated as rather distinct paths. So, for example, when scholars have discussed Charles Darwin's relation to utilitarianism, they have tended to do so with reference to Darwin's own (rather limited) discussion of moral philosophy (Richards 1989, 234–51). But Darwin makes use of use in discussing the principles of natural selection, as well as in his use of the laws of use and disuse articulated by Lamarck (see chapter 2). We can consider how natural selection might itself be treated as a utilitarian method: what is selected is what is useful to an organism in the struggle for survival. What is of use changes in time, although organisms do not necessarily change at the same time, which means parts of an organism that are no longer of use may still exist (however dwindled). In this book, I explore the intimacy of use and selection as a way of reflecting on what I think of as *the strange temporalities of use*.

One of my specific aims is to put use back into utilitarianism. Even when maximizing utility is treated as the proper end of government, it remains dependent on the activity of use. In chapter 3, I show how Bentham defines idleness, unemployment, and nonuse as the cause of degeneracy, unhappiness, and even death.[10] It is not simply that Bentham emphasized use as an activity. He also developed plans for a Chrestomathic School, which was to be organized under the rubric of "useful knowledge." Although Bentham's plan for a school did not come to fruition (rather like his more famous plan for a prison), it has much to teach us about how useful knowledge was predicated on use as an activity.

Many utilitarian thinkers were in fact involved in educational projects in the early nineteenth century. The middle part of this book focuses on this specific period of time. The book could thus be described as more grounded than my earlier two books that are part of the same trilogy and had more wandering archives.[11] This groundedness might be a result of following use, which has kept me closer to the ground. It is the grounded nature of use that explains why historical materialism provides us with a useful archive: as Karl Marx noted, "Usefulness does not dangle in mid-air" ([1867] 1990, 126). I will return to this quote in chapter 1. The work also became more grounded because of my interest in the emergence of useful knowledge as a project, which meant attending to the labor of those involved in that project. I became especially interested in the history of monitorial schools (see chapter 3) as well as the role of utilitarianism in shaping the modern university (see chapter 4). Monitorial schools were introduced in poor and working-class areas of England and also throughout many British colonies. The schools provided me with a way of considering how utilitarianism traveled throughout empire not only as a body of ideas or as a way of justifying colonialism as increasing happiness, as I explored in *The Promise of Happiness* (2010), but also as a set of practices aimed at creating "a useful class."[12]

This book explores the development of educational techniques for directing subjects toward useful ends. I thus consider how usefulness became a requirement. I understand my work as participating in wider critiques of utilitarianism as an educational framework. Some of these critiques have taken the form of valuing "useless knowledge," that is, knowledge that is not deemed useful in accordance with existing (often narrow) criteria. Nuccio Ordine, for instance, affirms the usefulness of the useless: "I wished to place at the center of my reflections the idea of the usefulness of those forms of knowledge whose essential value is wholly free of any utilitarian end" (2017, 1).[13] Ordine also describes "utilitarian ends" as "the dominant usefulness," which is about "exclusively economic interest" (4). In such a "universe of utilitarianism," he adds, "a hammer is worth more than a symphony, a knife more than a poem, a monkey wrench more than a painting" (4).

It is always worthwhile to ask *where* worth is located. My task is to think from *where*. We can ask not only where usefulness is found but also how the requirement to be useful is distributed. My consideration of the general will in *Willful Subjects* (2014) had already led me to consider how the requirement to be useful, while often presented as general or even universal, tends to falls upon some more than others. I consider the following passage from Pascal's *Pensées*, along with the quote from Eliot I shared earlier, starting points in my journey along the path of use.

> Let us imagine a body full of thinking members. . . . If the foot and the hands had a will of their own, they could only be in their order in submitting their particular will to the primary will which governs the whole body. Apart from that, they are in disorder and mischief; but in willing only the good of the body, they accomplish their own good. . . . If the foot had always been ignorant that it belonged to the body, and that there was a body on which it depended, if it had only the knowledge and the love of self, what regret, what shame for its past life, for having been useless to the body that inspired its life . . . ! What prayers for its preservation in it! For every member must be quite willing to perish for the body, for which alone the whole is. (Pascal [1669] 2003, 132)

Here a foot is evoked, a foot as part of a body. If the foot was to have a will of its own, it would or should be like Silas's pot, willingly helpful, which means it should be willing to submit its particular will to the will of the whole. A foot has a use, and in having a use, the foot acquires a duty; we might call this will a duty—it should be willing to be used. If a willingly helpful pot allowed a body to carry something, a willingly helpful foot would allow a body to stand. We can note how an instrumental relation can be predicated on sympathy: to be in sympathy with the whole body is to be useful to that body. An instrument can also thus be understood as the loss of externality: *becoming useful as becoming part.* Pascal suggests that usefulness is a form of memory: to be useful is to remember what you are for. Not to be useful is to forget you are part of the body, to forget what *embodiment* you are for. For Pascal the foot refers to human beings, who must remem- *imp. to* ber they are part of God's kingdom. It implies we are all parts and that *"use"* as parts we must be willing to be of use or of service to the whole. But as I explored in *Willful Subjects* (2014), some individuals come to be treated as the limbs of a social body, as being for others to use (or more simply as *being for*). If the workers become arms, the arms of the factory owner are freed. If some are shaped by the requirement to be useful, others are released from that requirement.

My exploration of use as an idea is thus also an exploration of how use became a technique that differentiates between subjects without necessarily appearing to do so. In considering use as a technique, I build upon Michel Foucault's discussions in *Discipline and Punish* (1977), as well as work by Anne Brunon-Ernst (2012b), who offers an important series of reflections on the relationship between utilitarianism and biopolitics. I explore use as a technique for shaping worlds as well as bodies. I noted earlier that by the expression *uses of use* I am sometimes referring to how use is used in scholarly works. At other times I am pointing to the shaping effects of use. And given that to use something is to shape something, use can be a technique. What do I mean by this? When we hear the expression "use it or lose it," we might imagine a relatively organic process of something flourishing or withering away, or we might imagine that the fate of something, whether or not it is lost, is determined simply by our own actions. My book considers how things are sustained or lost as an effect of decisions that are not always consciously made or policies that do not necessarily take the form of explicit injunctions or prohibitions. Simply put, some things can be strengthened or kept alive by easing their use; other things can be slowed down or stopped by being made harder to use. In chapter 4, I explore how institutions are shaped by such uses of use.

When mechanisms work to enable or to ease a passage, they become harder to notice, especially for those whose passage is eased. Use can be how worlds are built for some, becoming available or ready for them. In the chapters that make up this book, I thus approach use as *having a history* insofar as use tends to become part of the background—use as how things are working. In *Queer Phenomenology* (2006), I suggested that "background" is one way we can combine genealogical and phenomenological methods. Drawing on phenomenology, we can understand the background as spatial, as what is around an object that appears distinct insofar as what is around it is "dimly perceived" (Husserl 1969, 102). We can also understand the background as temporal—as what is behind something or how it arrives. If to attend to use is to bring use to the front, we are fronting up to a history.

An Archive of Use

Research can be "hapfull"; we can be redirected by what happens along the way. I began the research for this book in 2013. But I took time away from the project after becoming involved in a series of inquiries into sexual harassment and sexual misconduct between 2013 and 2016. During this period, I wrote *Living a Feminist Life* (2017) and began a blog that took up the figure of the feminist killjoy. Feminist killjoys have already appeared in this book; they turned up as soon as I asked, what's the use?[14] I came back to my project on the uses of use after I resigned from my academic post. It did feel rather like picking up some shattered pieces! I wrote the first draft of *What's the Use?* in 2016, at the same time that I began a new empirical research project into complaint. I draw on some of this data from my research into complaint in chapter 4, alongside some of the data I collected from my earlier research into diversity.[15]

I did not at first expect that my research on complaint would connect so strongly with my project on the uses of use. Maybe I should have: as researchers we are the connection between our projects. Even so, the connections between our projects can still surprise us. And these two projects connected in part through the objects that I had already gathered: the doors, the paths, the postboxes, the signs of various kinds. I was not intending these objects to travel with me across the chapters, but that is what they ended up doing. Indeed, these objects helped me make sense of experiences I had during the writing of the book: that postbox became a filing cabinet, the well-used path a way of repicturing citational practices. I learned from the objects and their mutations. They certainly helped me thicken my account of use as an everyday activity. And they also became communication devices, enabling me to show how different parts of a system work together; in chapter 4, I describe this work as *institutional mechanics*. My book, which starts small, with the use of a thing, points to these larger histories: how spaces are occupied, how bricks form walls, and how barriers become physical.

And so, along the way the material came to matter in a different way. I noted earlier that when I arrived at the question of use, I thought I would be using the same method I employed in *The Promise of Happiness* (2010) and *Willful Subjects* (2014), of following words around *in and out* of their intellectual histories. Working on use redirected my work or perhaps helped me understand the inadequacy of this description for what I have been trying to do. Perhaps the problem is my use of "in and out," which implies a distinction between intellectual histories and other kinds of histories. The artificiality of any such distinction has been brought home to me by working on use. If I have followed use by following things, those same things often appear in academic writing to exemplify the effects of use. If things move between domains we might assume to be distinct, such as biology and architecture or design, *they carry use with them*.

Use also helped me appreciate the significance of how intellectual histories are themselves made up of used books that have a life insofar as they circulate or are passed around. Rather than following the word *in and out* of its intellectual history, I now think of use as *around and about.* All the materials I bring together in this work can be understood as used. I began deliberately choosing used books. I learned from the traces of past readers. Once these books became part of my archive, I began to relate to them differently; they became not only source materials insofar as they were *about* use but recording devices, recording histories I was trying to address. And I began to think more explicitly about how these works "worked" not just by housing ideas but by being made, being put together from different materials. In chapter 2, for instance, I explore how examples in academic writing have their own biographies of use, rather like the objects I gather in my opening chapter. My particular interest was in the rather striking figure of the blacksmith's strong arm, which has been used to exemplify Lamarck's laws of use and disuse.

I became interested not only in what was being argued—in how use became associated with specific values—but how use was put into circulation, becoming a conversation about the value of things. For the first I visited archives and museums as part of my research, including the archives of the Society for the Diffusion of Useful Knowledge (SDUK), which are currently held at the National Archives (though they belong to the University College London [UCL]); the British and Foreign School Society (BFSS), held at Brunel University; the records of early correspondence that led to the formation of London University, held at UCL; as well as the British School Museum at Hitchin, which has the only remaining monitorial schoolroom left in the UK.

These visits made such a difference to my understanding of how use matters as a way of making and shaping things. I began to think of a useful archive not only as something we assembled *around* use but as an archive *in* use. Kent Anderson, in his article "The Useful Archive" (2002), talks about the restriction of usability as part of the philosophy of stewardship. He wrote: "The philosophy of stewardship made the future itself a sort of metaphysical customer, and the archive was kept from current users by both its centralization and by specialist caretaking and storage requirements. This is the archive model that is most familiar—a few well-organized and redundant stockpiles maintained and protected from loss, so that unseen future generations may use them for research, literature, and historical perspective" (2002, 85). Already in archives are a philosophy of use or a philosopher of the user. A present use might be made harder because the user becomes the future. And yet archives become useful when they are being used. It is certainly, as Carolyn Steedman has noted, that in being used, an archive comes to life. She explains that "it [stuff] just sits there until it is read, and used and narrativised" (2001, 68).[16] When we take stuff out of folders, it comes to life. Archives can be more or less user friendly; they can be more or less open and closed. Before I left my job as an academic, I remember thinking that I better join the National Archives, assuming that having a professional status might make it easier to access. Access matters to using archives not only in the sense that you have to go through a process before you can use them but also because you have to learn the rules of use. At the National Archives, you are required to watch a video before you can join, which is basically an instruction manual on how to use the archive. Archives hold materials that are deemed worthy of being preserved; and yet, as I discuss in chapter 1, use can compromise the preservation of materials. An archive in use is an archive that could disappear if care is not taken in using the archive.

When I visited the archives of the British and Foreign School Society held by Brunel University, I had my own table, but I was placed in a shared office. I was looking through the minute books of the organization. They contained mostly what you would expect from books written to record the activities of an organization; they provided an administrative history. I remember feeling rather bogged down by the detail; it was slow, heavy.[17] As I was reading through details of financial transactions, meticulously recorded, I overheard a conversation. One archivist said to another, "We have more records about who would pay for the tea and biscuits than more important legal matters." So much of the paperwork that is necessary can feel like a distraction from what is necessary. I was reading about paperwork. So much of use is about paperwork. A history can be around us, when we shuffle through papers, overheard as conversation, as well as what is being recorded and preserved in papers.

On my first visit to the National Archives to look at the correspondence for the SDUK, I was overwhelmed. I remember walking up to that big, shiny building; it was a cold, frosty morning, and ducks were playing on the frozen water of the pond. It was cold and the building was warm. I saw there was a restaurant, busy and humming with life; I sensed that this space was organized around users, to make their visits comfortable and pleasant. I remember sitting down by myself in a room with large windows, with the three boxes I was allowed in front of me. I had the room all to myself—it was a room used just for the UCL archives, which were temporarily being housed at the National Archives. There were no signs of dust in these archives. Everything was clean and tidy, even shiny.

As a user I felt addressed: the user of the archive was prioritized in how everything was stored and made available. I sat there with my notebook and my pencil (pens are not allowed; marks must be temporary). I was not really expecting to find stuff that I would use in my book on use. This organization was interesting to me, but it was a tangent in the story I had been telling thus far (and remains a tangent in the book). When I opened the first page of the minutes of the first SDUK meeting, when I touched the paper, the tips of my fingers tingled. I was surprised by how much I was affected by seeing the extravagant curves of the handwriting. I felt closer to what I was writing about, more of a sense of that writing as happening, as coming out of something that was happening in a present. The very first sentence of the very first minute of the very first meeting had a line crossed out (I will share the content of that line in due course). I would not know of the hesitations, the deletions, without having read the minutes firsthand. I had a sense of a world coming into existence through the conversations that had been minuted about usefulness, conversations that do not flow smoothly but involve tussles and disagreements that are sometimes ironed out in how things are written up; things can be written out in being written up.

There is so much material to wade through. The archive too is stuffed. I will return to the significance of the stuffy nature of the archives of the SDUK in chapter 3. The more effort to make something, the more material we end up with. There are 121 boxes of materials for the SDUK, and most of these boxes contain correspondence (both correspondence sent by readers to the organization as well as correspondence sent by the organization). I went through only some of them. The letters sent to the SDUK included cancellations of subscriptions, statements from lawyers with concern about defamation, letters of thanks from happy readers, letters of complaint from less happy readers, letters from readers asking if they could meet with the secretary, letters from publishers, and letters from authors (including some folded-up copies of page proofs). Some letters were hastily written notes; they are scraps. They are preserved in the archive, because of *who* they were sent *to*. An addressee becomes an archive. What I got a sense of from reading the correspondence was how valuing use (and useful knowledge in particular) involved a range of actors who in becoming part of a conversation left evidence behind: from readers to authors to publishers. A conversation generates stuff— material that can be read, stored in a box, and can then be opened; once we reach this point, history is what spills out.

It is interesting what caught my attention. It was one word, the word *use* itself. When I picked up one letter in one file in one box, it held my attention. Words always seem to capture my attention; words still, words spill. As a researcher at the archive, I was the same kind of researcher I was before arriving at the archive, following the words. I noted before how when I did qualitative research for the first time, interviewing diversity practitioners about their work, I was the same kind of researcher that I was when I was doing text-based research, following words (Ahmed 2012, 9–10). This might not surprise us in the slightest; again, we are the connections between our projects. But if it does surprise us, it would not be that surprising: methods are often taught generically as if you use a different method in order to create a different output. Maybe methods are not simply tools, or if they are tools, maybe they do different things depending on who uses them, with this *who* being understood as not simply an individual but someone shaped by many histories—intellectual, social, other.

This is a handy point: it was still the words that captured my attention. And in this case, it was one letter that really stood out, a letter sent by William Adamson in 1830 (figure I.1). In the letter the word *use* is underlined twice (figure I.2). The word *use* jumps out not simply because it was used. It is hard to write a letter without using use; use is a rather ordinary kind of verb and is often hard at work, a sweaty verb. The word jumped out because the author had given emphasis to the word.

Exploring the uses of use has led me to the question of emphasis. In chapter 1, I discuss how the overuse of emphasis can stop an emphasis from working. An emphasis has much to teach us about the temporality of use—use as wear and tear. An emphasis can also be what stands out. In chapter 2, I will discuss marginalia in a published text that also stood out to me because of the emphasis given to use. It is not simply that we tend to notice what has been emphasized. When an emphasis is shared, a connection is made. If I had not had my own emphasis on use, I might not even have noticed the double underlining, even though the double underlining is used in order to catch attention. To follow a word allows you to see what is there, to pick up on something, even on significance. You have a bond when an emphasis is shared. An emphasis can mean an intensity of expression. In time, it came to mean the extra stress given to a word or phrase. It is a way of showing or displaying significance. Sometimes, you emphasize something because you perceive it has been overlooked. Perhaps you are trying to stop something from being passed over.

I.1. Fragment of letter sent by William Adamson to SDUK, 1830, SDUK Papers, UCL Library Services, Special Collections.

I.2. Detail of letter.

Why does this letter emphasize use through double underlining that word? Adamson writes, "The 'Schoolmaster's' instructions have hitherto been chiefly confined to infants and adults, but there is a large class between these that call loudly for his assistance. I shall confine my remarks to reading, as taught in country day schools. In most of these some other book is used along with the Scriptures, Murry Readers and Goldsmiths Histories. The art of reading is taught but not its *use*." Adamson goes on to suggest how teaching reading for use would be quite different, as a way of teaching how words are put together to create meaning. Adamson is suggesting that for knowledge to be useful, we need to think of how words are used. He makes an argument that I am making in the book: that we need to put use in its everyday sense, as a dynamic activity, back into utilitarianism.

The history of useful knowledge includes these moments in which use comes up as something that has been forgotten, when use is emphasized because or when it is not given enough emphasis. In following use, a loose thread, fragile even, we have much to pick up on. In the book I consider how use matters by combining three registers: philosophizing from the everyday (chapter 1), a genealogy of an idea and an apparatus (chapters 2 and 3), and an ethnographic description of an organization (chapter 4). The book thus draws from diverse fields and follows a rather queer and idiosyncratic path. To describe the work as queer and idiosyncratic, a peculiar mix of things, is to locate my work in relation to others. I write this book in mixed company. I am inspired by scholars working on questions of race, colonialism, gender, sexuality, and disability who write from or about "bodies out of place," "misfits," or "troublemakers," including Judith Butler, Rosemarie Garland-Thomson, Alexis Pauline Gumbs, Aimi Hamraie, Alison Kafer, Heidi Mirza, Aileen Moreton-Robinson, Nirmal Puwar, Shirley Anne Tate, Gloria Wekker, as well as many, many others. Those who are not quite at home—in a body, a discipline, a world—have much to teach us about how things are built, that is to say, have much to teach us about the uses of use. Who is housed by a world? We could think of Gloria Wekker's (2016) description of "the house that race built" or Aileen Moreton-Robinson's (2005) description of the nation as a "white possession" and as "the house that Jack built." We might recall Audre Lorde and think of *that* house as "the master's house" (1984): the house built with the master's tools. Before you can dismantle a house, you need to know how it is built, which means learning about use, learning from how those tools have been used.

An archive too can be built; we can be more or less at home there, even if we assemble our own archives from bits and pieces that are available because of where we have been. A useful archive could be thought of as a form of memory, a way of holding onto things. To use an object is to create a memory that is shared. Each time something is used, we accumulate more stuff to remember with. And to create an archive is to make a body, each part being of use to that body, although how a part is to be of use remains to be known. The act of building such an archive is not exhausted or exhaustive; there are things forgotten, paths not followed. A history of use is also a history of that which is not deemed useful enough to be preserved or retained. I have tried to pick up fainter trails, to find in the materials other ways of telling stories about use. These fainter trails, as I explore in my conclusion, can be described under the rubric of queer use. A fainter trail is what is left behind when you leave the official routes.

and also how to shed new light on these very things

1

....

Using Things

Use can be a way of being in touch with things. We make use of a knife when we need to cut something. Which knife we use might tell us something about the task at hand: a sharper knife might make a thicker piece of cardboard easier to cut. We learn from past experiences about what to use for what; we might know *this* knife is sharper, *this* knife is blunter. Use gives us a sense of things: how they are; what they are like.

It is noteworthy that use is often framed within philosophy as losing sight of things: "Matter can be used in such a way that it *vanishes into its uses*" (Wall 1999, 68–69, emphasis mine). Martin Heidegger's discussion of the broken hammer suggests that when the hammer is working, it disappears from view. When something stops working or cannot be used, it intrudes into consciousness. We might call what cannot be used *broken*. A break can be how something is revealed: for Heidegger a break is how we are "given any access to *properties* or the like" ([1927] 1962, 200). My discussion of using things in this chapter will include scenes of breakage: objects that are "out of use" or that have become "unused" and "unusable."

When we are absorbed in a task at hand and things are working, we can indeed stop noticing things. But use can also be revealing of things; use can even involve heightening our awareness of things. This is what I find so evocative about Silas Marner's relationship to his pot, referred to in the introduction. George Eliot catches something in how she describes

their relation. The pot is a useful thing; it is described as a "precious utensil" ([1861] 1994, 17). Silas's affection for the pot is filled with purpose just
as the pot can be filled with water: "The impress of its handle on his palm
gave a satisfaction mingled with that of having fresh clear water" (17).
The impression of the pot is an impression on his hand. An impression
can be a memory. An impression can be a reminder of what the pot is for:
the cold water it allows him to carry from the well to the house. Sherry
Turkle suggests thinking of the evocative object might take us away from
our usual way of relating to things "as useful or aesthetic, as necessities
or vain indulgences" (2007, 5). We can bring Turkle's insights together
with Eliot's description by considering how usefulness can be evocative:
use as how we handle things; use as how we mingle with things.

A mingling can be a transforming. When we are using something, it is
being transformed. The transformation is not simply what we are aiming
for, what we are trying to achieve. It is not just the cardboard that is affected when we use the knife to cut the cardboard, although how it is affected might be more noticeable because it is more dramatic—one piece
becoming two pieces—and more obvious, given it was the point of the
action. Using a knife affects the knife; it can make the knife less sharp, or
blunter. To keep using the knife, you might need to sharpen it; and then
you need to make use of something else, a sharpener or something that
can be used as a sharpener. In a relation of use, there is a kind of transfer:
as the knife becomes sharper from contact with the sharpener, the sharpener becomes blunter.[1]

When something becomes blunt from being used, it is being shaped
by use. Use offers a way of telling stories about things. We can ask *about*
objects by following them *about*. My examination of using things in this
chapter is indebted to Igor Kopytoff's work on the biography of things.
To offer a biography of things is to follow them "as they move through
different hands, contexts and uses" (Appadurai 1986, 34).[2] I also follow
things as they change hands. But rather than taking one object and exploring how it moves "through different hands, contexts and uses," I
explore a number of objects and try to catch them at different moments
of use, thus considering how use moves through things.

Use can be treated as a record of a life: use as a recorder. I proceed in
this chapter by considering the *use status* of things. We learn about something by considering how it *is* being used, *has* been used, or *can* be used.
But what seems to point to the future (can be used) can just as easily refer
back to the past (has been used). And what has been used in the past can

just as easily point us toward the future; if use records where we have been, use can also direct us along certain paths. In this chapter, I tease out the strange temporalities of use.

[handwritten margin notes: "as separate / diff. as assumed?", "'Use' of characters", "author", "reader", "text"]

Use

The word *use* is a busy word. To start with use is to start small and to start simply. Use when used as a verb can mean to employ for some purpose, to expend or consume, to treat or behave toward, to take unfair advantage of or exploit, to habituate or accustom. Use is a relation as well as an activity that often points beyond something even when use is about something: to use something points to what something is for. Some objects are made in order to be used. We might describe these objects as designed. A cup is made in order that I have something to drink from; it is shaped this way, with a hole as its heart,[3] empty, so that it can be filled by liquid. In the case of designed objects, what they are *for* seems to bring them into existence.

Drinking fluids is in the realm of necessity, something we need to do to be.[4] Because we need to drink, it is useful to have vessels for holding liquids. We do not only drink from things that have been designed as drinking vessels. I think here of Lucretius's philosophical poem on the nature of things. Lucretius writes there was thirst "before there were cups to drink from" (4, 156).[5] Indeed, Lucretius suggests the fact that "these inventions were devised for usefulness's sake" can give us a mistaken belief that nature too is designed. In contrast, he suggests, in life, "nothing is born so that we can use it. That which is born creates its *own use*" (4, 834–35). In another translation of Lucretius's words, use is made hap or happy: "What happens to exist is the cause of its use" (cited in Capra and Luisi 2014, 209).[6] I might drink from a cup or I might cup my hands to drink water from a stream. My dog, Poppy, might drink from a bowl, which I have placed by the door for this purpose. Or she might drink from a puddle, a small pool of water that can settle because of the concave surface of the land. Elements combine to make a puddle possible—enough rain has to fall, and the land has to be shaped in such a way that the water *can be held*, a shaping that might be affected by how and by whom the land has been used—that tractor, say, that created a furrow on its journey from the field to the shed.

The puddle does not exist in order that Poppy can drink from it. But once a puddle exists, it can come into use. Use can come after. A biography of use might explore the different moments in which use happens in the life course of one thing or another. When something is made in order to be used ("devised for usefulness's sake"), use seems to have temporal priority.[7] We might summarize the implied relation: *for is before*. In the case of drinking from a puddle, *for comes after*: when we make use of something because it exists, existence has temporal priority.

However, even if something is shaped around what it is for, that is not the end of the story. If for some things for is before, what happens to those things is not fully decided by what they are for. Howard Risatti notes in *A Theory of Craft*:

> Use need not correspond to intended function. Most if not all objects can have a use, or, more accurately be made usable by being put to use. A sledgehammer can pound or it can be used as a paperweight or lever. A handsaw can cut a board and be used as straight-edge or to make music. A chair can be sat in and used to prop open a door. These uses make them "useful objects" but since they are unrelated to the intended purpose and function for which these objects were made, knowing these uses doesn't necessarily reveal much about these objects. (2007, 26)

Use does *not* necessarily correspond to an intended function. This *not* is an opening. I am not so sure if uses are quite as unrevealing about things as Risatti implies ("knowing these uses doesn't necessarily reveal much about these objects").[8] I am being told something about the qualities of a sledgehammer that it can also be used as a paperweight. That a sledgehammer can be used as a paperweight tells me about the heaviness of the sledgehammer. This heaviness still references *for*; it is heavy enough for me to use it to hold down the paper.

When use can be separated from function, use seems to come after. But starting with use might require going back even further, before something became functional, before a cup came to be a cup, a utensil, a thing from which we can drink. When would a story of use begin? Perhaps the starting point for use is always arbitrary; use takes us back to how such-and-such thing came to be recognizable as such-and-such thing. We could think of paper as the material we use for writing, though paper has many other uses that are indicated often through naming: wrapping paper, toilet paper, wastepaper.

That paper gets around might have something to tell us about the usefulness of paper. That a paperweight becomes necessary teaches us about not only the heaviness of a paperweight but also the lightness of paper. We can learn about objects from the objects they are near, from their traveling companions. Objects can be in time with each other, traveling *in* time. Objects also travel *through* time. Paper came into existence partly because the heaviness of bamboo made it inconvenient to handle.[9] The lightness of paper meant it was more suitable than bamboo for wrapping things that needed to be transported. Henry Petroski in *The Evolution of Useful Things* replaces the usual expression "form follows function" with "form follows failure." He explains, "The form of made things is always subject to change in response to their real or perceived shortcomings, their failure to function properly" (1994, 20). Inventiveness comes from the fact—or the perception—that things are not functioning as well as they could be. In one chapter, Petroski asks how the fork got its tines. He gives us an answer: "Frustrations with knives, especially their short-comings in holding meat steady for cutting, led to the development of the fork" (7–8). Petroski cites the work of the architect Christopher Alexander on misfitting: "Misfit provides an incentive to change; good fit provides none" (30).[10] The failure of things to work creates an incentive to make new things.

Experiments with design are made because objects that are available to use do not allow us to do something as well as they could. Use thus brings things into existence through gradual modifications of form; *to form is to transform*. Things are transformed by being useful. In *Capital*, Marx notes, "It is absolutely clear that by his activity, man changes the forms of the materials of nature in such a way as *to make them useful to him*. The form of wood, for instance, is altered if a table is made out of it. Nevertheless the table continues to be wood, an ordinary, sensuous thing" ([1867] 1990, 163, emphasis mine). We need to look at things with a view to this history. As Marx explains further, "Every useful thing, for example, iron, paper, etc., may be looked at from the two points of view of quality and quantity. Every useful thing is a whole composed of many qualities; it can therefore be useful in various ways. The discovery of these ways and hence of the manifold uses of things is the work of history" (125). What is important here is that discovering the "manifold uses of things" requires work. Historical materialism places a strong emphasis on use because of how use requires attending to material conditions: "The usefulness of a thing makes it a use-value. But this usefulness does not dangle in mid-air. It is conditioned by the physical properties of the commodity, and has no existence apart from the latter" (126). If the usefulness of a thing gives it a use value, the value does not originate simply in that thing. For Marx, something acquires *use value* through labor: use values are understood as *combinations* of materials and labor (133).[11] Some things have utility without use value; that is, they are furnished by nature without being "mediated by labour" (131).

If labor shapes how some things take shape, things are shaped in order to be used. Staying with something is about grasping what it allows us to do. We can return to paper. Once paper has materialized—that is, been mediated by labor—paper can be used for different things. Use teaches how we pick things up because of their material or physical qualities, which is to say, given what they allow us to do. Even if intentions do not exhaust possibilities, even if there is something queer about use, something cannot be used for anything. Use is a restriction of possibility that is material. Even when we use something in ways that were not intended—a cup as a paperweight, for instance—we do so *given* the qualities of a thing. Perhaps when we use something in ways that were not intended, we are allowing those qualities to acquire freer expression. The keys that are used to unlock a door can be used as a toy, perhaps because they are shiny and silver, perhaps because they jangle. Queer uses, when things are used for purposes other than the ones for which they were intended, still reference the qualities of things; queer uses may linger on those qualities, rendering them all the more lively.

In Use

An object has been shaped by the requirements of use. A surrounding too can be shaped by use by how objects are gathered around. If I am a writer, I may have certain objects around me—a computer, a keyboard—that are placed on my writing table, which itself is placed in the corner of my study, the room I use for writing. These objects are near enough; they are ready to be used. A phenomenology of usefulness would attend to how use involves a way of arranging worlds as well as ourselves. We are in this sense already "in use" before we pick up objects; to inhabit a world is to be inhabited by use. In *Queer Phenomenology* (2006), I described proximity as oriented; that which is placed near enough to a body can show its leanings, and the things that are placed so they are convenient to use tell us how you are usually occupied. Proximities are not only revealing of our own occupations. Objects too exist in relations of proximity: an object might be near another object as they are used together; use is how things come to share a location.[12]

Attending to use allows us to explore the oriented nature of spaces, including public spaces. Objects that surround us, which become familiar features of a landscape, might be there because of what they are *for*. We can be surrounded by *for*. I think of postboxes, which are sometimes described as "street furniture," as well as aesthetic objects that liven up the landscape. One article explains, "For many communities, they are a reassuring presence—a cheerful, red splash that has stood out on British streets for a [*sic*] more than a century and a half."[13] Another article claims, "Our post boxes are true landmarks and their history is imprinted on them."[14] Postboxes are, of course, not just decorative features of a landscape; they are objects with a history. They matter because they are "regularly used by most as it had been for generations." Indeed, we know what they *are* because we know what they are *for*. An object can be how you encounter a system. Postboxes are *in use* because they are part of an existing arrangement that requires them to work. They are part of a communication system, which is also a transportation system. When we post our letter into a postbox, the postbox is in use. We can do so with confidence, without thinking; we assume that letter will not just be sitting in a box but be picked up and sent on its way. A letter can reach its destination because of what is in use.

To say something is in use does not only mean that it is currently being used. In fact, when I say the postbox is in use, I could be referring to the fact that I *am* currently using it, or that I *could be* using it. A coin that is *in use* is circulating but it could still be in my pocket. It can come out and come into use, current as currency, because its circulation was only temporally suspended.

How do we know things are in use? Is it obvious that something is being currently used? Consider the sign *Occupied*. The fact that we sometimes require signs to tell us that something is in use tells us that use is not always obvious.[15] We are familiar with such signs. The sign *occupied* on a toilet door is an address to potential users, telling them that the toilet is being used by somebody else (figure 1.1). The sign is telling us that we need to wait before we can use the toilet. When we say something is *in use*, it can also mean that it is not available to use right now. Most of us have had the experience of opening the door of a toilet stall and finding someone else in there. The failure to lock the door, to signal that the toilet is

1.1. A sign indicating a toilet is in use.

in use, can be deemed an insult or injury, causing embarrassment because users are not meant to coincide on such private matters. Maybe you did not lock the door properly, and then you say sorry in mortified embarrassment when someone else walks in. Having a sign to signal something is in use is a convention. It is like a polite form of speech, a way of maintaining bodily as well as social boundaries. If the status of something as being in use or occupied requires a sign, we learn that is not always clear whether something is in use.

Use often comes with instructions. And I am not just referring to user manuals that accompany many objects, especially technical objects (the more complicated it is to use something, the longer the manual tends to be). The word *use* is often used in instructions. Instructions can be about *when* you can use something, *how* to use something, or *who* can use something. Restrictions of use can be enforced. Another familiar sign is "doors are in constant use" (figure 1.2).

This sign makes a claim that the doors are in constant use in order to justify a use instruction, that is, an instruction not to park a car or a bike in front of the door. If persons were to use the door to park their bikes, they would be using the door incorrectly in at least two ways: it is not being used *how* it is supposed to be used (the door is for passing not parking)

1.2. A use instruction.

nor by *whom* it is supposed to be used (the correct users of the door might be the owners of the building, or their guests, who need to be able to open and close the door, to get in as well as to get out). Use instructions are perhaps more likely to be made and enforced when incorrect uses make correct uses impossible: if the door were to be used for parking, it could not be used for passing. Use instructions might be deemed necessary because of a past history of incorrect use: you might have to insist that people do not use the door to park their bikes or cars, because they have used the door for that purpose before. If persons were to refuse that instruction, they would become an obstruction. Becoming an obstruction describes the fate that awaits some users. The status of the door as being "in constant use" is thus an affirmation of the priority of some uses and users. Intended functionality can be a reference not only to *what* something is for but *who* it is for. Ownership would here imply not only a right to use but a right not to use something, however constantly what is being used is being used; use is constant if framed as potential.

In creating a public space, however, it might seem that anyone can use something; use as what is released by a public from a restriction, from privation, could be called *common use*. Let us return to the occupied sign. It is a sign that is familiar: it is placed on the door of a toilet. The

1.3. Addressed by a sign on a door.

sign is also a lock: it is how you lock yourself in and lock others out. The use of a facility also references the use of a category. A public bathroom is a highly regulated as well as contested political space partly because you are performing a private function in a public space.[16] We could think here of the person addressed by the sign on the door as the *user*. The user is an anonymous figure rather like the figure of the stranger (Ahmed 2017, 34). It seems you become a user by virtue of using something. But can anyone become a user? Before you get to this door, you usually have to enter the room by going through another door, upon which signs are placed: men or women (figure 1.3). We know about use from use: the signs are not referring to the toilets themselves as men and women but to the *users* of the facilities. A use instruction also functions as *an address*. If you are addressed by the sign women, you go that way, you open that door.

Who is supposed to use a toilet can also be a matter of who is supposed to reside within a category. A social category is a category that is in use and of use. You use the women's toilets because you identify as a woman. You use the toilet because of where you reside. Some women do not appear to others as women. If you do not appear as you are expected to appear, your use of a facility becomes deemed an obstruction. This is why for some would-be users the public toilet is a space of trauma and difficulty. When she walks into the toilet, she might be stopped, harassed because she is not seen as she. She might be told: you are not supposed to be here, you are not supposed to use this facility. She might be directed toward another facility—another gender, another door.

When your use of a facility is questioned, you are questioned. When you are questioned about your right to occupy a space, you are being questioned about your right to occupy a category. It is not just then a question of turning up, of being able to use something because the facility is vacant or free. This means that a facility can be occupied even when it is free. *In use* can describe how worlds are occupied by bodies for which they are *assumed* to be intended. You can have trouble making use of facilities when you fail an assumption. And remember: you go there because you *need to go*; if you cannot use the toilet, you cannot perform a necessary function. Not being able to perform a necessary function in a public space is how a public space becomes unusable.

Out of Use

Something can be taken out of use. Maybe the sign on the toilet door says vacant. It is empty. But there is another handwritten sign pasted on the door: out of use. This sign is a command: do not use the toilet! The toilet is not available for you to use even though someone else is not using it. Usually this means that the toilet is broken. Out of use can register that something is not working. When it is not working, using something could clog up the system.

A breakage can also be a transition moment: why something is taken out of use; how it is taken out of use. Say my cup loses its handle (figure 1.4). Or we might say the cup has flown off the handle. The handle was how I held the cup; without a handle, the cup can hold the water but maybe it is harder for me to hold the cup. A breakage might be that transformation of a quality of a thing while being experienced as a change in a relation. Remember Silas's pot? The story I shared in my introduction was only part of the story. Silas, when he is carrying the pot that carries the water, stumbles. And the pot breaks: "One day as he was returning from the well, he stumbled against the step of the stile, and his brown pot, falling with force against the stones that overarched the ditch below him, was broken in three pieces. Silas picked up the pieces and carried them home with grief in his heart. The brown pot could never be of use

1.4. A broken cup.

to him anymore, but he stuck the pieces together and propped the ruin in its old place for a memorial" (Eliot [1861] 1994, 17).

When an object breaks, it can no longer be of use. It can take up its place by becoming memorial: a holder of memories, not water. In becoming a memorial, Silas's pot does not become rubbish or waste; the fragments are put back together, not swept away. But there is still something sad and empty in the account. Silas is left with a hole in his heart, a pot-shaped hole, a sense of being empty. If you can fix something but still feel broken, then what is broken is not only a thing. If a connection is made possible by use, a connection can be broken when something breaks.

Sometimes to fall is to fall out of use. But something can fall out of use without being broken. An out-of-use word has become *obsolete*. It might be out-of-date, old-fashioned, or outmoded. When it is no longer living, it is no longer acquiring new meanings, like Silas's pot is no longer being used to carry the water; use becomes the possibility for picking up more stuff along the way. I think of how words can be picked up. You can hear how words are being picked up; you can hear the buzz, how they are becoming busy. It is harder to hear how words are put down; it can be hard to notice how things fall out of use when falling is gradual. But once words become obsolete, they sound differently, curious, out of time, strange, queer, and startling. We could offer a biography of use by giving an account of how words fall out of use or are taken out of use.

Something can fall out of use, almost by accident, although a falling can appear as an accident even when it is the result of design.[17] Or something can be taken out of use *in order to be preserved*. We could think of museums as where objects are stripped of use and put on display. It is not just that objects are stripped of use but that the communities for whom objects matter are stripped of what matters to them. The word *strip* points to the violence of this history: it derives from the West Saxon *bestrypan*, meaning to plunder. When you preserve a life by stripping something from use, what you are preserving is not a life but the rights of some to decide what and who counts as life.[18] The politics of preservation so often involves the rights of some to appropriate what is of use to others, because they assume they alone have the technologies needed to preserve things. This assumption of the right to withdraw things from other people's use is how some people become the guardians—who often speak of *taking care*. Taking care can mean *taking things*. Thefts are justified as taking care of things by taking them out of use.

You can also take something out of use because it is being used by someone else. Take the example of an out-of-use postbox (figure 1.5).[19] There are many reasons a postbox can be taken out of use. It might be claimed that the postbox was not being used enough.[20] Usage here would be a sign of importance or value: more people making use of something can be used as a retrospective confirmation that it needs to exist. We can sense an injustice: if something is taken out of a system because it is not used enough, those who use that something *become not enough*.

This particular image does not tell *that* story, though that story does need to be told: the story of those whose use of something is not deemed enough to justify the continuation of something. There is a sign on the postbox that indicates it has been taken out of use, by giving a use instruction (please do not use this box). We are also given the reason for that instruction; it has been taken out of use because the postbox is *occupied*. The postbox has provided a home for nesting birds. If the toilet is occupied when it is in use, the postbox is out of use because it is occupied. But, of course, at another level the postbox is in use; it is just not in use *as* a postbox.

I have noted that intended functionality can refer to whom something is for as well as what something is for. The postbox is not being used as it was intended to be used: it is providing a home for nesting birds. In

Would be interesting to think of her conception of "use" in relation to "uses of critique" or "uses of literature"

1.5. An out-of-use postbox.

being used by the birds, the postbox has become a nest. Queer use can also mean when something is being used by those for whom it was not intended. That a postbox can become a nest still tells us something about the postbox. It can provide such a home because of its shape and form; the same shape and form that enables it to function as a postbox enables it to function as a nest (there is a hole to enable entry and empty space to enable a home for those who are small enough to fit). We learn about form when a change in function does not require a change in form. Different uses of the same thing change how we refer to the thing: a *who* change as a *what* change. When the postbox becomes a nest, it ceases to be a postbox. A sign is needed to register the transition (otherwise the letters would dislodge the birds).

We might note that a decision could have been made to eject the birds in order to enable the postbox to stay functional. But the birds were not ejected; they were given rights of residence, which means the postbox is *currently* a nest and is *out of circulation* as a postbox. When the birds leave, the thing we called a postbox might return to being a postbox. Something is what it provides or enables, which is how what something "is" can fluctuate without changing anything at the level of physical form.[21] So we could say the real thing is the postbox and that it has withdrawn (a real postbox might always be withdrawn because even when it is being used, it is more than what it is for).[22] Or we might say that the postbox has become a nest temporarily but *really* it is still a postbox. Neither ways of addressing the relation of being and use capture what I am trying to suggest here. To refer to something as a postbox is to refer to a use of a thing or even a use not a thing. The use of a thing can bring that thing into existence: *for is before*. Just because something comes to exist for a purpose, we should not confuse what it was intended for with what it is or can be. Describing what something is for is a partial account of what it can be. *Forness helps reveal the partiality of an existence. For* can be loose enough to accommodate others; for can be an opening just like the opening of the postbox can allow the birds to enter.

Intended use and potential use are not the same thing

Use can involve comings and goings. And we can think too, then, of the story of the pot that has broken, that has to be taken out of use, because it can no longer be of use. To be taken out of use means that the pot has become stationary, as well as remaining empty, filled with memories but not water. And now, another story of use can begin: a broken pot can provide a home for an insect; a stationary pot might provide a safer home than a pot that was still being used to carry water.

Used

When something has been used, it becomes a *used thing*. Use seems to inevitably lead to used; use seems to mean something can no longer be unused. Sometimes the word *used* is used to mark the devaluation of something. I can buy a book new or secondhand. If a used book is secondhand, we might say a new book is firsthand, as if my hands are the first hands to touch it (even though we all know many hands had a stake in a book becoming a book). If I bought the book from a bookshop, others might have picked it up, but they put it down again. I could take that book out of its packet; just removing it from a packet can be enough to become a used book, even if I have not read it. This means that something can become used before it is used. How quirky.

I bought a used book on hands that was handy (figure 1.6). You can tell the book is used; the user has left many traces: underlining, circles around words such as grief (figure 1.7). If the book had been new, it would have been more expensive. If the book had been less marked, it

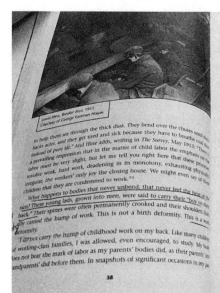

1.6. A secondhand book.

How to carry this memory without betraying it? It would be a violation of family trust if I told my story for rhetorical effect. I tell it because I know there are some readers who will recognize in it their own family legacies of missing fingers, uneven shoulders, varicose veins, deafness, blinded eyes, enlarged hearts, swollen hands—an encyclopedia of ailing or phantom body parts, work-related injuries, that collectively attest to untold stories of labor. These missing body parts and inscriptions on the body are crucial to our understanding of cultural formation and academically sanctioned knowledge. I also wish to expose the connection between culture and the "g" word—grief. How is grief culturally represented and negotiated? The *New York Times*'s "portraits of grief," paragraph-sized obituaries and photos of the victims of 9/11/01 is one way.[4] The

39

1.7. You left a trace.

Use assoc. w/ traces, which then influence your use of the product and become part of web would have been more expensive (unless the user is esteemed, in which case the value of the user might rub off onto the value of the book; I will return to marks left by an esteemed user in chapter 2). To use something well requires keeping signs of usage to a minimum. I did not just buy a used copy because it was cheaper. I love used books; I love the traces of earlier readers. I want readers to leave parts of themselves behind.

Why did you circle the word *grief*, I wonder? I feel a connection to the circle, through a circle. Even the underlining of words can give me comfort, a sense that others have been here before, that others will follow. So this is what you thought was important, I think. I try skipping the words that are not underlined and work out if I can work out how you were reading, what you were reading *for*.

When an object is bought, there is a suspension of use. Marx suggests that when something becomes a commodity, it becomes a transcendental: when it is exchanged, a table ceases to be a mundane object, "an ordinary sensuous thing," that wooden object, upon which my used book rests, a table that is in use ([1867] 1990, 163). To make use of the table is to bring it back down to Earth. Indeed, Jacques Derrida returns to Marx by turning to a table that might be in use or out of use: "This table has been worn down, exploited, overexploited, or else set aside, no longer in use, in antique shops or auction rooms" (1994, 149).[23] The table becomes worn down by use whether or not it is in use. The scratches on the table might tell us something about what the table was used for. We might think of the scratches left behind from use not as signs of degradation or the loss of value but as testimony. The table might testify to its own history.

Use might offer a resistance to the transcendental, a way of getting back to the materiality of things. To value use might require a change of values. We might value worn things, broken things, for the life they lived, for how they show what they know: the scratch as testimony; the wrinkle as expression. The secondhand shop is a place to go if you are curious about used things, the old and the worn, if you value them for the stories they have to tell, and not just where you go if you wish to purchase something that is cheaper. Matthew Rowlinson suggests that in a secondhand shop, objects are "not only objects for sale; they are also objects that have already been used. If in a classical model of exchange the notion of use identifies the terminal point of the commodity's circulation as the moment when its value is consumed, the objects in the curiosity shop belong to the afterlife of commodities" (2010, 350). An object enters the secondhand shop because it has been used. Perhaps it stays there for some time; it might be picked up only to be put down again. But then the object might be taken home and be used all over again, with this second story of use being part of the biography of the same thing even if the users do not meet, even if what is shared is not experienced directly by those who experience the object as belonging to them. Use: how we can be touched by those we do not meet. A used object preserves a life even after it appears a life has been terminated.

A used object is shaped by comings and goings, even though those who come and go in the life of a thing do not encounter each other directly. Peter Stallybrass in his moving meditation on Marx's coat suggests use can indeed be an ethics of proximity, a worldly ethics. Stallybrass refers to the coat that is being worn. Such a coat might end up in a pawn shop, becoming traded for money in a time of scarcity. Stallybrass explains, "From the perspective of the pawnshop, any value other than exchange value is *sentimental* value, a value of which the object must be stripped if it is to be 'freely' exchanged on the market" (1998, 195). The stripping of sentimental value is required for the thing to be free to enter the market; freeing as abstraction is a forgetting of how something matters and a sign of how something matters. To hold onto things is a memory project, a way of preserving not just a thing but the intimacies that make things what they are; it is not simply to hold onto the containers of our memories but their memories too. Stallybrass describes how "in the language of nineteenth century clothes-makers and repairers, wrinkles in the elbows of a jacket or a sleeve were called memories. Those wrinkles recall the body that had inhabited the garment. They memorized the action, the mutual constitution, of person and thing. But from the perspective of commercial exchange every wrinkle or 'memory' was a devaluation of the commodity" (196). An object's memories can be of a body that is wearing the thing, a memory as an acquisition of shape. A worn coat recalls the body that wore the coat: use as recall, as being called again; use as companionship. Our companions have their own companions. The coat that is kept in the wardrobe might encounter a moth, becoming nourishing for another, but a nourishing that leaves the coat in tatters. Perhaps it is at this point, the point at which something is left in tatters, that uselessness becomes part of a story. If use can make something useful, to be useful as to be full of use, use can also make things useless, no longer full.

Using something can mean wearing it out. In everyday life, decisions about use can also be decisions about value. You might put the best china

1.8. Scruffy from use.

away in the cupboard; it does not matter that it is harder to reach because you do not intend to use it much. You might decide not to use (or to use less) what you consider your best things to increase the chance of preserving them. Using something less can mean handling it less. Value can also be sentimental. If we use something more because it has our affection, loving more can mean lasting less. That is my own relation to used things: my bag, for instance, has become scruffy from use, worn and weary because it has been a constant companion, traveling with me whenever I travel (figure 1.8).

When objects change hands, we mingle with them and through them. But we could also think of how things change our hands, how we are shaped by what we handle. Mingling becomes intermingling. We can use different words to describe this intermingling. Contact would be one; friction is another. I return to friction in due course. The skin at the tips of my fingers touches the paper; the paper touches the tips of the fingers. In the case of a very old book, perhaps the paper is parchment, the skin of sheep; the preservation of the book might depend on not being touched by skin with its natural oils. Contact would be erosion—and indeed damage. Damage cannot be incorporated into the memory of a thing if that thing ceases to be. A memory of being might be lost when a being is lost. To preserve an old book, one might be required to introduce a third

1.9. The more a path is used, the more a path is used.

mediating element, such as gloves, which prevent contact between skin and parchment or paper. Sometimes the preservation of something requires minimizing contact, which means trying to stop use from leaving traces. I have already described how museums can strip objects of life by taking them out of use. Preservation without use can mean preservation without life. The question of use becomes a life question; a question of whose life matters is bound up with who gets to use what.

Use can also be a sign of a life being lived, which is to say, use involves coming into contact with things. Use could be described as a contact zone. A contrasting image to the used book would be that of a well-trodden path (figure 1.9).[24] The path exists because people have used it. Use is not the only reason for its existence: the path might be there because it is sensible for it to be there; it might be on the edge of a hill; or it might be the most protected route from one busy town to another. A path might be maintained by someone being employed to maintain a path or by volunteers who care for the environment. This maintenance work might be necessary for the path to be usable: that tree that fell over might need to be moved, that rubble pushed to one side, those prickly thorns cut back. We can think of this maintenance work as care; to keep something usable requires taking care. Bonnie Honig (2017, 48–49) discusses how public things are not always "in use" but provide a holding environment, drawing on the work of Hannah Arendt and Donald Winnicott. The maintenance of such useful things is work: for something to remain of use is thus a form of public care and concern.

individual is made into something public

Sometimes use can be sufficient to maintain something. If the image of a used book and a well-used path are contrasting, they are connected. A line on a page is left by a pen held by a hand; a scruff mark is made by a shoe that holds a foot. Use leaves traces in places. Use involves friction: things rubbing up against each other. Friction is the resistance the surface of an object encounters when moving over another. The more people travel on a path, the flatter and smoother the surface becomes. When something is smoother, it is clearer; the more a path is followed, the easier it is to follow. Once something has become used, you are encouraged to go in that direction: your progression would be eased. Used involves not only a description of a condition but an invitation. *The more a path is used, the more a path is used.* How strange that this sentence makes sense. There is more to more; more creates more. However much usedness is shaped by the past usedness points toward the future: used as being directed toward that which has become easier to follow.

A path can appear like a line on a landscape whether or not there is a sign indicating a path. But a path can be how thoughts and feelings are directed. Within empirical psychology, this idea of a well-trodden path was certainly in use. John Locke, for example, suggested that thoughts "once set agoing, continue in the same shape they are used to, which, by often treading, are worn into a smooth path, and the motion in it becomes easy and as it were natural" ([1690] 1997, 531). Locke here uses "used" in another sense; the difference is audible but not visible. We say that we are used to something. Used becomes an idiom for being accustomed or habituated. Used can mean previously used, shaped by comings and goings; becoming used can refer to how an activity has become customary. A history of use is a history of becoming natural. With effort, things seem effortless. A wrinkle in a performance can be ironed out by a performance. If history can be how a gesture is smoothed, a history can be how history is smoothed over.

The idea that use smooths a path has been central to work in neuroscience. William James noted, "The path once traversed by a nerve-current might be expected to follow *the law of most of the paths we know*, and to be scooped out and made more permeable than before," such that "once a current has traversed a path, it shall traverse it more readily still a second time" ([1890] 1950, 108, emphasis mine). The law of most paths: following a path makes a path easier to follow. The implication of this relationship between use and easiness is that use can be quite a conservative phenomenon; thoughts can function on well-traveled paths, such that you think the same thoughts, over and over again. Edward Thorndike in his discussions of animal intelligence discusses two laws: the law of exercise (which I take up in my discussion of Lamarck in chapter 2) and the law of effect. He suggests that some behavior can be about the strengthening or weakening of neurons: "the wearing smooth of a path in the brain, not the decisions of a rational consciousness" (Thorndike 1911, 74). Neural pathways are often compared to paths in a landscape, especially in popular texts: "Neural pathways become easier to follow, like a well-used trail in the woods" (Vickery, Matson, and Vickery 2012, 182). Each time a path is used, it becomes easier to use, such that over time we can call it well used or even used well.

Use can be restrictive as well as a directive or restrictive by virtue of being directive. If the same paths are used more, the fewer paths are available to be used. The emphasis on plasticity within neuroscience is partly an explanation of how use is not only about conservation, how deviation is always possible, even when connections have become strong. Other paths can be created by being used: use does not make deviation impossible. Deviation is hard. Deviation is made hard.[25]

Something might become less likely the harder it is. And often, as work on neuroplasticity has explored, the potentiality for change comes from trauma, damage, or crisis, from something breaking down that was previously in use (Malabou 2012). However, neuroplasticity is also used in optimistic accounts of therapies such as mindfulness, as we can note from this statement: "The analogy I often use to explain how mindfulness and other therapies enhance Neuroplasticity is to imagine a path through the forest; The more we use a specific path, the deeper and smoother that path becomes and being so, following it is easier tha[n] traveling through the forest any other way. Our minds are the same—we develop neural pathways in our brain by repeated use and if those pathways lead us to depression, anxiety, or disordered thinking we feel stuck on those paths."[26] Knowledge of the effects of use on the easing of pathways can lead to a self-consciousness premised as consciousness of use.[27] You might start using a path that would be helpful but is hard to follow in the hope that by using it, it would become easier to follow. Of course, the difficulty of this viewpoint is that it renders subjects responsible for ill-use or nonuse, as if their failure to make new paths by altering patterns of use is why new paths have ceased to be possible.

It is interesting to consider how work in psychology makes use not only of well-used paths but other used objects in explaining the acquisition of tendencies. William James cites the work of a M. Léon Dumont on habit: "Everyone knows how a garment having been worn a certain time clings better to the shape of the body than when it was new. . . . *A lock works better after being used some time*; at the outset a certain force was required to overcome certain roughness in the mechanism. The overcoming of their resistance is a phenomenon of habituation" ([1890] 1950, 105, emphasis mine). Taking his second object first, the lock works better after being used because roughness is eliminated by use; the passage of the key has become like that well-worn path: smoother, easier. It is important that the role of use in easing the passage is about the reduction of force needed. For James, habituation is the overcoming of resistance, the lessening of the force required to do something. Small acts of use are the building blocks of habit: if we took habit as our unit, we would miss these smaller steps, which accumulate to take us somewhere.

If a garment becomes more attuned to a body that uses it, attunement is a consequence of use. We can glimpse in the story of the garment that clings better the more it is worn the beginning of another story: *use can mean the lessening of receptivity to others*. The garment that clings to the shape of a body wearing it might cling less well to those with a different shape. This is why I call an institution a well-worn garment: it has acquired the shape of those who tend to wear it such that it is easier to wear if you have that shape. Easier to wear: a clinging can be experienced as comfort. We can think of comfortable chairs. In earlier work, I suggested that social norms can operate rather like comfortable chairs (Ahmed 2004, 148). Comfort can be about the fit between body and object: my comfortable chair might be awkward for you with your differently shaped body. Comfort is about an encounter between more than one body, the promise of a sinking feeling. I now realize how much this way of thinking of spaces was about the shaping effects of use. The surface of a space is impressed upon by those who are using it. You can witness these impressions rather like you can witness an indent on the surface of a chair; an indent is created when a body leaves, telling us someone was there once they have gone.

Could chairs have something else to teach us about the relation of use and function? André Leroi-Gourhan in his reflections on the history of objects suggests that the functional quality of "human made" objects is an inversion of an "absolutely natural process" ([1964] 1993, 299). His example is a chair: "You need only take a cast of the body of the person to be supported in a seated position in order to obtain a purely functional concave object, a seat in the form of a shell which judiciously oriented supports, its shape strongly reminiscent of a seashell's" (300).[28] Here a thing would be useful for a body by inverting the shape of that body. But in fact it is not useful to design chairs that perfectly invert a singular body. Leroi-Gourhan concludes that functional aesthetics is "rarely perfect," as a chair "can never achieve perfection in terms of strict functionality, for to do so, it would have to be designed for just one individual sitting in just one position" (301). Corporeal diversity loosens the relation of function and form. And by corporeal diversity, we would be referring not only to differences between bodies but differences within bodies: how bodies have more than one position. Functional plasticity means more can fit because the relation between form and function is made less precise. We might say that a chair is made so that more can sit upon it; each person fitting less well means more can fit.

Of course, some bodies will still not fit by virtue of their form. I return to not fitting as a matter of formality in due course. But if something is supposed to function by fitting imperfectly, then repeated use of something can make something fit less imperfectly. *Use can thus lessen the plasticity of function.* When spaces become more comfortable by being repeatedly used by some, they can also become less receptive to others. I will develop this point in chapter 4, exploring how spaces become occupied because of how they are being used. I have suggested that use can be queer; use can roam around objects. Queer use might refer to how things can be used in ways other than how they were intended to be used or by those other than for whom they were intended. I am now suggesting use can be how things become more restricted in time. Use can be how the queer potential of use is lessened. Simply put: use can make use less queer.

Unused

Unused might refer to that which has yet to be used. But something can also become unused: the "un" here is acquired when something is stopped. Perhaps a child's favorite book is well used, scruffy. It cannot lose the history of having been used; that history is all over the pages. But *and in how it continually to affectively move us, surely?* maybe the book is placed on a higher shelf because the child has moved on to new books more suited to her age. You can outgrow books as well as clothes. The well-used book, tattered by use, becomes unused in the sense of no longer read (to make use of a book is to read a book). Unused can be a moment in a biography; as I noted earlier, that same book might end up in a charity shop or that secondhand shop where another story of use can begin.

What about an unused path? What story of use can be told? An unused path might refer to the path that is no longer used as a path. To become unused can mean to unbecome. If we stop using a path, it might cease to be usable as a path. I will return to usability as a fate in due course. The path might become overgrown: you can hardly see the sign for the leaves. If using something can be what keeps something going, not using something can involve cessation. Not using: not being. We can return to the expression "use it or lose it" discussed in my introduction. That expression can be offered as a mantra in personal training, but it can also become a philosophy of life: using as being, not using as not being. When using becomes what you must be doing in order not to lose something, use becomes a moral duty, what you must do to keep something alive.

In the case of the unused path, more effort is required to use it (figure 1.10). You might have to push your way through the growth. A consciousness of the need to make more of an effort can be a disincentive. You can be dissuaded by perpetual reminders of how hard a route would be. So although you are not stopped from using an unused path, although the sign might make you feel relatively confident that you could get through (signs are directive), you might decide to find another path. The less a path is used, the less a path is used. How strange that this sentence too makes sense.

I have implied that use is an activity that leaves traces (more or less). *need to remember that affectives changes a trace, too* These traces can become outlines for something: invitations to do something, to proceed in a certain direction. However, something might appear unused while being used. A pad of paper seems crisp and empty; there are no traces of usage. We might assume the pad is unused. But it

1.10. You can hardly see the sign for the leaves.

might be that we cannot see the evidence of past use, that a pencil was used and the marks erased (we might make use of things *because* they leave less permanent traces), or that the marks left were not at the front of the pad where you would expect them to appear. Something can thus appear unused while having been used if that use did not leave traces where they usually appear. Use is a frame: not all activities appear as uses if not all uses appear.[29]

Frames of use have uses. For example, many uses of land were not counted as uses because land use in Western culture is primarily understood in terms of cultivation. The labor theory of property was also a theory of use. Indeed, John Locke's *Two Treatises of Government* makes extensive use of use and in particular of the expression "made use of." If the world is given by God in common, common as potentially of use to all, the land must still be made useful. Locke elaborates, "It cannot be supposed [the land] should always remain common and uncultivated" such that "he gave it to the use of the industrious and rational" ([1689] 1824, 149). Use is defined as cultivation. Land that has not been cultivated becomes wasteland, unused, and thus available to be appropriated. Indeed, Locke argues, the more the land is cultivated, the more value is derived from the land for the benefit of all: "He, who appropriates land to himself by his labour, does not lessen but increase the common stock of mankind" (150). Agriculture is framed not only as the use of land but as its improvement, an increase in stock. That Locke is justifying the colonial project as making better use of land is clear: he argues that a thousand acres of "the wild woods and uncultivated waste of America, left to nature, without any improvement, tillage or husbandry," would yield less to its "needy and wretched inhabitants" than "ten acres of well cultivated fertile land in Devon" (151). It is labor, Locke concludes, that "puts the greatest part of value on land," to labor "that we owe the greatest part of all of its useful products," and without that labor, the land "would be scarcely worth anything" (152). Appropriation is justified as getting the most use from what is available to use (a *most* implying here a many), as stopping what is held in common from being wasted or becoming waste. It is important to add that waste is understood by Locke as an active process of neglect, and that to waste what is one's own is to cease to have property rights. As Barbara Arneil notes, "Locke's use of neglect is important, for it implies that one can judge in the case of property which has been used by other people, whether they had in fact neglected the land and thereby made it nothing more than waste and available again for appropriation by the labour of others" (1996, 142). Locke does recognize that use can involve degradation, that having too many things can mean not making use of them before they spoil. Indeed, he supports the project of accumulation by justifying the invention of money; capitalism requires the use of a system for exchanging perishable goods.

Accumulation also refers here to the appropriation of common land. Edward Said describes how colonialism as practice made use of use: "Imperialism was the theory, colonialism the practice, of changing the uselessly occupied territories of the world into useful new versions of European metropolitan society" (1979, 28). *Colonialism is justified as using what is unused.* And use is then imposed in that justification: the colonial gesture is to rename places with names that refer back to the colonizer's territory; the requirement to use those names is to alienate the land from original inhabitants all over again.

Occupation, however violent, is narrated as taking care of things. In "Zionism from the Standpoint of Its Victims," Said writes specifically of how Palestine was appropriated by being rendered a place that needed a caretaker, a place that was unappreciated as well as unused. Said describes through close readings of Zionist narratives how Palestine is rendered "a whole territory essentially unused, unappreciated, misunderstood . . . *to be made* useful, appreciated, understandable" (1979, 31). And Said notes how to be "made useful," while a forceful utterance, remains written in the language of care. Palestine becomes "an empty and patient territory, awaiting people who show a proper care for it" (31). Brenna Bhandar explains how "the physical occupation and use of the land as the basis of ownership has been defined quite narrowly by an ideology of improvement in settler colonial contexts" (2018, 34). The narrowness of this definition of use is useful. It is clear, I think, how and why the word *useless* is a powerful tool, a way of designating some beings as being without value, a way of discarding people as well as things. The word *unused* is also a word that is deeply political, as a frame, as a technique, all the more the moment it appears to be used as mere description. You can declare something unused or ensure something becomes unused as the grounds for justifying an appropriation.

It is not simply that use makes something "mine" or "ours" but that use is understood as a particular kind of activity, a way of getting the most from things; a way of framing activity *is* an activity. Land became occupied by virtue of not recognizing those who already existed on the land as using the land; the land is occupied by being rendered unused and thus wasted. We could respond by stressing that use describes only one way of relating (to land and things). Or we could respond by showing that the restriction of use to cultivation and cultivation to ownership is how other uses disappear as ways of relating (to land and things). If the expression "ground clearing" can refer to the removal of traces of those who were here before, then paths as well as people can be *made to disappear*. What appears as an activity (use as becoming used) provides a way of framing an activity (an idea of use as being used) and can become a technique (how something is stopped from being used).

Overused

There is a certain point when using something ceases to make that thing easier to use, a moment that is "too much," when a well-used thing breaks down. At that moment, use might become overused. Snap. Even with a well-used path there can be a point—maybe under certain conditions, say it is wet and the terrain is heavy—when too much use makes the path less usable or even unusable. You would get stuck. Or a muscle that is used more might become stronger, but after a certain point that muscle might become tight and vulnerable to injury: overuse as becoming strained. Use: from stains to strains. When something is overused, we have reached a tipping point. A biography of use is a biography of tipping points. Using something might require local knowledge; to become intimate with something is to acquire a sense of how far you can go with something before you reach that point when it stops working. At some point you might have to reach a tipping point, to overuse something, to know how far you can go with something.

Something has become overused when the use of something stops it from being usable for something. The *over* relates in some way to *for*. In some cases, what something is for seems clear; *for* seems to name that clearing. We use the path to get somewhere; we use the book to read. We might call these digital uses: you use it or not; something is switched on or off. Let us think of use in terms of communication. To communicate, we make use of signs. Sometimes a sign is used to indicate a path. The message might still be clear even if the path has become overgrown. Use can also be more delicate; uses can involve differences in gradation, combinations that make use a matter of inflection. Before I return to the specific question of overuse, I want to consider what it means to think of signs as things that can be used. Let us take an exclamation point.

!

This image is not really of a thing. It is a sign. Perhaps use teaches us that a line between a sign and a thing is thin or tenuous. This sign is an exclamation point. An exclamation point is a vertical line with a point below it. An exclamation point is a form of punctuation. It is a way of ending a sentence. We need to know the usage of something to recognize what it is. Ludwig Wittgenstein thus encourages us to rethink about words in terms of their use: "the meaning of the word is its use in a language" ([1953] 1958, S 43, 20).[30] He suggests that words are as diverse as tools in a box: "Think of the tools in a tool-box: there is a hammer, pliers, a saw, a screw-driver, a rule, a glue-pot, glue, nails and screws. The functions of words are as diverse as the functions of these objects" ([1953] 1958, S 11, 6). Some tools can be used because of how they point. An arrow, for example, is a weapon consisting of a thin, straight stick with a sharp point, designed to be shot from a bow. An arrow is also a symbol with a sharp point. The sharpness of a symbol can be borrowed. What objects enable us to do (to throw something sharp in a certain direction) can be taken on by language (how we point sharply in a certain direction). We come to know what arrows mean by learning how they are used. Wittgenstein notes: "The arrow points only in the application the living being makes of it" (S 454, 132). We learn over time that the point is to follow the point of the arrow (if the point is on the left, and the stubby end on the right, the arrow means, *go left*). If we did not know how to use signs, we might end up going the wrong way. To learn is to learn how to use something: use as how we go the right way. When we learn to use a sign, we are following a convention. This means that to learn how to use something, a sign or a thing, is to exercise a prior history of use. That the arrow can point in this direction depends on other arrows, thrown before we got here, thrown forward toward something. Learning how to use words and signs is how we come to inhabit what Wittgenstein called "forms of life." He describes how when people are in agreement, they are in agreement "in the *language* they use," such that agreement "is not in opinions but in forms of life" (S 241, 88). When an agreement is in forms of life, those forms tend to disappear from view. Perhaps forms of life do not appear as forms because we are used to them, where "used to" references a time before our immersion in a world with others. A convention: how a *used to* becomes crisp, a sharp outline, a clear outline, of what to do to make sense.

To understand words as performatives, as J. L. Austin (1975) was to explore with reference to speech acts, is to consider the utility of words; how we use words to do things. We instruct, we warn, we perform: with words. When words are in use, they too might become well-worn paths, words as a route you follow to get somewhere. Use is also about how words combine. If we keep using one word with another word, the association between them becomes stronger. This strengthening of an association seems to follow the same principle as the smoothing of a path. Once an association has become strong, one word seems to follow, almost automatically, the other.[31]

When we consider the use of exclamation points, we can ask what they usually follow. An exclamation point is usually used at the end of a sentence.[32] It seems to indicate strength of feeling or an increase in volume. One understanding is that exclamation points come from the Latin for joy: "its origins are thought to be medieval, where the word *io* meaning hurray was written at the end of the sentence to indicate joy. Over time, the 'i' moved above the 'o' to form a symbol" (Seddon 2016, 37). In earlier uses, the exclamation was seen as a positive inflection expressing wonder and admiration. An exclamation point can now be used to end a sentence with an intensification of feeling, whether positive or negative. You can shout in writing, by using capitals or by using a series of exclamation points!!! An exclamation point teaches us how a line and a point can be used to express a range of feelings. In the past, exclamation points have also been described as "shriek marks." I like the idea that you can shriek in a text. Really I do!! I have often made use of exclamation points in my own academic texts—even though I know they are understood as informal or sometimes even an inappropriate way of giving emphasis. Sometimes, I feel like I am an exclamation point, as if in being I am shrieking. I will return to the use of exclamation points in diversity work in chapter 4.

In my introduction to the book, I referred to the use of underlining as a way of giving emphasis to a word. I noticed underlining because of use: I picked up a letter in the archives of the SDUK because it double underlined the word *use*. The exclamation point is also a tool we use in order to give emphasis. You emphasize what you think is more important. An exclamation point can appear without a deliberate decision: it can come out of you like a shriek. Or you can use one because you want a sentence to be heard in a certain way; an exclamation point becomes a clue, what you want someone else to pick up on.

We can begin to understand why analyzing emphasis can teach us about overuse. If you underlined all the words in a paragraph, you would no longer be emphasizing specific words. At this point we might say underlining has been overused since the point of underlining is to give emphasis. Overuse would not simply refer to how much something is used even when how much is too much. If you use exclamation points at the end of every sentence, they seem to stop working. The *Chicago Manual of Style* says the exclamation point "should be used sparingly to be effective." The word *sparing* is itself a use word: it suggests not using something too much. A spare is something held in reserve or kept for a later use. The expression "an heir and a spare" reminds us that a spare only becomes heir when we lose an heir. A spare is what we can use when other reserves have been exhausted.

Thinking about the overuse of exclamation points teaches us that finitude is not reducible to finite numbers. If we overuse exclamation points, it is not a question of having a certain number in a basket, such that each time you use one, you have one less to use. Finitude can refer instead to capacity—how much can be received before something stops being effective. Only so much emphasis can be received before an emphasis stops emphasizing, before a sign is tired out (or the receiver becomes tired out). Overuse has implications for a theory of performativity: it implies that even explicit performatives, in which "the verb names precisely the act" (Sedgwick 2003, 4), do not always succeed. An apology can cease to apologize when an apology is overused. If you are always using the word *sorry*, sorry becomes tired or worn out, which probably means that the one who receives the apology has become tired or worn out. When something is worn out, it has been degraded by use.

The overuse of exclamation points provides a different way of giving a biography of use. Earlier I suggested that use tends to smooth a passage; more use leads to more use. But here to use something more can mean something does less; use can even weaken or lessen the effect or impact of something. In the case of a sign used to indicate an increase in intensity or volume, such as an exclamation point, it seems to become less intense when it is used more.

We learn from lessening. Words seem almost the opposite of muscles. The more you use words, the floppier they become—the less precise, the less sharp. This is not necessarily true for all words. As I have already noted, associations can become stronger because of how words combine. An insult might become even sharper from being used; a history of use can be carried by a word: traveling as impact. In other cases, the more a word is used, the less impact it has. That use *can* weaken or lessen the impact of something contradicts the law of exercise, which assumes *as law* that to use is to strengthen. This contradiction needs to matter to a theory of use that is robust enough to explain different uses of use.[33]

It is not only words that can be used to contradict the law of exercise: we could return to one of my opening examples of the knife that becomes less sharp through use. Use has different effects on things. Some of the effects of use considered thus far include sharpening, blunting, loosening, smoothing, strengthening, and weakening. The effect of use is not always the point of use. If something becomes blunt as an effect of use, the effect of use can enable or compromise the action because sometimes you need to be blunt, other times not.

The times of use can be strange. Perhaps this strangeness can be part of the point. Sometimes it might seem clear what the point is. The point of a knife is to cut or the point of an exclamation point is to create intensity or to give emphasis. But the point is not always clear. To use a word so much that it has become loose does not necessarily mean that the word has ceased to be effective; it might have only ceased to be effective if the point was to be precise. Floppier words can have their uses. Even overuse might have its own uses—weakening the impact of something can be intentional. I will return to the use of overuse with reference to the word *diversity* in chapter 4. Overuse then is not simply a point you reach when things stop working. Overuse can operate as a judgment that is not shared, including by the user. The use of multiple exclamation points might be judged as overuse because the exclamation points are no longer working as they are *supposed* to work, to give emphasis or to add intensity. But the person who is using exclamation points unsparingly might be using them for reasons other than to give emphasis. The current president of the United States, Donald Trump, could be understood as overusing exclamation points in his tweets, because they (and they are usually they!!!) end almost every utterance made. But perhaps by being used in this way, exclamation points are used for other ends. These multiple exclamation points appear to be marching, rather like an army, an army of signs: operating as a kind of linguistic aggression. The greater use of signs for intensity does not always lessen their intensity; more use can even amplify intensity, like a shout that is sustained, becoming more and more piercing until it cuts the atmosphere like a knife.

We might say here that degradation by use can be purposeful. When someone is judged as overusing a sign, we mean it has ceased to be effective for a specified purpose. But that cessation can be the point of how something is used; the point can be to stop something from working as it usually works, to repurpose a tool. Overuse may still be a tipping point, a point when something stops working as it usually works, but a tipping point can be what is intended. To question use is to question whether we can know how things are working or how they are supposed to be working.

Used Up

Overuse is not simply a matter of amounts, of having a finite amount of something (energy, capacity) that has been depleted. Overuse can still imply exhaustion: we might say a word is overused *because* it has become tired and flops about. The expression "used up" also implies exhaustion but in an even stronger sense of numbers being up.

Think of toothpaste that has been all used up (figure 1.11). How we relate to an image of used-up toothpaste might tell us something about our

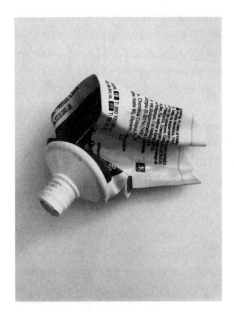

1.11. All used up.

relation to use. When I see such an image, I think: how sad, that toothpaste all curled up without anything left. You can feel like that yourself: that you have given all that you have to give and now you are just limp and wasted. You can feel like: I have spilled all my contents. The toothpaste when it has finished being useful can remind you of the feeling of being finished. This might be a case of projection, of an object being vacated by a subject putting herself in its place. But I think projection is more open to otherness than it might be assumed. To project: to throw something. Projection can show up how subjects and objects are thrown together right from the beginning.

Different people might relate to an image of used-up toothpaste quite differently. When my toothpaste is almost finished, I want to throw it away. I see its lifeless, limp body and I wince. I want a nice, new, plump body, filled with its own content, full of potential. But others might not feel like that at all. Some might want to get every last bit out of the toothpaste, and see the limpness as an invitation to get just a little bit more. For some, using up is about getting the most out of things: not wanting to give up on things until the very end. For others, using up is a reminder of how use itself can involve depletion: how to use something, to consume something, can also mean to take the life out of something.

The meaning of use might change when using means using up. Here we might sense that even to use something can be to lose something; we might be eating something and try to make it last as long as possible, and we might even feel sad before we have finished that it is nearly finished. When something has finished, it becomes waste. To use something can also be how something becomes waste, or at least parts of something, by traveling another course through a body. A body discards what is useless by consuming what is useful. The word *waste* is hard and heavy. To waste can also mean not to make use of what you have been given. When you waste time, you have not used that time well. Waste is also that which is discarded. To become waste is to be judged as not being worth being kept. Waste: to be judged as useless. I will turn to the judgment of uselessness in due course.

Perhaps when use becomes using up, it is a question of time. We all know how waste is often rendered alarming through time—to waste time as to become a waster, to waste time as to waste your life. Wasters are reminded of just how short life is. Such a judgment depends on an idea of making use, as if time is wasted unless it is used properly or used well. We might want to challenge what uses count as proper or good uses. But we could also think here of how time is shared. Perhaps you have two hours for a seminar, and there are three speakers. You each have twenty minutes, leaving time to spare for questions. If one speaker goes over time, the other speakers have less time. Inequality here becomes manifest in how much some take up time; time taken up can be time taken away from others.

Use as using up can be a matter of energy. We use a certain amount of energy from the energy that is available to use. Efficiency is determined by the following formula: *the ratio of useful work relative to the output of energy.* To consider using up is to reflect on use as a system: when efficiency is something that is valued, it becomes a value system. Marx offered one of the most powerful analyses of who pays the cost of this value system, which is at once a system for extracting value (what he called surplus value) from living bodies and machines. In chapter 15 of *Capital*, Marx attends to the role of machinery in transforming the factory. The laborer is no longer in intimate relation to a tool that he handles but becomes part of a mechanized process, henceforth losing any connection to what he is making. But Marx also attends to the significance of "wear and tear," that is, the tendency of machines to wear out, whether by use or nonuse. He notes, "The material wear and tear of a machine is of two kinds. The one arises from use, as coins wear away by circulating, the other from non-use, as a sword rusts when left in its scabbard" ([1867] 1990, 528). The point becomes to get the most use out of something before it is worn down.

The introduction of machinery might appear to be labor saving.[34] This has historically been a hope afforded to new technologies, that is, machines as reducing the time and energy necessary to accomplish a task. I return to this question of labor and muscle in my discussion of the figure of the blacksmith's arm in chapter 2. But Marx showed how the machinery *intensifies* labor and enables the extraction of greater surplus value from upping the requirements of a system. Marx cites Mr. Ashworth, who says to Professor Nassau W. Senior: when a laborer "'lays down his spade, he renders useless, for that period, a capital worth eighteen-pence. When one of our people leaves the mill, he renders useless a capital that has cost £100,000.' Only fancy! making 'useless' for a single moment, a capital that has cost £100,000!" ([1867] 1990, 529). Note that to get the most use of what is valued becomes a duty, which can be enforced by discipline on the factory floor. The worker cannot be allowed to rest because the machine cannot be left idle: such rest would amount to a theft of potential; value becomes here exhaustive of potential.

I have suggested that use can be a record of a life. To value use would not be to romanticize what is preserved as a historical record: signs of life can be signs of exhaustion, which is to say, signs of life can be signs of how a life has been extinguished. The cost of the machine becomes a capital investment that requires even greater use to be extracted from the bodies of workers in order to repay that investment and more. The extraction of use is intensified by a mediating thing. Marx argues that the machine suffers from *moral depreciation*: an immediate loss of value that may yet be compounded by further loss of value given the introduction of new and better machines. This depreciation of value takes time, which means that the extraction of value from the machine must be achieved as quickly as possible. Most equals fast, an equation with deadly consequences. Marx established the intimacy of exploitation and exhaustion: to exploit something or somebody you must exhaust their potential. A potential becomes that which must be exhausted. Amy E. Wendling describes how "from the perspective of capitalist production, value is calculated solely by the amount the machine is able to produce before wearing out. If a well-made machine wears out rapidly, it means it has produced well or been used up with the maximum amount of efficiency. Here too the machine and the worker are similar: they fulfil their function only in working themselves to exhaustion as quickly as possible" (2009, 114). When using something becomes necessary because of the cost of something, those who are using something are those who are being used, whose own labor becomes necessary to get the most out of something. Used up is thus a relationship of expenditure, in which some are required to give themselves up by giving themselves over to ends that are not their own. Being used up can be an experience of being used, becoming a means to someone else's ends. Some become used up in order to allow others to achieve their ends.

Usable/Unusable

Usability seems to reference the status of the object. We would describe the object as usable when it *can be* used (for something). Usability can be hard to picture because it tends to be assumed by virtue of the proximity or placement of something. Usability might be assumed unless there are signs indicating otherwise, such as if an object appears broken or damaged or if there was a sign indicating "out of use." So we might assume a door is usable because there is no sign indicating that it is not (figure 1.12).

An assumption of usability might affect what we do in the present: we use something because we assume it is usable. It is noteworthy that Risatti suggested "it is more accurate" that something is usable because it has been "put to use" (2007, 26). We might assume usability as possibility precedes use as actuality. But actuality can precede possibility if something becomes usable from being used. This reversal of the usual sequence matters. We are glimpsing the strange temporalities of use.

In the literature on design, usability refers not only to the fact that something can be used. It refers to a kind of communication through design: a usable object is one that gives the user more clues about how to use the object. For user-centered design, improving usability becomes the goal. Donald Norman in *The Design of Everyday Things* describes usability as a key factor in design, noting how errors tend to be viewed by users as their own fault rather than design fault ([1988] 2013, v). But he notes how a failure of design is often a failure of communication: the large and unfriendly instruction manual is an expression of a prior lack of friendliness to the user in the design of an object.[35] In the case of a well-designed object, it should be obvious *from* the object how to use it.

1.12. We might assume a
door is usable.

As is often the case, we know what it means for something to be as it
should from the failure to be as it should; we know usability from unusability, which is why I am discussing them together. One of Norman's
most used examples is the unusable or difficult-to-use door. In fact, he
used the example of the difficult-to-use door so well that such doors
have been named after him; they are called Norman doors. He asks:

> How can such a simple thing as a door be so confusing? This door would
> seem to be about as simple a device as possible. There is not much you
> can do to a door: you can open or shut it. Suppose you are in an office
> building, walking down a corridor. You come to a door. How does it
> open? Should you push or pull, on the left or the right? Maybe the
> door slides. If so, in which direction? I have seen doors that slide to
> the left, to the right, and even up into the ceiling. The design of a door
> should indicate how to work it without any need for signs, certainly
> without any need for trial and error. ([1988] 2013, 1–2)

A usable door might be one where you do not need to try to work out how it works. So we could describe our door as not usable or as difficult to use; the use of a push sign is evidence of a failure of design. Usability is not simply a property of something. Norman uses the term *affordance* to emphasize the relational nature of usability: "An affordance is a relationship between the properties of an object and the capabilities of the agent that determine just how the object could possibly be used" (11). His example is a chair: "A chair affords ('is for') support and therefore affords sitting." But a chair also needs to be lifted: "If young or relatively weak people cannot lift a chair, then for these people, the chair does not have that affordance" (11).

A chair could be unusable if it is too heavy to lift. A door too can then be unusable if it is too heavy to push or pull. It might be usable in the sense that it is obvious from the door whether you would push it or pull it without being usable in the sense that you can make use of a door by opening it to enter a room. Our door might not be as usable as it could be given the need for a push sign, but it is more unusable than it should be because it is too heavy for those in wheelchairs or for those with limited physical strength in their arms. What is usable to some is unusable to others.

In treating usability as communication, we would be thinking not only of whether it is obvious *how* to use something but *who* can use something. I noted earlier that you can be addressed by a sign on a door. *You can also be addressed by a door*. Scholars in disability studies have developed some of the most important insights into the uses of use, through exploring how the world has been designed for a body with assumed capabilities. As Aimi Hamraie describes in *Building Access*, "Examine any doorway, window, toilet, chair, or desk . . . and you will find *the outline of the body meant to use it*" (2017, 19, emphasis mine). Hamraie usefully names this outline "the normate template" (19). Intended functionality is about the creation of such outlines: *for whom something is supposed to function*. An outline is not simply an idea of who is the user. An outline is an enabling or a disenabling of somebody. If an outline of a person is intended, then those who are outlined can use something; those who are not cannot. Usability can thus be reframed as a question of accessibility: it is not just *whether* an object or environment can be used but *who* can use an object or environment *given* how it has been designed and who cannot.

I noted earlier that in the literature on design, misfitting is understood as an incentive for design; the misfit between an old thing and a function can generate a new thing. But misfitting can also be how a body does not fit the requirements. Rosemarie Garland-Thomson describes not fitting, or misfitting, as follows: "A misfit occurs when the environment does not sustain the shape and function of the body that enters it. The dynamism between body and world that produces fits or misfits comes at the spatial and temporal points of encounter between dynamic but relatively stable bodies and environments. The built and arranged space through which we navigate our lives tends to offer fits to majority bodies and create misfits with minority forms of embodiment, such as people with disabilities" (2014, n.p.).[36] You have a fit when an environment is built to accommodate you. You are a misfit when there is an incongruous relation of your body to thing or body to world.

When modifications have to be made to enable people with disabilities to be accommodated by an environment, we learn how that environment assumes a certain kind of body, an able body. In an earlier article, Garland-Thomson describes misfitting as "an incongruent relationship between two things: a square peg in a round hole" (2011, 592–93). When you try to fit a norm that is not shaped to fit your body, you create an incongruity. I have already noted that even when intentions do not exhaust possible uses of a thing, the uses of a thing are restricted by its material. There are more angles to this restriction: the use of something is restricted by virtue of how it is arranged or made. A restriction can be about who can use something, not just what something can be used for.

Talking about doors returns us to the example of the lock that works better after being used. If we turn to locks, we are led to doors. You might use the lock to lock the door, to stop the wrong people from entering. Doors are not just physical things that swing on hinges; *they are mechanisms that enable an opening and a closing*. We might assume that a door is in use when it is being opened. But if the point of a door is to close as well as to open, a locked door is in use. Indeed, when those who do not have the key cannot open the door, the door is in use. The very point of something can be to stop someone from using something. This means that a door can be in use and unusable at the same time. Indeed, if we think of how an object is also a mechanism, then the point of a door can be to be shut to some and open to others. For those without the key (and a body can be a key), a door functions as a wall: what stops your progression. If a body can be key to whether you can open a door, a door can be locked without the use of a lock. According to the Fair House Act Design Manual, usable doors should be "designed to allow passage into and within prem-

1.13. Access signs have their own biographies of use.

ises" and be "wide enough to allow passage by . . . persons in wheelchairs" (3.3)[37]. Doors that are in areas of "public and common use" are required to be accessible, and doors that are interior to dwellings are required to be usable. A manual becomes necessary to make doors more usable and accessible, to counter the history of doors that are not.

It is known that many doors are not usable to those who have mobility restrictions, such that signs are used to indicate when doors are accessible. These signs are usually, as Tanya Titchkosky describes them, a "white stick figure against a blue background," which has become a "symbol of a wheel chair user" (Titchkosky 2011, 61, figure 1.13).

Access signs have their own biographies of use. Titchkosky also notes how if you have to use a sign to indicate access, then "there must be an assumption of a general lack of access" (2011, 61). Earlier I suggested that the usability of a door might be assumed unless there is a sign indicating otherwise. For other users, the unusability of a door might be assumed unless there is a sign indicating otherwise. If a door or route into a building has to be marked as accessible, other doors or routes into a building can be assumed to be inaccessible. *A building can be built around an assumption.* Jay Timothy Dolmage (2017) explores "retro-fitting," when adjustments are made to enable buildings to become accessible, like ramps that are placed alongside stairs. The use of ramps teaches us who is given affordance by stairs. The necessity of an addition teaches us who the building was *not* built for. Those who are *not* have to fight for inclusion.

Starting with the needs of those who are not included rubs up against the very idea of inclusion. Aimi Hamraie offers an important history of the project of "building access," including a history of Universal Design. Universal Design was coined by the architect Robert Mace in 1985 in an effort to go beyond a politics that aims to eliminate barriers. Universal Design refers to "the design of products and environments to be usable by all people, to the greatest extent possible, without the need for adaptation or specialized design."[38] As Hamraie notes, experiments with product designs "that could benefit multiple types of users, including disabled users," became "testing grounds" for Universal Design (2017, 193). Hamraie explains how the lever handle became the focus of much experimentation, quoting Mace: "The front door is made easier for everyone to open by one simple change—a lever handle in place of the traditional knob" (193). Universal design is premised on the principle that making buildings more accessible makes them easier for everyone to use. But, as Hamraie notes, the problem with this approach when translated into practice is the use of "everyone," which can work to enable the needs of differently abled users to disappear.[39] Hamraie explains that "a designer unaware of the need for disability access could miss the imperative for spatial inclusion entirely" (201).

The very use of access signs demonstrates the failure to meet the principle of Universal Design (which is why Universal Design became a principle). And even the use of an access sign on a door does not always mean the door is accessible. Tanya Titchkosky gives a number of examples of how access signs are placed on inaccessible doors. She notes how the justification of these signs is often made with reference to historic use: use as past tense; use as a reason for use. She gives an example of an access sign placed on a "narrow, thick and heavy wooden door" (2011, 63). An attendant explains, "For many years this was the only way into the building for anyone who had any problems" (63). She asks, "Why hang onto a useless—no, not useless—*misleading* sign?" (63). The use of an access sign does not necessarily mean that space is accessible or usable to those with disabilities; disabled users can be directed the wrong way by the signs that are supposed to direct you the right way. Even a door with an access sign can function as a means by which some are enabled to progress; others not.

Modifications of spaces to enable their use can themselves function as historical records. Modifications can also be reorientations. Margaret Price interrogates how access signs often point disabled users somewhere else (think of the arrow; we know the point from use). As Price further describes, "This sign delivers a familiar message to wheelchair users and others who cannot use stairs: the accessible entrance is somewhere else, probably around back, and quite likely at the other end of a winding maze of pathways and passageways" (2016, 152). Those who need modifications to enable them to access spaces are directed away from the paths that are busiest, the paths where things usually happen.[40]

We can return here to my use of the well-used path. The well-used path shows us how a route can be a routine, how busy can become business. If the more-used path is where business is conducted, when you cannot use the more-used path you are removed from a business. To be directed to the back of the building might be how you end up not being in the places where decisions are made; you are being taken away from the paths that lead not just *through* but *up* the organization. What is usable is about *where* you can enter a building and *how* you can proceed along a path.

I will develop this argument about the function of the well-used path with reference to universities in chapter 4. We could also think more literally about paths as nature trails. The role of use in shaping the landscape shows how natural environments are also social environments. Alison Kafer argues that "the natural environment is also built" (2013, 138), with nature trails being a case in point: "They are mapped, cut, and maintained by human beings with tools and machinery" (139). Nature trails can be made more accessible by alterations in how they are built. Kafer discusses how some protest the building of accessible trails as being too invasive for the environment. She suggests that "the rhetoric of ecoprotection then seems to be more about the discomfort with the artifacts of access— ramps, barrier-free pathways—and the bodies that use them" (138).

An artifact is usually defined as a human-made object. And of course inaccessibility also involves artifacts, which is to say, when a path is accessible for able-bodied users, they too are using things that have been made. It might be that something is treated as artificial and unnecessary when it is not necessary for the progression of those who are assumed as the users. In other words, when things are made to enable the progression of an assumed user—who is singular, fit, upright, and able—they seem not artificial but natural.

Even paths that are made smooth by use, without the use of tools or machinery, are made.[41] Physical and social landscapes are both shaped by use. Use offers a connecting thread, a trail that crosses between worlds, showing not only *that* they are made but *how* they are made. If the path that is used more becomes smoother through use, it does not follow that everyone can use that path. In other words, a path can be used, even well used, without being usable. The smoothing of the path is also a matter of affordance; what might be smooth to some and enable the easing of a passage can be too bumpy for others. "You are making a molehill out of a mountain." We can appreciate how little that saying is saying. What seems like a molehill for some, a small bump, what hardly matters, or what should not matter, might as well be a mountain for others, as it would take a huge amount of energy to get over or to get around. If smoothness is an effect of use, smoothness does not necessarily mean the path has become more usable for all users.[42]

We can return to my analysis of being used up. If a world has not been built to accommodate you, it takes much more out of you to do the same thing compared to those who are accommodated. Opening a door, for instance, might require more of your energy if you have less strength in your arms. You can be used up by what you need to do in order to complete what might seem to be a simple task, such as entering a room, or sitting at a table, or going to the toilet. If the same task can be much more easily completed by some because they meet the requirements, use becomes used up more quickly for others.

 Simply put: the more you are attuned, the more your progression is eased. It can be wearing to inhabit a world that is not built for you. Bodies can become worn—words too, things too. Annette Kuhn describes how, as a working-class girl in a grammar school, she feels "conspicuously out of place" ([1995] 2002, 115). She describes this sense of being out of place by giving us a biography of her school uniform (another biography of use); by the time her ill-fitting uniform came to fit, it had become "shabby" and "scruffy." The well-worn garment is being used to tell another story in Kuhn's hands. Garments might be used more, becoming shabby, becoming scruffy, when they cannot be discarded because you cannot afford to keep replacing them. The word *wear* originally derives from the Germanic word for clothing. It then acquires a secondary sense of "use up, gradually damage" from the effect of continued use on clothes. It is not always the case that when something is used more, it fits better.

That a garment becomes scruffier can be a sign of how you do not fit. Use does not always smooth a passage, or enable a better fit, but can lead to corrosion and damage. This difference—between use that smooths and enables and use that corrodes and damages—could thus be understood as distributed.[43]

A Useful Assignment

In this chapter I have explored how objects can be caught at different moments of use. My task has not been to offer a history of use but to think *from* use, from how and when and where we use things, do not use things, find them useful or not. Use provides a way of philosophizing from the everyday, a way of thinking about what we are doing as we are doing it. When we say something is being shaped by use, we are also talking about *who* can use *what*, *when*, and *where*. A consideration of use allows us to show how a world can be shaped by what seems to be the smallest thing: how worlds are shaped from the bottom up.

In this chapter, the words *useful* and *useless* have come up at different moments in biographies of use. These words can be used to indicate whether something can be used: a cup is useful when it can be used to drink; a cup is useless when it cannot. The word *useful* can mean to be able to be used for a number of practical purposes as well as to be able or competent. *Useful* is an adjective with a job description. The word *useless* can mean not fulfilling an intended purpose or having no ability or skill in a specified area. *Useless* as an adjective still has a job to do even if that job is to describe a failure to do a job. As adjectives, *useful* and *useless* tend to have companions or nouns—what or who is being described. They also work effectively as *judgments* by designating the quality of something: when we apprehend something or someone as being useful or useless, that thing is given positive or negative qualities.

We can relate these different uses of *useful* and *useless* if we think of usefulness as an assignment. An assignment can be a value that has been given to something or someone. An assignment can also be a task indicating what needs to be done. A useful assignment can thus mean receiving the (positive) value of being useful from completing a task. Something can be assigned useful in advance of completing a task. Uselessness comes up when an assignment fails. A useless assignment can thus mean receiving the (negative) value of being useless from not completing a task.

Usefulness as a judgment thus tends to follow usefulness as an assignment. The negative value of not completing what has been given as a task can travel through a system. Edward Johnson notes:

> Some minute difference from the ordinary arrangement in the organization of parts is fully sufficient to account for the effect, great as it is. How exceedingly slight is the variation in the arrangement of organized parts, which is nevertheless sufficient to elevate what would otherwise have been little better than an idiot into that magnificent thing, a man of genius, is proved, I think conclusively, by observing how slight is the derangement—how minute the lesion of cerebral structure—which is sufficient to reduce the man of genius to a drivelling idiot. You make but an exceedingly slight change in the organization of a watch by removing the hands—yet this change, slight as it is, reduces a rare and most important machine to a useless bauble—and so, by an equally slight alteration made in a different direction, viz. that of adding the hands, the useless bauble becomes at once a most useful instrument of the highest importance. (1842, 194)

A slight transformation can lead to a useful instrument becoming a useless bauble (and vice versa). The whole thing is made useless. A useless part is not simply a part that is missing or broken but is that which stops the whole thing from working. Not all alterations to a thing have the effect of stopping it from working. We can sense why the judgment of uselessness is useful: it allows something or someone to be made responsible for that which is not working, for the transformation of "a useful instrument" into a "useless bauble" or "a man of genius" into an "idiot." This is why uselessness tends to be leaky; a judgment can be a leaky container, getting everywhere.

How can a judgment be leaky? Let us go back to my bag (figure 1.14). Even though my bag was scruffy from constant use, it was useful; it was full of use. But now the zipper has broken and I have left it in a corner, limp and waiting for me to fix it. We might say it has become useless for carrying things. But we do not always qualify the judgment of uselessness in our modes of description. We might not say that the bag has become useless for carrying things but rather "it is useless." Or you might say "I am useless" when you cannot do something; the very feeling of not being good enough can be overwhelming. A person might feel useless in advance of trying to do something; bodies can shake from the effort not to confirm that judgment that they will not be able to do something. That

1.14. Become useless.

shaking can be what stops someone from doing something; a judgment can be confirmed by an effort not to confirm it. Uselessness can travel through us from the fingertips where we touch a surface, shaking the core of our being.

The useless part can thus be understood as a killjoy or as willful, to use the terms from my previous works in this trilogy (Ahmed 2010, 2014). The useless part is that which is deemed to cause a breakage, to stop something from working, to prevent an action from being completed; it is what gets in the way of a progression. If uselessness is what stops the whole thing from working, eliminating uselessness can be morally justified *as the restoration of functionality*. And by eliminating uselessness, we can be referring to the elimination of those who have received the assignment. In order to make sense of where, and in whom, usefulness and uselessness are found, we need to travel back. To track the uses of use, we need to offer a genealogy, which is to say, we need to learn from how, and for whom, usefulness became an assignment. In the following two chapters, I explore the uses of use in biological and social thought as well as educational practice in the early nineteenth century. Along the way, we find out more. We find out for whom usefulness was an assignment and for whom uselessness became fatal.

[handwritten margin note: think through this more in relation to character]

2

....

The Biology of Use
and Disuse

what Ahmed's doing essentially is tracing use's web

Statements about use have histories of use. "Form follows function" is such a statement. It is a statement of use that is so well used that it can be hard to think of it as having its own history, its own story of coming into use. Of course, it has such a history. The statement was first used by the architect Louis Sullivan in 1896. We might assume that "form follows function" implies a normative commitment as a principle of design: that form *should* follow function; how a building is built *should* be determined by the function of that building. However, in making this statement, Sullivan was in fact describing what he called simply "the law," that in life, form follows function; indeed, form *ever* follows function.

> Whether it be the sweeping eagle in his flight or the open apple-blossom, the toiling work-horse, the blithe swan, the branching oak, the winding stream at its base, the drifting clouds, over all the coursing sun, form ever follows function, and this is the law. . . . It is the pervading law of all things organic and inorganic, of all things physical and metaphysical, of all things human and all things superhuman, of all true manifestations of the head, of the heart, of the soul, that life is recognizable in its expression, that form ever follows function. This is the law. (1896, 408)

The idea that form follows function is a natural law is a commitment to a principle: that use and life are entangled. Use is treated as a generative or life principle, that is, as a principle that shapes the very forms of life. We might describe such forms of life as biology. The word *biology* is used for the study for living organisms, including their structure, function, growth, evolution, distribution, identification, and taxonomy. As Sarah Franklin has noted, biology can refer to both a "body of authoritative knowledge (as in the science of reproductive biology) and a set of phenomena" (2001, 303). Biology can thus refer both to studies of living organisms and to the living organisms themselves. It is noteworthy how early studies of living organisms made use of use to explain a set of phenomena. Jean-Baptiste Lamarck, the first scholar to use the word *biology* in a scientific sense, describes the laws of use and disuse as "laws of nature which are always verified by observation" ([1809] 1914, 113).[1] This primacy is pedagogy: biology and use coevolved right from the beginning.

In this chapter, I compare how Lamarck and Darwin made use of use in their explanation of the origin of species. Why this comparison? I noted in my introduction to this book that *use* is a much-used word: if we follow the word, we would end up all over the place. But when use is used in order to explain phenomena, use is being channeled in specific directions. Comparing Lamarck and Darwin's uses of use provides a way of *zooming in*, allowing me to explore what use is doing when exercised as a conceptual tool. A comparison between Lamarck and Darwin provides a particularly effective case study of the uses of use because the differences and similarities between them have already been framed in these terms. For example, Ernst Mayr counted the number of times Darwin evokes "use and disuse" in *The Origin of Species* as a way of demonstrating the extent of Lamarck's influence on Darwin (Mayr 1972, 78).[2] That the relation between two scholars can be decided by counting the number of times one made use of the other's law of use and disuse has much to teach us. In this chapter, I consider how Lamarck and Darwin mobilized the vocabulary of use before discussing how the figure of the blacksmith's arm was used to exemplify Lamarckian principles even though Lamarck himself did not use this example. The figure of the blacksmith's arm provides a handy way of showing how and why biological and sociological thought in the early nineteenth century invested so much significance in use not only as a generative or life principle but as a method of social improvement and advancement.

The Law of Use and Disuse

In *Zoological Philosophy*, Lamarck makes a case for a functionalist approach to biology rather than what would typically be characterized as a structuralist approach. He argues, "Naturalists have remarked that the structure of animals is always in perfect adaptation to their functions, and have inferred that the shape and condition of parts have determined their use of them" ([1809] 1914, 113). Lamarck argues against any such inference. He suggests from observation that "the needs and uses of the parts that has caused the development of these same parts, which have even given birth to them when they did not exist, and which have consequently given rise to the development of these same parts" (113). A need and use for a part not only shapes a part but can bring it into existence. I call this principle as it is articulated in relation to designed objects "for is before."

What Lamarck presents first as an observation provides the basis of a law, what he calls the law of use and disuse: "*In every animal which has not passed the limit of its development, a more frequent and continuous use of any organ gradually strengthens, develops and enlarges that organ, and gives it a power proportional to the length of time it has been so used; while the permanent disuse of any organ imperceptibly weakens and deteriorates it, and progressively diminishes its functional capacity, until it finally disappears*" (113). The laws condense some of the arguments discussed in chapter 1 about how using something strengthens it (here "something" refers to an organ), and how the disuse of something can lead to its weakening and eventual disappearance. Lamarck's thesis is explicitly framed in terms of time; use refers to the length of time being used. And time is related to power: the more time something is used, the more power it acquires; the less time something is used, the less power it retains. Power is time in proportion. To make use of a part is to take time: use as strengthening and preserving; disuse as weakening and withering.

It is important to note that Lamarck's first law about the effects of use and disuse was not introduced by Lamarck. He himself observed that "the law of the effects of exercise on life has been grasped for a long time by observers attentive to the phenomena of organization" (cited in Burkhardt [1977] 1995, 166). The law of exercise simply suggests that the more something is done, the better it is done, or the more an association is made, the stronger it becomes. Note here how the law of exercise is referred to as central to the "phenomena of organisation," such that use and disuse can be understood as organizational principles.

Lamarck's law of use and disuse is presented as empirical observation: what can be grasped from attention to the organization of life. Use and disuse are also used to explain how individual organisms gradually come to take their shape over long periods of time; such shaping by use and disuse is not easily perceptible from the vantage point of the present. The second law is that of use inheritance. Simply put, Lamarck argues that the effects of use and disuse are inherited by future generations if certain reproductive conditions are met: "*All the acquisitions or losses wrought by nature on individuals, through the influence of the environment in which their race has long been placed, and hence through the influence of the predominant use or permanent disuse of any organ; all these are preserved by reproduction to the new individuals which arise, provided that the acquired modifications are common to both sexes, or at least to the individuals which produce the young*" ([1809] 1914, 113). Use inheritance is the inheritance of form acquired as a result of repeated use. Use and disuse are themselves understood as *acquired modifications* that can be transmitted over time, which is how use and disuse come to shape not only individual being but species being.

It is important to note that for Lamarck, use and disuse are *effects*, however much they affect the structure of organisms. "Form follows function" thus describes only one aspect of Lamarck's thesis; even if function is given precedence over form, function comes after or even follows the environment. By "following" here we would be concerned with *influence*. Lamarck describes the influence of the environment on the habits and activities of animals, and the influence of habits and activities of animals on their organization and structure. Use and disuse are thus framed as "habits and activities." I have described use as the building block of habit, the "small steps" that take us in a certain direction. Habit is defined by Lamarck as "*second nature*" ([1809] 1914, 114). When use is repeated, becoming a pattern, use becomes second nature.

For Lamarck, habit is shaped by habitat. And habitats are dynamic. This means that for Lamarck, use and disuse are not first principles; that is, they do not start the endless process of modification, which is evident from the letter of the law: "*hence* through the influence of the predominant use or permanent disuse of any organ" ([1809] 1914, 113, emphasis mine). Use and disuse are how animals are, as it were, under the influence; they could be described as how organisms receive a message from the environment in the form of needs. It is important to Lamarck's argument that the environment's effect on structure is not direct: "Whatever the environment may do it does not work any direct modification whatever in the shape and organisation of animals" (107). In other words, he is not suggesting that the environment causes in an efficient manner changes to biological structure.[3]

I would suggest that Lamarck makes use of use in order to make sense of how modifications are achieved *indirectly*. Even if the environment does not directly modify the structure of organisms, the environment is decisive because it shapes what an organism *needs* in order to survive. Lamarck writes, "New needs which establish the necessity for some part really bring about the existence of that part" ([1809] 1914, 108). I do not think there is a claim here that a need for something is an efficient cause; it might be more useful to understand the claim with reference to what Aristotle called a final cause.[4] Although Lamarck is primarily discussing use as activity or employment (*emploi*), his emphasis on needs (*besoin*) could also be understood as referring to use in another sense.[5] The English word *use* can be used as an idiom to refer to need (to have a use for something as a need of something), which means in English we can use the same word (*use*) to refer to need and to employment.[6] By emphasizing need, Lamarck is making another use of use. Simply put: for Lamarck, a part is used more *because* there is more of a use for it; use as employment follows use as need.

So already we have two levels in which use is understood as generative: use as an activity that modifies an organism (a modification that can be inherited) and use as directing activities in this way or that (use as a requirement). It is the environment that makes certain activities necessary for survival, which is to say, which determines what would be more or less useful for organisms to do and to have. If the use and disuse of parts shape the form of organisms, use and disuse are shaped by what would be useful or not useful *given* an environment. It is given this given that use and disuse are themselves not given, in advance, as it were.

Use in both the senses of need and employment is thus an effect more than a cause, or an effect that becomes a cause: an emergence might be triggered by a state of emergency (for example, by a change from an existing habitat or migration to a different habitat) in which something that is necessary does not yet exist. *Use is a way of showing how what is necessary is contingent.* Simply put: it is because environments are dynamic and changing that organisms need to be dynamic and changing. Indeed, the emphasis in his description is how environmental change requires alterations in activities: "Great alterations in the environment of animals lead to great alterations in their needs, and these alterations in their needs necessarily lead to others in their activities" ([1809] 1914, 107). The environment is put in the position of the subject who is doing things (in an earlier sentence, Lamarck describes how "*it* produces in course of time corresponding modification in the shape and organisation of animals"). Once a new habit is formed, habit shapes form: "If a new environment, which has become permanent for some race of animals, induces new habits in these animals, that is to say, leads them to new activities which have become habitual, the result will be the use of some one part in preference to some other part, and in some cases the total disuse of some part no longer necessary" (108). For Lamarck, use is how a body receives *and* how it acts: a body receives the influence of an environment in the requirement to act in a certain way, to make use of some parts more than others. This "making use" is transformative.

One of Lamarck's most famous examples is that of the giraffe's long neck. I return to the status of this example in the third section of this chapter. Lamarck suggests that the giraffe's neck becomes longer over time as an effect of the sustained effort to reach the higher foliage that the giraffe needs to reach (122). This is not a question of willing what is necessary.[7] It is question of the *effects* of doing what is necessary to survive. Use is both how an organism receives a message from the environment about what it needs as well as how an organism is directed to act in particular ways. We can bring these arguments together: *reception is direction.* Indeed, lengthening would be understood as how effort shapes form in the sense of giving direction: "Efforts in a given direction, when they are long sustained or habitually made by certain parts of a living body, for the satisfaction of needs established by nature or environment, cause an enlargement of the parts and the acquisition of a size and shape that they would never have obtained, *if these efforts had not become the normal activities of the animal exerting them*" (Lamarck [1809] 1914, 123, emphasis mine). When an effort becomes normal, a form is acquired. When a form is acquired, less effort is needed.

In the previous chapter, I contrasted a used and an unused path, suggesting that the use can smooth and ease a passage. When a path is used more, it is easier to follow. The well-used path provides a pictorial snapshot of the *longue durée* described by Lamarck. Behavior can be understood as a path, a route that is being followed. The incentive to create new paths, *to do what does not come naturally*, derives from the pressures of environmental change. Gradually, over time, a path becomes easier, which is to say, the effort required is lessened. This lessening *is* the acquisition

2.1. A longer neck.

of form. A form such as a longer neck is a well-used path, *an effect of use that eases use* (figure 2.1).

The implication of Lamarck's argument is that changes in behavior triggered by environmental changes precede changes in form. Stephen Jay Gould argued that it was this aspect of Lamarck's thesis that should be understood as his "primary contribution" (1985, 36). Gould also suggests that the lag between behavioral change and formal change accounts for some of the "oddest" and most "curious" of animal inventions. Gould's examples include flamingos that dwell in hypersaline lakes: "Few creatures can tolerate the unusual environments of these saline deserts" (24). The flamingos have an unusual way of feeding "with their heads upside down" (25). This "flip flop" is described as "complete and comprehensive" not only in form but also in motion (32). The action is also described as "topsy-turvy" (32). Gould concludes that a "peculiar reversal in behavior has engendered a complex inversion of form" (32).

Such curious reversals and complex inversions offer another lens with which to explore the queerness of biology. Scholars not only have explored queer biology by finding evidence of homosexual pairings in the animal world or by pointing to organisms that can change sex or to nonsexual forms of reproduction but have also shown how these forms of diversity can attune us to other forms of social complexity and creativity (Bagemihl 1999; Roughgarden 2004).[8] We can follow their lead by using queer biology to refer to what Gould calls a "peculiar reversal in behavior" and a "complex inversion of form." The word *inversion* was used in the nineteenth century to describe homosexual attachments: in the language of sexology, the inverts felt internally that they were the "opposite sex." The word *invert* was used because it implied being *turned* in the wrong direction. We can pick up on the old meanings of that word, just as we can pick up on the old meanings of queer. An inversion can teach us about how the right direction is achieved or how the upright becomes the right way up.[9] In order to survive in an unusual environment, the flamingo's beak ends up the wrong way up. An implication of such curious cases might be that usual orientations or even a sense of there being a "right way up" are effects of habits; straight or upright become second nature in time.

Something becomes queer, odd, noticeable, or curious when it reverses how things exist usually or by challenging how things are expected to be. When something has become usual, the unusual is striking. It is not surprising that the queerness of biology is brought out by attending to uses of use. After all, adaptation could itself be described as a process of fitting (*adapt* comes from Latin, *adaptāre*, to fit or adjust), which means *not fitting* acquires originary status (in the sense that not fitting is what requires adaption). In chapter 1, I discussed how not fitting is understood as an incentive to design new objects. In biology, not fitting is given a similar role as "an impetus to change," to borrow Gould's terms. He elaborates, "An organism enters a new environment with its old form suited to other styles of life. The behavioral innovation establishes a discordance between new function and inherited form—an impetus to change" (1985, 36–37). A discord is temporal, between past and present as well as being a discord between form and function. If organisms and environments are always changing, they are not changing at the same time. *The nonsimultaneity of change is how biology and time become queer at the same time.* The queerness of biology, the existence of curious reversals and inverted forms, can be exposed through the queering of time, the nonaccordance of past and present. We can draw on Elizabeth Freeman's (2010) work on queer temporality as "temporal drag." Forms could be thought of as "temporal drag"; the visceral pull of a past is evidenced by how they drag behind functions, a dragging that is expressed queerly in "imperfections and odd solutions cobbled together from parts on hand" (Gould 1985, 37).

this sort of coincides with what I was thinking about as attunement as productive discomfort

If norms *become* forms in time, then norms are not *always* forms. Organisms become more attuned to their environment over time, which means nonattunement—not fitting the requirements—is a necessary part of a struggle for existence. I noted in chapter 1 how attunement can reduce the effort required to complete a task. Attunement can also mean the reduction of the effort to do what is necessary to survive. The implication of use inheritance is that a reduction of effort is transmitted *as form*, which means that organisms, by inheriting a history, are *inheriting an effort*. I return in chapter 4 to the implications of this argument for an understanding of social inheritance.

how?

does attunement clarify our perception?

Usefulness and Selection

Lamarck certainly implied that use can be a reason for existence: a use for something can bring it about. Charles Darwin seemed to deviate from Lamarck because of the implication he heard that organisms can bring about what they need.[10] Richard Burkhardt's *The Spirit of System* refers to the following sentence by Lamarck: "The forces brought into being by a newly felt need will necessarily give rise to the proper organ for satisfying this new need if the organ does not exist already." Burkhardt notes, "In his copy of the second edition of Lamarck's *Histoire naturelle*, Charles Darwin responded to Lamarck's claim by jotting on the page where the claim appeared: 'Because use improves an organ, wishing for it, or its use, produces it!!! oh'" ([1977] 1995, 178).

It is interesting how Darwin parts company from Lamarck on the specific question of use. And we can pause here with the punctuation, that is, with Darwin's own use of three exclamation points.

!!!

In the previous chapter, I explored how exclamation points are used in order to give emphasis, or to give more intensity to an expression. When exclamations are overused, they might cease to function as they are supposed to. One could consider how a history of use can be expressed as a series of exclamation points. That Darwin makes use of three exclamation points has something to teach us about how he judged the book he was reading. The jot is available to read by virtue of digital reproduction; we cannot see the inscription (it is too faint to be reproduced), but we can read the translation (figures 2.2, 2.3).

loi par l'observation je ne conserve aucun doute sur le fondement que je lui attribue, la nécessité de son existence étant entraînée par celle de la troisième loi qui est maintenant très prouvée.

Je conçois, par exemple, qu'un *mollusque gastéropode* qui, en se traînant, éprouve le besoin de palper les corps qui sont devant lui, fait des efforts pour toucher ces corps avec quelques-uns des points antérieurs de sa tête, et y envoie à tout moment des masses de fluides nerveux, ainsi que d'autres liquides; je conçois, dis-je, qu'il doit résulter de ces affluences réitérées vers les points en question, qu'elles étendront peu à peu les nerfs qui aboutissent à ces points. Or, comme dans les mêmes circonstances, d'autres fluides de l'animal affluent aussi, dans les mêmes lieux et surtout parmi eux, des fluides nourriciers, il doit s'ensuivre que deux ou quatre tentacules naîtront et se formeront insensiblement, dans ces circonstances, sur des points dont il s'agit. C'est sans doute ce qui est arrivé à toutes les races de *gastéropodes*, à qui des besoins ont fait prendre l'habitude de palper les corps avec des parties de leur tête.

Mais, s'il se trouve, parmi les *gastéropodes*, des races qui, par les circonstances qui concernent leur manière d'être et de vivre, n'éprouvent point de semblables besoins; alors leur tête reste privée de tentacules; elle a même peu de saillie, peu d'apparence; et c'est effectivement ce qui a lieu à l'égard des *bullées*, des *bules*, des *oscabrions*, etc.

Sans m'arrêter à des applications particulières, pour faire apercevoir le fondement de cette deuxième loi, application que je pourrais multiplier considérablement, je me bornerai à la soumettre à la méditation de ceux qui suivent attentivement les procédés de la nature à l'égard des phénomènes de l'organisation animale.

2.2. Darwin's copy of Lamarck's *Historie Naturelle*, 157. Courtesy of Biodiversity Heritage Library.

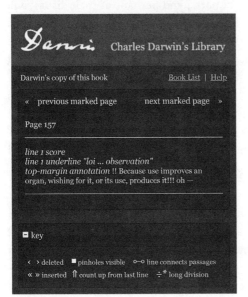

2.3. A disagreement with Lamarck's use of use. Courtesy of Biodiversity Heritage Library.

One thinks of the erasure of use as part of the history of use: the faint marks that might gradually disappear; traces left behind by a user whose own value means the trace is of value. Digital reproduction can allow us to keep track of what otherwise might have faded from memory as well as from view. We might think again of used books and how they matter as recorders of a history. A message scrawled in the margin by Darwin, which was a scrawling *about* use as well as a sign *of* use, teaches us about how Darwin distanced himself not only from Lamarck but from Lamarck's use of use. A used book, as I explored in chapter 1, can tell us many stories. The traces left behind of Darwin's reading of Lamarck, the rather scornful utterance that shows how he read him, offers another trail in our short history of use.

A widely held (but not universally agreed) view that Darwin became progressively more Lamarckian over his career was in part due to the increasing use of use in the revised editions of *The Origin of Species*, as well as in the stronger claims made in *The Descent of Man*, which not only made use of Lamarck's first law but also the second; he stated explicitly that the effects of use and disuse are "probably inherited."[11] We can consider Darwin's own use of use in the first instance by considering how he employed Lamarck's law in relation to his thesis of natural selection. Take the following quote:

> We should keep in mind, as I have before insisted, that the inherited effects of the increased use of parts, and perhaps of their disuse, will be strengthened by natural selection. For all spontaneous variations in the right direction will thus be preserved; as will those individuals which inherit in the highest degree the effects of the increased and beneficial use of any part. How much to attribute in each particular case to the effects of use, and how much to natural selection, it seems impossible to decide. . . . I may give another instance of a structure which apparently owes its origin exclusively to use or habit. The extremity of the tail in some American monkeys has been converted into a wonderfully perfect prehensile organ, and serves as a fifth hand. ([1859] 2009, 188)

In this combination of sentences, Darwin offers the law of use and disuse and natural selection as two differing explanations of biological form. One is not presented as true, and the other false; rather, each is offered as a limited or partial explanation of more or less the same phenomena. Darwin notes, "When a variation is of the slightest use to any being, *we cannot tell* how much to attribute to the accumulative action of natural selection, and how much to the definite action of the conditions of life" ([1859] 2009, 107, emphasis mine). This inability to tell how much a variation that is of use is due to natural selection is telling. In both quotes, attribute is not a noun but a verb: some things (variations) can be attributed more or less to conditions of life, which include the effects of use and disuse, or natural selection. What is interesting here is the implied *combination* of effects, as a combination that will cohere differently in different parts. The effects of use and disuse are "strengthened" by natural selection because spontaneous variations in the right direction will be preserved. In his later book *The Descent of Man*, Darwin describes natural selection as "aided" by the effects of use and disuse: "Natural selection would probably have been greatly aided by the inherited effects of the increased or diminished use of the different parts of the body" ([1871] 1992, 39). So while natural selection and the law of use and disuse are often represented as competing theories, it is important to note that at least some of Darwin's own description implies their status as companion theories: natural selection and the law of use and disuse support each other, because they explain how things end up going in more or less the same direction.

Comparing Lamarck and Darwin might lead us to assume that natural selection as an alternative thesis to the law of use and disuse does not make use of use. But natural selection could be understood to offer an *alternative thesis of use*. The law of use and disuse and natural selection could be described as offering different approaches to the relation of use, variation, and time. For Darwin, variations in the structure of organisms are not explained as an effect of environmental changes. Rather, variations are "spontaneous," or a matter of "chance," though both these terms are treated with caution (for a discussion, see C. Johnson 2015). So for Darwin it is not that a part comes to exist because it would be of use but that a part that happens to exist that would be of use is more likely to be preserved. Even if Lamarck and Darwin explain variation differently, both understand use as a *mode of directionality.* For Lamarck, an organism is directed by its own patterns of use that are made necessary by the environment. For Darwin, spontaneous variations in the right direction will be preserved, whereby the rightness of the direction is a matter of what *happens* to be useful in the struggle for existence.

Darwin's reflections on domestication give us more insight into his uses of use. He writes that "the key is man's power of *accumulative selection*: *nature gives* successive variations; man adds them up in certain directions *useful to him.* In this sense he may be said to make for himself useful breeds" ([1859] 2009, 22, emphasis mine). Darwin made use of the word *selection* in *natural selection* because of its use in animal breeding: the term that was already in use was *methodical selection.* Darwin sometimes refers to domestication as "artificial selection." Natural selection strengthens the effects of use and disuse because it preserves the parts that are more useful to an organism. In domestication or methodical selection, humans take the place of nature by doing the selecting; they breed the animals that have the characteristics that would make the animals more useful to them (and not to the animals themselves). Even if domestication is modeled on natural selection, usefulness is determined as a different kind of relation. Humans select what is useful *to them*; nature selects what is useful *to the organism.* The "to" in "useful to" is redirected away from the organism and toward another organism that is making use of it (instrumentality here could be understood as a *technique of redirection*[12]). The organism is directed in order to create "useful breeds," that is, breeds that will be useful to humans in their own struggle of existence. Human beings do not create something from nothing: rather, they have a hand in it, the "breeder's hand." They direct how organisms come to be from selecting the variations that are advantageous to them. Darwin describes, however, the artificial selection of useful breeds as an inferior activity to that of natural selection, "Natural Selection . . . is a power incessantly ready for action, and is as immeasurably superior to man's feeble efforts, as the works of Nature are to those of Art" (49). Natural selection and methodical or artificial selection both rest, however, on what Sarah Franklin has usefully called "biological plasticity" (2007, 43; 2013, 51). As she describes: "The analogy of the breeder's hand so important to Darwin's account of biological plasticity has been considerably extended in the form of animal populations bred and manipulated as models of what this plasticity can be made to do—that is, how it can be differently managed and disciplined" (2013, 51). Plasticity, the capacity of organisms to receive an influence, is instrumentalized. I return to how selection can function as a technical apparatus in the following chapters.

As we have noted for Darwin, a part does not come into existence because it would be useful. The relation of "what is of use" to "what is" is still rather and perhaps rather strangely intimate: the implication is that nothing comes to be without having been of use at some point in time. One section of chapter 6 of *The Origin of Species* is called "Utilitarian Doctrine, How Far True; Beauty, How Far Acquired." This section is written in response to naturalists who challenge "the utilitarian doctrine that every detail of structure has been produced for the good of its possessor" ([1859] 2009, 159). The challenges emphasize the role either of beauty or of the Creator in determining structures; Darwin cautions that both challenges would be "fatal" for his theory if they were found to be true. His defense is a utilitarian case: "Natural selection will never produce in a being any structure more injurious than beneficial to that being, for natural selection acts solely by and for the good of each" (162–63).[13] Insofar as what is useful is what is preserved, then biological structures themselves can be treated as "useful archives": what is selected was useful at one point or another in the biological life of a species such that each body carries traces of past uses. Use becomes an accumulated somatic history, a history of qualities that are acquired over time, even if what is of use now might be different from what was of use before.

The Origin of Species thus gives considerable time to the existence of useless, rudimentary, or vestigial parts, parts for which the organism has no obvious use in the present, parts that are of no obvious benefit. One of Darwin's examples was the small eyes of a blind mole: the eyes remain even though the mole no longer uses them, but they have dwindled or diminished; perhaps they are on their way to ceasing to be. The small eyes of a blind mole are an example of a vestigial part of a body that persists despite no longer being in or of use. The appendix and the tonsils are obvious human examples, although there are some who argue that these organs that have apparently become useless do have a function.[14] Vestigial organs allow us to witness what I have been describing as the strange temporalities of use; that a part can still exist even if there is no use for it implies that use can be *out of time* with a body. What is no longer of use can linger or leave traces as parts of an organism. Such parts are often referred to as *leftovers*.

I noted in the previous section how attending to use can expose queerness of time as well as biology. We can consider how a body is the site of such an exposure; a part can take time to disappear after it has ceased to be of use. Thinking about useless parts might allow us to explore the queerness of use in another way. Darwin writes:

> I presume that lowness here means that the several parts of the organisation have been but little specialised for particular functions; and as long as the same part has to perform diversified work, we can perhaps see why it should remain variable, that is, why natural selection *should not*

have preserved or rejected each little deviation of form so carefully as when the part has to serve for some one special purpose. In the same way that a knife which has to cut all sorts of things may be of almost any shape; whilst a tool for some particular purpose must be of some particular shape. Natural selection, it should never be forgotten, can act solely through and for the advantage of each being. Rudimentary parts, as it is generally admitted, are apt to be highly variable. . . . *Their variability seems to result from their uselessness,* and consequently from natural selection having had no power to check deviations in their structure. ([1859] 2009, 118–19, emphasis mine)

Darwin makes use of a used object in giving an account of the emergence of life. Objects can be used to tell stories about all manner of subjects. James made use of a lock and a key to show how repeated use or habituation leads to the overcoming of material resistance; Darwin makes use of a knife to address how more variability is enabled when something is less specialized. Knives themselves can be used to tell different stories about use; they can become blunt from use, as I noted in chapter 1. Darwin is making a different point by making use of a knife. The point is not whether it is sharp or blunt but that a knife is released from the requirement to be a particular shape when it is intended to cut "all sorts of things." If variable forms are enabled by a diversity of uses, *then specialization can be understood as the stabilization as well as restriction of form.* Indeed, returning to my discussion of Leroi-Gourhan's example of the chair that fits more bodies by fitting each body less perfectly, we could argue that advancement is understood by Darwin as the gradual loss of functional as well as biological plasticity: each part is *stabilized* by becoming more *specialized* for a particular purpose.[15] However, natural selection also depends on variability; natural selection is indifferent toward those parts that are not useful, and those parts tend to be variable. I return to the queer implications of this connection between variability and uselessness in my conclusion to this book. Suffice to say here the suggestion that uselessness enables variability makes queer a motor of history, *a freedom to deviate as a freedom from function.* To be useful is to be more subject to *checks* carried out here not by agents but by an invisible force, although one thinks of how a breeder's hand can function as a checking force.

If what would be useful changes, then an organism too must change, otherwise it would expend energy on retaining that which would not be profitable or advantageous. Darwin describes how "natural selection is continually trying to economize every part of the organization. If under changed conditions of life a structure, before useful, becomes less useful, its diminution will be favoured, for it will profit the individual not to have its nutriment wasted in building up an useless structure" ([1859] 2009, 117–18). This model of natural selection as an "economiser" might be how and why Marx understood Darwin to be an "apologist for industrial capitalism" despite the extent to which Marx modeled his own social history on Darwin's natural history, as Sarah Franklin has persuasively demonstrated (2013, 13). We can ask how the argument that the most useful is what is selected differs from Lucretius's example of the cup designed for usefulness's sake, mentioned in the previous chapter. Lucretius's philosophical poem demonstrated how building a theory of life from the example of designed objects leads to the mistaken fallacy that nature operates on design principles. Darwin also dismisses the idea that something is shaped for or by use, an idea that is sometimes called "finalism" as well as creationism.[16] But despite this, Darwin does in fact make use of the metaphor of the architect in describing the mechanism of natural selection. Surely this very metaphor risks the implication of nature as design? Darwin was aware of these risks (for a discussion, see C. Johnson 2015, 124–25). In the second volume of *The Variation of Animals and Plants under Domestication*, Darwin offers an interesting adoption of the architect metaphor that clarifies how he understands the relation between use and contingency. He notes:

> Throughout this chapter and elsewhere I have spoken of selection as the paramount power, yet its action absolutely depends on what we in our ignorance call spontaneous or accidental variability. Let an architect be compelled to build an edifice with uncut stones, fallen from a precipice. The shape of each fragment may be called accidental; yet the shape of each has been determined by the force of gravity, the nature of the rock, and the slope of the precipice,—events and circumstances, all of which depend on natural laws; but there is no relation between these laws and the purpose for which each fragment is used by the builder. In the same manner the variations of each creature are determined by fixed and immutable laws; but these bear no relation to the living structure which is slowly built up through the power of selection, whether this be natural or artificial selection. . . . The shape of the fragments of stone at the base of our precipice may be called accidental, but this is not strictly correct; for the shape of each depends

on a long sequence of events, all obeying natural laws; on the nature of the rock, on the lines of deposition or cleavage, on the form of the mountain which depends on its upheaval and subsequent denudation, and lastly on the storm or earthquake which threw down the fragments. *But in regard to the use to which the fragments may be put, their shape may be strictly said to be accidental.* (1868, 248–49, emphasis mine)

We have in this quote a fascinating account of use. An architect is usually a designer and not a builder. But Darwin compels the architect to build, to make use of stones without cutting them in order to fit a design (the way a cup may be designed "for usefulness's sake" to borrow again from Lucretius's poem). The stones are thrown up, or available, according to natural laws. Determination is here a combination of events that makes things available as things to use, or even that makes some things useful for specific purposes. But use itself is described as accidental. These stones were not made in order to be used. Stones become useful to the architect *once he has begun building*: this fragment fits here, that one there; because of the shape they have, these stones happen to meet the requirements of a building that is being built. But even if they are chosen with reference to their physical properties or material qualities, which have been acquired in accordance with natural law, they were not designed to fit. *You are more likely to use a stone that happens to fit that space.* The architect is here, by analogy, natural selection: natural selection selects that which is most useful from what happens to exist. If what is selected is what would be useful, to select is to use or to put to use ("in regard to the use to which [they] may be put"). The moment of use is hap: use as happenstance; use, even, as happy. I return to the implications of Darwin's happy use of the architect metaphor in chapter 4.

I opened this chapter by nothing that the well-used expression "form follows function" came from architecture but was articulated as a law of life. The traffic between architecture and biology goes in both directions.[17] Stephen Jay Gould and Richard Lewontin introduce the concept of *spandrels* from architecture to explain biological structures. They describe spandrels as follows: "Every fan-vaulted ceiling must have a series of open spaces along the midline of the vault, where the sides of the fans intersect between the pillars. *Since the spaces must exist, they are often used for ingenious ornamental effect*" (1979, 582). They argue that spandrels are a consequence of a structural design, created because of how fans and pillars intersect. For Gould and Lewontin, spandrels demonstrate that use can be secondary: "a necessary by-product of fan vaulting; their appropriate use is a secondary effect" (582). They conclude, "The immediate utility of an organic structure often says nothing at all about the reason for its being" (583). In Darwin's use of the architect metaphor, even if what is selected is dependent on what would be useful given the requirements, what is built is still in accordance with what is of use; while for Gould and Lewontin, a use can be what is acquired after a structure has been built.

In this much-cited article, Gould and Lewontin are in fact calling for a return to Darwin *and* a more pluralistic account of the origin of species; in other words, a pluralistic model is understood as Darwin's legacy. As I have noted, Darwin tends to position Lamarck's law of use and disuse as a companion model to natural selection despite how he distances himself from Lamarck's use of use. This means that for Darwin, natural selection is not offered as the only mechanism to explain the origin of species. Perhaps we can think of pluralism as a *pluralism of use.* If we put these different uses of use together, they would show how use can go all the way down because use can matter at any moment of time. Use can shape what is (use as past tense); use can explain how something is selected from what is (use in the present tense); and use can be what is possible given what is (use as future tense). Use might have strange temporalities because use is how time *comes to matter.*

*[handwritten margin note: this is int. *(and also int. to think about in relation to uses of criticism)]*

The Blacksmith's Arm

Most of the examples used by Darwin and Lamarck in developing their approaches to use refer to the parts of nonhuman animals. Indeed, in *Zoological Philosophy*, Lamarck's main reference to humans in exemplifying his first law of use and disuse is to diet and its effects on the size of stomachs.[18] However, a human example that is often referred to as Lamarckian is the blacksmith's strong arm. This arm has been used to illustrate both of Lamarck's laws: that what is used will be strengthened in proportion to time spent; and that the effects of repeated use will be inherited by future generations. The argument is an argument about paternity as well as generation: the sons of the blacksmith will inherit stronger arms. The strong arm becomes another well-used path, use as a direction taken that is enabled by past use, an enabling that is inherited; sons inherits the efforts of their fathers by being born with stronger arms (figure 2.4).

The blacksmith's arm is in fact so well used as an example of the effects of use that it has achieved a somewhat iconic status. Indeed, considering

2.4. A stronger arm.

how the blacksmith's arm has been used as an example has much to teach us about the role of use in shaping fields of knowledge. Examples could be thought of as having their own "biographies of use." An example can be used as evidence *of* something. Examples can also be used as guides to help readers, by giving flesh to what might otherwise remain abstract or obscure principles. Some examples are used more than others—they are given more work to do, perhaps because they are more affective as well as effective; some examples might be remembered more easily than others.

When examples catch or become catchy, they can distract readers from the principles they are intended to exemplify. This was indeed Steven Jay Gould's concern about Lamarck's examples. Gould notes, "Every classical example—from eyeless moles, to webbed feet of water birds, to long legs of shore birds, to the blacksmith's strong right arm—ranks as a lateral deviation, not a stage on the main sequence" (2002, 188). He thus encourages readers not to overstate the significance of specific examples to Lamarck's overall argument. Gould was particularly concerned that Lamarck's example of the giraffe's long neck had become distracting. Gould even describes Lamarck's use of the giraffe's long neck as a "throwaway example" (305), implying that the giraffe's long neck not only has assumed too much importance but should be disregarded by careful readers. I suspect Gould describes the use of the giraffe's long neck as overuse because that example has often been used to dismiss or mischaracterize Lamarck's argument as implying voluntarism, that a part of the body can be lengthened at will or by will.

But what then did Gould have to say about the blacksmith's arm? It is here that something curious seems to have happened. In *Eight Little Piggies: Reflections in Natural History*, Gould refers to "the blacksmith's big right arm" as Lamarck's "Amanaesque metaphor" (1993, 216). When Gould discusses Aldous Huxley's *On Our Knowledge of the Causes of the Phenomena of Organic Nature*, he discusses how Huxley does not make use of the giraffe but rather the blacksmith's strong right arm as one of the two examples "emphasized by the Frenchman himself" (1999, 306). The example of the giraffe's long neck is used only once by Lamarck. However, the blacksmith's arm is not used by Lamarck at all. Lamarck does not use the example that Gould implies he emphasized. This is particularly curious given that Gould criticizes how the example of the long neck of the giraffe has been overused. His preoccupation with how the giraffe's long neck has been stretched as an example seems to have something to do with how he did not notice that Lamarck does not use the example of the blacksmith's arm at all. It is possible (given how much Gould was influenced by Darwin) that Gould was following Darwin's own emphasis. It was Darwin who used the blacksmith's arm as an example of Lamarck's law of use and disuse, which is another fascinating footnote in how use came to matter in framing the relation between Lamarck and Darwin.[19]

It is also important to note that the blacksmith's arm was widely employed throughout the nineteenth century to demonstrate the first of Lamarck's principles—the law of exercise—without reference to Lamarck. In one educational treatise, the blacksmith's arm is evoked because that is the arm that is usually evoked: "The blacksmith's arm is the standing illustration: it is said that the young lad who lifts with difficulty the sledge the first day soon finds his arm growing strong by use, and his muscles taking on the might of the steel he forges" (Yocum 1876, 545). This is an interesting instance of the principle explored of how more use can lead to more use; and by this I am referring not only to the effects of use on an arm but to *the use of the arm as an example of the effects of use*. An example is used because it has been used ("a standing illustration"). The blacksmith's arm could be considered a much-used or even overused object in the sense that it is being used as a figure to do a certain kind of work *whether or not the arm appears.*

Perhaps it is because the blacksmith's arm is assumed to be there that it is not noticed that the arm is missing. We could even understand Lamarck's blacksmith's arm as a phantom limb.[20] A phantom limb would typically be understood as a limb that is felt to be there after a real limb has been lost. The blacksmith's arm is not a phantom limb in this sense: the arm was not cut off. The blacksmith's arm operates as a phantom in the sense that the use of the arm covers over not only the absence of the arm but that the arm was never there. We can treat the absence of a reference to the blacksmith's arm in Lamarck as a teachable moment; we learn how *what is missing comes to matter.* The history of the use of the blacksmith's arm is a history of an impression of an arm being there. As I noted in chapter 1, the law of exercise as articulated by the psychologist Edward Thorndike suggests that an association becomes stronger through use. I also discussed how use leaves impressions with the example of the impress or indent left behind on a chair after somebody gets up.[21] The blacksmith's arm is an impression in the sense that it creates the effect of a body having been there. When an impression is shared, it becomes stronger or more distinct.

What is used most can be mostly missing. To notice that the blacksmith's arm is missing from the corpus of Lamarck's work is to learn how what is missing can still become material. In *Bodies That Matter*, Judith Butler offers a powerful exploration of the temporality of matter.[22] Butler defines matter as a "process of materialization that stabilizes over time to produce the effect of boundary, fixity, and surface we call matter" (1993, 9). Butler's approach to materialization as a process creating the effect of matter is helpful in considering the status of the blacksmith's arm. *The arm materializes as an effect of how it has been used to exemplify the effects of use.* Butler references Aristotle's discussion of matter (*materia* and *hyle*) as potentiality. She notes, "The Greek *hyle* is wood that already has been cut from trees, instrumentalized and instrumentalizable, artifactual, *on the way to being put to use*" (31–32, emphasis mine). The blacksmith's arm provides material in the sense that the arm is "on the way to being put to use." References are material; they involve a "putting to use." When the arm is constantly referred to, the references are *becoming substantial.* The references to the arm become the arm, fleshy things: a materiality created as impression, a materiality that is missing something. We could draw too upon Butler's (1990) arguments about gender as imitation to make sense of the use of the figure of the blacksmith's arm. Butler suggests that to perform gender is to become a copy without an original. It is not that behind the copy/reference is an original but that the copy/reference creates the impression of an original. An arm became Lamarckian without being used by Lamarck.

The arm is a phantom limb not only in the sense that it is missing from the corpus of Lamarck's work. A blacksmith's strong arm still matters or even becomes matter despite its absence because it has been exercised to do certain kinds of work. Noticing that the arm is missing allows us to ask *what the arm is doing*; the blacksmith's arm is called into existence by being called upon to work. Others before me have asked similar questions about the use of the blacksmith's arm. Archibald MacLaren in *MacMillan's Magazine* notes:

> In illustration of this, I would but point to the familiar example so frequently adduced when the value of exercise in the acquisition of strength is asserted—the Blacksmith's arm. Why is the Blacksmith's arm more powerful than that of the Clerk who uses his pen, of the Artist who handles his pencil, of the Tailor who plies his needle, or of the hand-loom Weaver who drives his shuttle? On account of the greater amount of exercise to which it is subject. Just so; but, if mere movement constituted exercise, the arms of the Clerk, Artist, Tailor, and Weaver ought also to be powerful, which we know they are not. In the wielding of their instruments their muscles have encountered comparatively no resistance, whereas the muscles of the Blacksmith's arm have had to resist the weight of a 20-lb. hammer every time they whirled it aloft; they had to arrest it in its upward flight, and to make it descend to the anvil with a speed quadruple that attending the law of gravitation. (1861, 36)

According to MacLaren, reflecting on the law of exercise, the blacksmith's arm comes to matter because of the strength required to work with the tools necessary for the task; the hammer is heavier than a pen or needle. The heaviness of the tool also relates to the hardness of the material that is being worked upon: metal rather than, say, cloth or paper. What is heavier and harder is more resistant; more force is required to work with what is more resistant to transformation. The blacksmith's arm comes to stand not only for physical or manual labor but for *how* that labor shapes or impresses upon a body. A body becomes attuned to the requirements of a job, when an arm is *becoming stronger*. It is noteworthy that the word *job*, suggesting "something to be done" or a "task, piece of work," is a word of uncertain origin. It is understood by some to be a variant of *gobbe*, or "mass, lump," via the sense of "a cartload." A job carries this implication forward, of heavy work. If hammering metal is a necessary part of a job, given how someone is employed, a stronger arm is *acquired as well as required*. The blacksmith's arm was thus widely used as evidence of the law of exercise, which is why it might be assumed that Lamarck used this example in making this law his first law.

When we consider how the blacksmith's strong arm is used to support Lamarck's second law about use inheritance, we can deepen our understanding of why the arm has been usefully employed. If the sons of the blacksmiths are born with stronger arms, the implication is that they have received before birth what they would need to complete the work better or more easily; the strong arm lessens what the blacksmiths' sons would need to survive or thrive within an environment. But here, through the use of this example, the environment becomes a job description: the implication being that a stronger arm would lessen the effort required by a blacksmith to do his work. The strong arm is not only how a work load is eased *but how a work load is acquired*. *For* becomes an inheritance. *For as before* is translated here into a gender and class fatalism. Fatalism can be represented as the straight line of genealogy: sons will become their fathers; they will follow in their footsteps. A description (they have strong arms) becomes a prediction (they will have strong arms) and also a command (they must have strong arms). Genealogy could be understood as a technique for straightening things out: the sons in having stronger arms are already on the way to becoming their fathers.

In receiving an expectation, the blacksmiths' sons might indeed acquire what they are assumed to possess: stronger arms. An effect becomes a cause. So it is not just the references to the blacksmith's arm that have become substantial. An arm too is required to *become substantial*. For the blacksmith's son to inherit the effects of use is *to inherit a work load*. In having stronger arms, the blacksmith's son is already equipped to become a blacksmith; his arm has a hand in deciding his future. The requirement to make use of the arm, to become a blacksmith, can thus function as a recovery mechanism: a strong arm, created as an effect of use, covers over an absence. If the blacksmith's strong arm can be understood as a phantom limb, what is received is *an idea of direction*, an idea that is all the more powerful as the body can be shaped by receiving that idea. If in becoming a blacksmith a strong arm is acquired, what is reproduced is an idea of inheritance.

If in this chapter I have primarily considered different *ideas of use*, I am now exploring the *uses of an idea*. Use inheritance is used to suggest that individuals receive at birth what is necessary for them to fulfill their station in life: *reception as direction*. Use inheritance is thus translated into a requirement to reproduce an inheritance. We need to ask: what else is being reproduced by such a requirement? The blacksmith's arm matters as a way of figuring not just the effects of use and disuse on organic life but the improvement of humanity. Herbert Spencer's work on use inheritance as a biological principle becomes a way of understanding how society develops as an organism. In the following quote the blacksmith's arm appears alongside other examples.

> As surely as a blacksmith's arm grows large, and the skin of a laborer's hand thick; as surely as the eye tends to become long-sighted in the sailor, and short-sighted in the student; as surely as the blind attain a more delicate sense of touch; as surely as a clerk acquires rapidity in writing and calculation; as surely as the musician learns to detect an error of a semitone amidst what seems to others a very babel of sounds; as surely as a passion grows by indulgence and diminishes when restrained; as surely as a disregarded conscience becomes inert, and one that is obeyed active; as surely as there is any efficacy in educational culture, or any meaning in such terms in habit, custom, practice; so surely must the human faculties be moulded into complete fitness for the social state; so surely must the things we call evil and immorality disappear; so surely must man become perfect. (1851, 65)

Here the blacksmith's arm appears first in a series of images, which appear as rather striking, as poses of confidence. Each person modifies their faculties by using their faculties: that the blacksmith's arm grows larger is part of the story of the perfectibility of humanity as such. The acquisition of greater skill, we must note, is directive for each subject in this list, as they exercise their faculties in accordance with their role in the social state. The eyes of the student and the eyes of the sailor are adjusted by the very nature of what they do: this is what Spencer means by "habit, custom, practice."

Use here is understood as a measure of social progress because use is strictly limited. Use increases power in accordance with function: an arm that grows stronger from being used allows the blacksmith to function would this also be about becoming more attuned?

better *as* a blacksmith. We can note as well how use is tied to best: to use one's faculties more is to become better at something, with betterment understood as a molding, as being shaped by function. Two uses of use operated alongside each other: an organ or limb is used by a person, such that it becomes stronger and better; a person becomes better at fulfilling their function because of the strengthening of an organ and limb. Intended functionality can be used to refer to uses of the body: parts of the body are used in order that a body can carry out a function *for which it is assumed it was intended*. The blacksmith in acquiring a stronger arm from the inherited effects of use becomes the arm of industry.

This adaption to function is understood by Spencer as a form of social as well as biological advancement.[23] How individuals become more adapted to their specific function within social organisations is likened to how different organs of a physical body become specialized.[24] Reginia Gagnier has usefully described Spencer's thesis as "the biologization of Progress" (2000, 98). As Spencer elaborates: "differences of function, and consequent differences of structure, at first feebly marked, slight in degree, and few in kind, become, as organization progresses, definite and numerous; and in proportion as they do this the requirements are better met" (1871, 597). Spencer makes use of Lamarck's first law to suggest that each part to be strengthened must be used, and that the strengthening of the part would enable the whole body to perform better: "Each limb, viscus, gland, or other member of an animal, is developed by exercise—by actively discharging the duties which the body at large requires of it; and similarly, any class of labourers or artisans, any manufacturing centre, or any official agency, *begins to enlarge when the community devolves on it more work*" ([1860] 1981, 413, emphasis mine). The idea that use increases capacity is used to justify workers being given "more work." The more work they are given, the more the whole body is enlarged.

If using something is understood to enable progress and refinement, then what is refined is not only an individual capacity to fulfill a function but an existing system for allocating functions. We can call this system by its name: industrial capitalism. And it is clear that when Spencer refers to "the social organism" and "the physiological division of labour" he is referring to capitalism. He describe capital as the blood that "facilitates the processes of nutrition" ([1860] 1981, 418). He also refers to large-scale manufacturing industries such as cotton, iron, and wool not only as the producers of commodities but as the sources of *nutrients* to the physical body (412–13). Indeed Spencer describes profit as the means by which the body is replenished and repaired: "what in commercial affairs we call *profit*, answers to the excess of nutrition over waste in the living body" (413). In other words, economic growth is understood by Spencer as biological repair. Wear and tear (to the worker's body or to the machines of industry) must be overcome in order to keep the system working.

Spencer's model of social improvement seemed to imply that all members of a society must make more use of their relevant faculties. But the task of improving humanity is made especially dependent on increasing the productivity of workers. The blacksmith's arm keeps appearing, or is given priority, as it takes up this task. In an anonymously written article from 1918, the task of improving humanity is made technical. The article begins by asking, "Did you ever watch a blacksmith at work, forging a horseshoe or some other object of wrought iron? With the tongs he draws the glowing metal from the bed of fire in the forge, and resting it upon the anvil he begins to hammer it into shape. His powerful arm turns, bends and twists to bring the hot metal into just the right position."[25] Here the "powerful arm" is in company with other objects of use: the hammer, the tongs, the forge, the anvil. These objects have a family resemblance and they work together to create another useful object: the horseshoe. The powerful arm is not the only agent in the story; it is not the only element in how things end up going in the right direction. This short description helps us deepen or thicken our account of the combination of energies and resources that enable an object to become available for use.

But the article then proceeds by suggesting that the blacksmith's arm is not powerful enough to deal with the heaviness of materials in big steel works: "A blacksmith's arm has not the strength to handle such prodigious weight." For this reason, "human ingenuity" has invented a machine. An image included with the article shows us this invention. The machine is presented as the blacksmith's arm, as extending his power and reach. The introduction of machinery to enable the increase of labor power is here narrated as the extension of the body of the laborer. The demand for him to be usefully employed is the demand for new ways for him to become the powerful arm of industry. The extraction of labor power is how use and disuse become principles of engineering.

The blacksmith's arm could be understood then not only as a phantom limb, that comes to matter, but as technology; the blacksmith's arm is a prosthetic. The blacksmith's arm becomes a living tool, teaching us how, in Sarah Franklin's (2013) terms, technology is biologized.[26] And the figure of the blacksmith's arm is used in order to tell the story of industrial capitalism as a story of refinement and progression—not only of bodies becoming fitter, more attuned to job requirements, but of the creation of machines that extend what bodies can do. To simplify, the blacksmith's arm was overused to tell a story of exploitation *as* a story of improvement. Challenging that story is made possible by recalling other effects of use: indeed, historical materialism made such a challenge by using use to do a different kind of work. Arlie Hochschild makes specific reference to the arm: "The factory boy's arm functioned like a piece of machinery used to produce wallpaper. His employer, regarding that arm as an instrument, claimed control over its speed and motions. In this situation, what was the relation between the boy's arm and his mind? Was his arm in any meaningful sense his *own*?" ([1983] 2003, 7; see also Zandy 2004). The laboring arm becomes not only stronger and more muscular from the requirements of work but also worn down or worn out. An arm becomes a piece of machinery to be used: use as being used; use as used up.

I noted in the previous chapter how Marx explores the history of technologies not as labor-saving devices but as systems of expenditure and exhaustion. It is living bodies that are exhausted by what they are required to do with things, with materials such as paper, metal, and cotton, in order for those things to become commodities, to create surplus value. And the materials themselves allow us to make connections between how lives are used and used up. We can think, for example, of how cotton traveled to factories in the North of England from the slave plantations in the American South. Marx notes, "As the export of cotton became of vital interest to these states, the over-working of the negro and sometimes the *using up of his life* in 7 years of labour became a factor in a calculated and calculating system" ([1867] 1990, 345, emphasis mine). The connection between slave labor and wage labor is material in many senses of material: the transformation of cotton from raw material into commodity depends on the exploitation of slave labor in the plantation as well as wage labor in the factories.

Marx is describing here the interests of the United States in *exporting* cotton. The materials that arrive at the factory to be turned into commodities are not only imported; they are already commodities that have been extracted or stolen from the lives of the enslaved. Cotton was required for the growth of the manufacturing industries and the acquisition of capitalist wealth; in other words, British manufacturing was dependent on slave labor, as Marx did recognize. Sven Beckert points out that British cotton manufacturing was "the first major industry in human history that lacked locally procured raw materials" (2014, 85). The history of cotton shows us how we cannot understand capitalism without reference to colonialism and slavery; the expansion of this industry depended on "slaves in the Southern United States growing cotton on land expropriated from Native Americans" (85). The necessity of slave labor and of expropriation of land from native peoples to the expansion of capitalism requires us to understand capitalism as "racial capitalism," to use Cedric J. Robinson's term. In *Black Marxism*, Robinson notes, "The British trade movement firmly seats slavery in the movement from mercantile to industrial capitalism" ([1984] 2000, 116). Marx's own descriptions of the using up of the lives of slaves need to be understood as continuous with his more frequent and familiar descriptions of the exploitation of workers in factories in the North of England. As George Shulman describes with reference to Saidiya Hartman's *Scenes of Subjection* (2002), the slave becomes "an empty vessel to be occupied, enjoyed, and used up" (2016, 35). A history of being used up is the history of racial capitalism: a history of those who are worn down, worn out; depletion *as* the extraction of surplus value or profit.

A history of the requirement to be useful is also a history of exhaustion. Use becomes for some a form of biological destiny as well as bodily depletion. What we learn from this history of use is that the idea that usefulness resides somewhere—in an arm or a body and thus also in a system—is directly related to use as being used up or overused. Race and class work together to create a set of expectations of who will be useful for what, of what some bodies are *for* or how some bodies become *for*, of who and what becomes available as resources to be used up.

The extraction of use from bodies by defining others as bodies to be used was justified as a mission to improve humanity: to become arm is to become body, to offer brawn or brute strength; *to become arm as to become biological*. A history of arms that are used, overused arms, including arms that are missing, that have been lost in service to the industrial machine, is a history of how some are used to benefit others. It is not simply that laborers are assumed to acquire stronger arms, arms that can do more because they do "do" more, but that others are *freed from that requirement*. Manual labor becomes distinguished from mental labor, a distributed distinction, a distinction that is distributed between persons and things, such that making use of mental faculties came to be understood as dependent on relative freedom from biological necessity. The blacksmith's arm was usefully employed as a means of extracting that freedom.

The Unused Arm

The figure of the blacksmith's arm is used to tell a story of progress and advancement as the increasing refinement of the division of labor; workers become more attuned to the system by increasing their productivity and strength as workers. The figure of the blacksmith's arm also helps us understand the relation between disuse, diminishment, and degeneracy. Henry Edward Crampton's *The Doctrine of Evolution* also refers to the blacksmith's arm but then turns to the question of disuse.

> Then there are the variations of a second class, more complex in nature than the direct effects of environment,—namely, the functional results of use and disuse. A blacksmith uses his arm muscles more constantly than do most other men, and his prolonged exercise leads to an increase of his muscular capacity. All of the several organic systems are capable of considerable development by judicious exercise, as every one knows. If the functional modifications through use were unreal, then the routine of the gymnasium and the schoolroom would leave the body and the mind as they were before. Furthermore, we are all familiar with the opposite effects of disuse. Paralysis of an arm results in the cessation of its growth. When a fall has injured the muscles and nerves of a child's limb, that structure may fail to keep pace with the growth of the other parts of the body as a result of its disuse. These are simple examples of a wide range of phenomena exhibited everywhere by animals and even by the human organism, demonstrating the plasticity of the organic mechanism and its modification by functional primary factors of variation. (1912, 112–13)

Crampton makes use of the blacksmith's arm as it is usually used: as evidence of the law of exercise. But he then notes the "opposite effects" of disuse: that when an arm has paralysis, it suffers a "cessation of its growth." We can also see this coupling of inactivity or disuse and cessation in the following statement: "*Inactivity is destruction throughout the universe of things. The human body as a whole, or as to any one part, is no exception to that boundless law. The unused arm dwindles to skin and bone; the unused lungs soon weaken, then rot away*" (Hall 1869, 224). When something stops being used, the implication is that it ceases to be. This is how use becomes an expression of a commitment to life.

The figure of the unused arm is rather striking. *Willful Subjects* (2014) began with another striking arm that appears in a Grimm story. In the story, a child disobeys her mother and is allowed to die. Her death is punishment for her willfulness. But her arm keeps coming up from the grave until it too is beaten down. The arm in the Grimm story inherits willfulness from a child; it keeps coming up despite the death of the body of which it is a part. Once I caught sight of the willful arm, arms had my attention; the book itself became a call to arms. And perhaps it was because arms had my attention that I was rather struck by the use of the blacksmith's arm and that I noticed that the arm was missing. Even if the willful arm and the unused arm appear very differently—one full of life and vitality, the other emptied of life and dwindling—they both can have deadly consequences. Arms that are too active, too alive, and arms that are too inactive, not alive enough, are called upon; they work as death threats, signaling that the consequence of not obeying the instruction to work would be deadly.

It is important then to think about how unused arms are used, what they are being asked to do.[27] Scott Nearing and Nellie M. S. Nearing's *Woman and Social Progress*, published in 1912, makes use of the figure of the unused arm.

> It is true of any animal that disuse means decay; the arm, held rigid for a year, would prove an indifferent member; this is equally true of any other faculty. Disuse involves decay,—physical, mental, spiritual.
>
> The powers of the will,—the positive forces of the individual which make up character,—are no exception to this rule. The man who idles becomes an idler; the women who make no effort become colorless. Like the unused arm, they degenerate through lack of functioning. (1912, 145)

The arm stands out or stands up in becoming rigid. The arm becomes an indifferent member of the body when it is not used; the failure to contribute to the whole body becomes the loss of the capacity to make a contribution. Not to function would be to cease to be functional. In exercising the figure of the unused arm, the text evokes both the promise of utility and the risk of degeneration. *What would stop an organ or a body from working is not working.* What would make an organ or body work is work. I return to how employment becomes a duty in the next chapter. We might note as well how the will becomes what must work to generate the character of an individual: if the unused arm is an indifferent member of an individual body, an unwilling individual would become an indifferent member of the social body.

So disuse becomes degeneracy when something is not being used that is *supposed* to be used. It is this "supposed to" that renders useful a morally weighted term even when it appears to be neutral or at least just a matter of what happens, like the stone that happens to be useful because it fits the space in a wall. We are back to how the blacksmith's arm appears in the form of an assumption and is given the form of an assumption. The strength of the arm becomes a measuring stick for the improvement of humanity because this arm is supposed to be laboring for that improvement. Disuse becomes degeneracy *when something that is assumed to be for is not being used for what it is for*. I noted in chapter 1 how an unused path reveals a paradox: for something to be usable, it must be used. An arm becomes the path for the laborer; you must follow the right path by keeping the arm in use, by strengthening the arm. The unused arm becomes a symbol of waste but also of death: the laborers who do not make use of their arms, who do not lend their hands to the master, cannot be supported without compromising the health of the social body.

Eugenics made such a profound use of use given how disuse was associated with death. Eugenics was first coined as a term by Francis Galton in 1883, deriving from "well born." Galton was Charles Darwin's cousin. One suspects this kinship story matters. Galton presented a paper on eugenics to the newly formed Sociological Society on May 16, 1904; the lecture was chaired by his student Karl Pearson, who became the first chair of eugenics at London University. This is another kinship story, a story of inheritance. I return to the significance of how eugenics was housed and inherited by London University in chapter 4. Both Galton and Pearson were committed to concepts of hard inheritance; indeed, Pearson was explicitly anti-Lamarckian, arguing against the inheritance of acquired characteristics. In coining the term *eugenics*, Galton was advocating for the improvement of humanity. He wrote, "The aim of eugenics is to bring as many influences as can be reasonably employed, to cause the useful classes in the community to contribute *more* than their proportion to the next generation" (1904, 1). Eugenics became a system for ensuring that the more useful are reproduced more.

It is not accidental (and I will return to the question of what is at stake in my use of accidental) that Spencer's commitment to utility as progress also led him in a eugenicist direction. He wrote, "Besides an habitual neglect of the fact that the quality of a society is physically lowered by the artificial preservation of its feeblest members, there is a habitual neglect of the fact that the quality of a society is lowered morally and intellectually, by the artificial preservation of those who are least able to take care of themselves" (1873, 606). Indeed, Spencer suggests that unworthiness ought to be deadly: "For if the unworthy are helped to increase, by shielding them from that mortality which their unworthiness would naturally entail, the effect is to produce, generation after generation, a greater unworthiness" (606). Spencer suggests that disuse would or should gradually lead to diminishment and death: "From diminished use of self-conserving faculties, already deficient, there must result, in posterity, the smaller amounts of self-conserving faculties" (606). Certain classes of people are assumed as unable or unwilling to use their faculties, and as such, Spencer argues, by the law of use and disuse, *they should cease to be*. The link made between disuse and unworthiness is fatal. In following these links, we are accounting for fatalities, even when we challenge how they were understood to be caused.

To track how eugenics made use of use would enable us to explore not how eugenics was an extreme position that can be held apart from wider social thought but how eugenicist ideas were widely diffused and disseminated: another history of use. Eugenicist ideas were *in use* in both senses I described in the previous chapter; they had currency and were in circulation, including within writing that might be understood as socially progressive. For example, Scott and Nellie M. S. Nearing's call for the education of women not only made use of use but also used the language of eugenics. They argued that middle-class and white women should make use of their faculties (that these women should not be allowed to dwindle like unused arms) so they could improve the race through making better reproductive choices. The call to make use of use was also about the dangers of uselessness spreading.

We can return here to how the laws of use and disuse were used to exemplify the success of social reproduction: the workers by working, by using their arms, shape the bodies of future workers. The danger in eugenicist writing is typically framed through reproduction—that useless parts would be too reproductive, thus spreading their uselessness throughout the whole social body. This reproductive success is explained as brought about by artificial means: the useless have been stopped from disappearing by the use of medicine and welfare. In Darwin's later writings (probably as a result of the influence of Galton—whom he cites—on his own work), this eugenicist impulse is also explicit. Darwin writes:

With savages, the weak in body or mind are soon eliminated; and those that survive commonly exhibit a vigorous state of health. We civilised men, on the other hand, do our utmost to check the process of elimination; we build asylums for the imbecile, the maimed, and the sick; we institute poor-laws; and our medical men exert their utmost skill to save the life of every one to the last moment. There is reason to believe that vaccination has preserved thousands, who from a weak constitution would formerly have succumbed to small-pox. Thus the weak members of civilised societies propagate their kind. No one who has attended to the breeding of domestic animals will doubt that this must be highly injurious to the race of man. It is surprising how soon a want of care, or care wrongly directed, leads to the degeneration of a domestic race; but excepting in the case of man itself, hardly any one is so ignorant as to allow his worst animals to breed. ([1871] 1992, 161)

It is still important today to challenge such an account of the history of poor laws. I will be referencing the inhumanity and cruelty of the poor laws in the following chapter; the very techniques that are represented here as checking "the process of elimination" led to elimination or the extraction of utility from death. Although Darwin does not argue for the elimination of the weak, the conclusions are stark: the reproduction of the weak (with weakness being defined, at least here, as constitutional) would weaken the species.

In order not to degenerate, a hand is called forth: the eugenicist hand as the breeder's hand; the strong must reproduce more. H. G. Wells's *Anticipations of the Reaction of Mechanical and Scientific Progress upon Human Life and Thought* also makes such a call to hands. This text frequently refers to the idea of the "social body," and how much the improvement of humanity requires the improvement of all its parts. It also frequently refers to "the abyss," a mass of unemployed people who are deemed useless and not worthy of being reproduced. Uselessness can be a deadly assignment. For Wells argues that the abyss can infect the whole body: "It has become apparent that whole masses of human population are, as a whole, inferior in their claim upon the future" and that their "characteristic weaknesses are contagious and detrimental in the civilizing fabric, and that their range of incapacity tempts and demoralises the strong" (1901, 314). Wells concludes, "To give them equality is to sink to their level, to protect and cherish them is to be swamped in their fecundity." The strong, according to Wells, need to select the strong by avoiding a politics of charity and equality that would artificially enable the weak to flourish. It is not just that what is selected is what is useful but that selection becomes a moral obligation of those already valued as strong: the "new republic" will be shaped by the procreation of "what is fine and efficient and beautiful in humanity" (314). The new ethics will "let die" a "multitude of contemptible and silly creatures, fear-driven and helpless and useless, unhappy or hatefully happy in the midst of squalid dishonour, feeble, ugly, inefficient, born of unrestrained lusts, and increasing and multiplying through sheer incontinence and stupidity" (323). Wells calls explicitly for the "euthanasia of the weak and sensual"(332).[28]

Use and uselessness (and their cousins efficiency and inefficiency) appear here as one value system among others such as happiness and unhappiness, beauty and ugliness, reason and sensuality. What matters is how they become attached to each other. I noted in *The Promise of Happiness* (2010) how the wretched have a history—how the history of happiness needs to be rewritten from the point of view of the wretch, of those deemed unhappy or, to use Wells's morbid terms, if happy, hatefully so. The language of utility, even if less binding or affective than happiness, is directive. Utility might be all the more directive for appearing all the less affective.

We can note that usefulness, unlike happiness, is not defined as a quality of the elite, those who have a power to enforce an assumption of being "the best part." Those who are designated useless are (mostly) those who are required to be useful, the laboring population. We have behind us strong critiques of the judgment of uselessness. We could take as an example Simone de Beauvoir's play *The Useless Mouths* ([1945] 2011). In their introduction to the play, Liz Stanley and Catherine Naji note, "The play deals with the ethical consequences of treating some persons as worthless and useless" (2011, 11). One thinks back to Pascal's useless foot that had forgotten it was part of the body. Here mouths are useless because of what they require from a body, to be nourished. There is a siege and people are starving. Beauvoir shows how ethical indifference toward, and violence against, those who need to be fed to survive is enabled by understanding that need as a deprivation of what should belong to others (to deprive others of something that is theirs to use). Tactics for demonizing others as useless turn violence into a moral right until a death of a population can be willed as the common good.

Useful is what some must become in order to avoid the consequences of being judged useless. In the following chapter, I consider how usefulness *interesting — I wonder, then, how recognition and use coincide?*

thus becomes a moral duty that required the full employment of the worker's limbs. We need to remember how the language of use, in biology as well as psychology, is the language of strength: to use something is understood as to make it stronger. The judgment of uselessness is brought to a eugenic conclusion, a conclusion that those who are weaker should be eliminated, in one way or another, by positive or negative means, a conclusion that was not necessary or inevitable but was not entirely accidental. Or perhaps we might say, following Darwin, that if its use was accidental, it still followed laws of determination in having become available to be used for this purpose.

3

....

Use as Technique

"*Active youths, when treated as cyphers, will generally show their consequence by exercising themselves in mischief.* I am convinced, by experience, that it is practicable for teachers to acquire a proper *dominion* over the minds of the youth under their care, by directing those active spirits to good purposes. This liveliness should never be repressed *but directed to useful ends*" (Lancaster [1803] 1807, 32, third emphasis mine). This statement from Joseph Lancaster, who introduced monitorial schools for working-class children in England in the early nineteenth century, has much to teach us about how use became a technique. For Lancaster, education was about directing or channeling the liveliness of the child toward what he called simply "useful ends." To direct the child toward useful ends is to redirect the child away from mischief without repressing the active spirits of the child. Lancaster's approach rested on a widely held view of the child as plastic and impressionable, capable of receiving an influence. Indeed, the child came to figure qualities—plasticity, impressionability—that were assumed to be gradually lost in time as an effect of use. If an effect of use is to shape and to mold, use becomes a cause: a way of directing subjects toward useful ends before they lose the capacity to receive an influence.[1]

In the previous chapter, I explored how the law of use and disuse informed biological and sociological approaches to the evolution of life and to the shaping of organic bodies. In this chapter, I explore the development of techniques intended to influence how bodies take shape. I consider use not simply as an idea with a history but as an apparatus, a series of technologies that worked together for specified ends. This chapter builds on Michel Foucault's important work on disciplinary power. Foucault defines disciplines in terms of the relation of docility and utility: "These methods, which make possible the meticulous control of the operations of the body, which assured the constant subjection of its forces and imposed upon them a relation of docility-utility, might be called 'disciplines'" (1977, 137). The dash between docility and utility abbreviates a history. When disciplining is about maximizing the uses that can be extracted from a given body, obedience is extraction. As Foucault describes, "In the correct use of the body, which makes possible a correct use of time, nothing must remain idle or useless: everything must be called upon to form the support of the act required" (152). Nothing must remain idle or useless: we can hear from the "must" the status of this speech act as prescription. Use becomes a technique that is exhaustive of the fullness of a subject's potential; correct use is when nothing is left idle. Use becomes a command as well as a threat: if to be idle or useless is not to support what is being accomplished, then to be idle or useless is not to be supported.

Foucault, of course, famously draws on the utilitarian philosopher Jeremy Bentham (and for some Bentham scholars, this "famously" would probably be replaced by "infamously") in elaborating the utility-docility relation.[2] Foucault makes use of Bentham's writings on the Panopticon to develop his model of how power is architecture: a way of organizing space as a series, a way of ensuring the prisoner is always seeable without always being seen such that the prisoner takes on the gaze of the prison guard by seeing himself. It is curious that Foucault in *Discipline and Punish* does not refer to Bentham's treatise "Chrestomathia," which also makes use of the panoptical principle among other principles in its design of a classroom. In this text, Bentham offers a plan for a school organized around a utility principle and modeled on the monitorial schools introduced by Andrew Bell and Joseph Lancaster. The absence of a reference is curious because Foucault himself discusses mutual improvement schools, which are also called monitorial schools, and Lancaster's method, which I will be considering at length in this chapter. Foucault describes monitorial schools thus:

From the seventeenth century to the introduction, at the beginning of the nineteenth, of the Lancaster method, the complex clockwork of the mutual improvement school was built up cog by cog: first the oldest pupils were entrusted with tasks involving simple supervision, then of checking work, then of teaching; in the end, all the time of all the pupils was occupied either with teaching or with being taught. The school became a machine for learning, in which each pupil, each level and each moment, if correctly combined, were permanently utilized in the general process of teaching. One of the great advocates of the mutual improvement schools gives us some idea of this progress: "In a school of 360 children, the master who would like to instruct each pupil in turn for a session of three hours would not be able to give half a minute to each. By the new method, each of the 360 pupils writes, reads or counts for two and a half hours." (1977, 165)[3]

The mutual improvement school is used here to demonstrate how education becomes like a machine: a way of combining forces, such that each student becomes a cog in the machine, working effectively together to maximize utility. The history of this school system can be understood as a history of machinery (as Foucault puts it, built up "cog by cog"). Bentham understood his own project "Chrestomathia," which was first published in 1816, as transforming the model of teaching and learning introduced by monitorial schools into a system of knowledge.

It is here that we can take the analysis in another direction, traveling in a direction that Foucault did not.[4] Monitorial schools were in fact a significant part of the history of education not only in Europe but also in the colonies. The educationalists understood to have invented the method are Andrew Bell and Joseph Lancaster. Bell was appointed by the East India Company as director of the Madras School for Eurasian Orphans of Soldiers in 1787. Lancaster's schools were primarily in working-class areas of London; he opened his first school on Borough Road in 1798. Monitorial schools thus embody a meeting point between colonial policy and domestic policy. As Alan Richardson notes, "The disciplining of England's colonial subjects and the internal colonization of its unruly 'industrial classes'—these twin problems inspired a single method or approach" (1994, 97). Twin problems: a history of usefulness as a requirement is also a history of uselessness as a designation, a history of the problem of who became the problem. In this chapter, I explore how use offered an educational and political technique by considering the history of monitorial schools with specific attention to the works of Joseph Lancaster, Andrew Bell, and Jeremy Bentham. I will focus on the significance of the figure of the monitor, the student or pupil who teaches the other students. The use of the monitor has much to teach us about the sociality of use: how use works through affectivity, through sympathy with others, and how sympathy itself can be repurposed as tool.

The Diffusion of Useful Knowledge

Useful knowledge could be described, in the first instance, as a project of diffusing knowledge. James Burns in his history of the transformation of polite learning into useful knowledge describes how "diffusion . . . remains at the heart of the enterprise. Whether by education, by publication, by exhibition and demonstration, by lectures, or by any other suitable means that might seem appropriate, what was known could not be truly useful unless it was widely known—available in principle at least to all" (1986). The suggestion is not that useful knowledge replaces polite learning but that useful knowledge is knowledge that should be available to many, if not all, while polite learning would remain available to an elite few. The idea of diffusing useful knowledge required new means for spreading that knowledge, "suitable means that might be appropriate," to use Burns's terms.

The *means* come to matter all the more when there is resistance to the *ends*. The efforts to expand education beyond the elite did indeed meet with considerable resistance from the elite. We might refer, for example, to the Parochial Schools Bill put forward by Samuel Whitbread in 1807. The proposal was to make parishes responsible for education, with every child having two years of schooling between the ages of seven and fourteen. These proposals were at least in part a response to poor laws, and were understood as a way of dealing with pauperism and crime. In other words, useful knowledge was proposed as crime prevention. However, the bill was defeated. To understand the defeat is to understand how high the stakes were: offering education to the laboring classes was deemed dangerous, even though many of the arguments for offering education rested on conservative ideas of law and order. We could take as an instructive example a speech made by Mr. Davies Giddy during a debate on the bill that took place on June 13, 1807. Giddy stated:

However specious in theory the project might be, of giving education to the labouring classes of the poor, it would, in effect, be found
to be prejudicial to their morals and happiness; it would teach them
to despise their lot in life, instead of making them good servants in
agriculture, and other laborious employments to which their rank
in society had destined them; instead of teaching the[m] subordination, it would render them factious and refractory, as was evident . . .
in the manufacturing counties[;] it would enable them to read sedi-
tious pamphlets, vicious books, and publications against Christianity;
it would render them insolent to their superiors and, in a few years,
the result would be, that the legislature would find it necessary to direct the strong arm of power towards them, and to furnish the execu-
tive magistrates with more vigorous powers than were now in force.
Besides, if the bill were to pass into law, it would go to burthen the
country with a most enormous and incalculable expense, and to load
the industrious orders with still heavier imposts.[5]

This speech gave expression to the anxiety articulated by the upper
classes about social upheaval in industrial Britain. It teaches us how the
happiness of the many was identified with accepting social rank as destiny; it shows us how education was deemed dangerous because it would
take people away from the cause of their happiness. Subordination and
service become virtues. A virtue, in other words, is understood as how
human beings acquire the qualities that would enable them to fulfill what
is assumed as their station. I will return to why *virtue* became such a crucial term in the diffusion of useful knowledge. Indeed, the speech implied
that education would lead to the "strong arm of power" being enforced
against laborers even more vigorously; it is implied that if educated, laborers would be forced to be subordinate because they would no longer
be willing to be subordinate.[6]

An implication can be a threat. It is against this rather threatening
background that the diffusion of useful knowledge was pushed forward
as a project by individuals as well as organizations. The Society for the
Diffusion of Useful Knowledge (SDUK) formed in 1826 is an example of
an organization set up to do this work. Attendees included well-known
utilitarian thinkers such as James Mill, George Birkbeck, Zachary Macaulay, and Lord John Russell in addition to Henry Brougham and Thomas
Coates, who acted as secretary. The minutes report that the aim of the
organization was to publish material to reach people who "did not have

the advantage of attending lectures at the mechanics institutions." The organization understood itself as a mediating link between publishers and readers, creating publications that were cheap and affordable. I mentioned in my introduction to this book the number of boxes left behind by the organization. The stuffed nature of the archive shows us the amount of work required to make knowledge useful. *The more work there is, the more material is left behind.* Useful knowledge was not simply an idea that was in circulation; it involved organizing and administrating—meetings, minutes, correspondence. We are reminded that ideas do not travel by themselves: ideas are picked up, put into papers, passed around, as an effect of work.

Even when the diffusion of useful knowledge was a core commitment, that commitment was difficult to express without ambivalence. The very first sentence of the minutes to the first meeting of the SDUK reads as follows: "At a meeting of Gentleman assembled at nb 7 Furnivall's Inn on Monday the 6th of November for the purpose of taking into consideration the propriety for the general diffusion of useful knowledge among the labouring population." This sentence is of interest because "among the labouring population" is crossed out. The decision not to refer to this population was probably because the remit was to include middle-class as well as working-class readers. That the laboring population appears only to be crossed out might be revealing of a tension in who the organization was *for*, and who it was *about*. The organization that was initiated to extend knowledge to the laboring population seemed to consider making an explicit reference to the laboring population a restriction to that extension.

Another key organization in the project of diffusing knowledge was the British and Foreign School Society (BFSS), which was initially formed as the Royal Lancastrian Society in 1808 to carry on the work of Joseph Lancaster but was renamed in 1813 after he fell into debt and disgrace. The BFSS was responsible for supporting the building of monitorial schools at home and abroad. Indeed, one of the primary methods of diffusing useful knowledge was through the monitorial schools themselves, which were established across Europe, North America, Latin America, Australia, India, and China. One of the reasons for the success of monitorial school systems was that they offered a cheaper way of teaching larger numbers of students; the students became monitors who taught the other students. The monitor provided a labor-saving device. The monitorial school movement still required key actors: it gathered pace and force through the work of societies such as the BFSS but also through "missionaries as well as teachers, and by the dispatch of manual and lesson sheets all over the world" (Aldrich 2013, 6). Paper travels.[7] The spread of useful knowledge involved the translation of manuals into a number of different languages. Jana Tschurenev describes how the BFSS pursued the "double mission of educating the poor in England as well as 'the Heathen' abroad" (2008, 249). Monitorial schools teach us how the diffusion of useful knowledge was justified as a civilizing mission.

It is worth pausing here and asking about the significance of how the main controversy surrounding the monitorial method was whether it was introduced by Andrew Bell or Joseph Lancaster; in fact, many utilitarian thinkers, including James Mill, as I will shortly discuss, weighed in on this controversy. Indeed, the monitorial school movement is now primarily remembered as "the Bell-Lancaster controversy." What does this fact tell us about the diffusion of useful knowledge?

We might need to think of diffusion as a "traffic of ideas," which like all traffic is directed. In the case of monitorial schools, the traffic of ideas included ideas about "the other," about "who" is being taught, with this "who" denoting not a person but a different race and class. The creation of ideas about the other did not require proximity to others. As Edward Said (1978) showed, orientalism did not require a traveling body to travel as a body of ideas. James Mill himself argued that his *History of British India* was more objective because he had never traveled to India, never been swayed by his firsthand impressions (Ahmed 2010, 123). Mill suggests that you can find out more about India in England than you could by traveling to India: "A duly qualified man can obtain more knowledge of India in one year in his closet in England than he could obtain during the course of the longest life, by the use of his eyes and ears in India" ([1818] 1997, 4). That "closet in England" functioned as a container technology, full of stuff, holding things: the other as stuffing.

Unlike Mill, Bell did travel; he made "use of his eyes and ears in India." He traveled on commission from the East India Company to take up a position as the first director of the Madras School for Eurasian Orphans of Soldiers. In *An Experiment in Education, Made at the Male Asylum in Madras*, Bell tells us about what he saw.

> I had, at first sight of a Malabar school, adopted the idea of teaching the letters in sand spread over a board or bench before the scholars, as on the ground in the schools of the natives of this country; a

practice which, by the bye, will elucidate a passage in holy writ better than some commentators have done. But till I had trained boys whose minds I could command, and who only knew to do as they were bidden, and were not disposed to dispute or evade the orders given them, I could not fully establish this simple improvement, which has since recommended itself to every person who has seen it. The same obstacles I found in every attempt I made to give the shape and form of method to this school, to adopt such practices as were established in the best regulated seminaries, or to introduce, as I went along, such as appeared to me improvements in the usual mode of instruction.

The advantages of teaching the alphabet, by writing the letters with the fingers in sand, are many. It engages and amuses the mind, and so commands the attention, that it greatly facilitates the toil, both of the master and scholar. (1797, 11)

Bell suggests here that the idea for the monitor derives from his imitation of a local practice: the colonizer as mimic. In his "Futurism of Young Asia" (1918), Benoy Kumar Sarkar used Bell's account as an example of how ideas travel back from India to England: "England's debt to India has been fitly acknowledged in the tablet to Westminster Abbey, which describes Andrew Bell as the 'eminent founder of the Madras system of education, which has been adopted within the British empire as the national system of education for the children of the poor'" (cited in Tschurenev 2014, 105). If Bell did not erase these signs of travel in describing how he came up with this method, he does, in having a dispute with Lancaster about who first conceived of the method, appropriate it as his own.

Imperial traffic might be assumed to be the traffic from the center to the periphery. But imperial traffic might also refer to how ideas end up *owned* by a center even when the traffic goes in the other direction. If Bell picks up ideas from "using his eyes and ears in India," those ideas become known as his own: use as appropriation. It is worth adding that the arguments for the development of schools for Eurasian children in colonial India were made in advance of Bell's own arrival. So, for example, Richard Wilson, in an address to colonial administrators in 1778, stated that he would "proceed to point in general the methods by which this vagrant Race may be formed into an active, bold and usefull Body of People, strengthening the Hands of Dominion with a Colony of Subjects attached to the British Nation by Consanguinity, Religion, Gratitude, Language and Manners" (cited in Love 1913, 179).[8] This description of the

Eurasian population as a "vagrant Race" was itself much in use. The word *vagrancy* suggests a "person who lacks regular employment, one without fixed abode, a tramp."[9] Throughout the empire, "the vagrant" was often exercised as a figure of criminality and to represent the danger of the unemployed. Lisa Lowe has demonstrated how "though differently employed and prosecuted, vagrancy became a criminalized category across the globe in the nineteenth century" (2015, 122). Education for Eurasian children was framed as a solution to crime, a way of rescuing a population from the vice of vagrancy and unemployment. This is how becoming "an active, bold and usefull . . . people" is about creating a people attached to "the British nation." Becoming useful *to* the colonizer was framed not simply as obedience but as an *attachment* to colonial culture.

Becoming useful was also offered as a solution to vagrancy. The Madras school was indeed established in 1778 after policies were passed by the East India Company that restricted the social as well as physical mobility of Eurasian children.[10] The mobility of a method can translate into the immobility of a class of persons. In this way, the diffusion of useful knowledge was profoundly linked to a racial and classed geography; the schools became container technologies, ways of preventing Eurasian children from traveling back to the imperial center. To be of use to the company was to be contained by a school. Bell describes his own project thus: "At Madras, my aim was to form such scholars, as the condition as that country required, as were wanted to fill the various occupations which presented themselves in the existing state of things there; to imbue the minds of my pupils with the principles of morality and of our holy religion, and infuse a spirit and habit of diligence and industry; so as at once to supply the necessities of the community, and promote the welfare of the individual—two objects indissolubly united in every well-regulated state." (1808, 7–8). I have already pointed out how a virtue was defined as what enables a human being to fulfill what is assumed as their station. Here a virtue is what is acquired when students have the skills required by the state. In other words, the moral ends of an individual are aligned with the political ends of a state. And at this point, of course, the state being referred to was the East India Company with its private armies as well as commercial interests. A virtue for Eurasian population is "a spirit and habit of diligence and industry." Virtue is how members of this population are transformed into willing workers, hands that will be handy for the company.

I noted earlier that education of the poor was understood by many to compromise the virtue of subordination. The diffusion of useful knowledge was defended by *using the same terms*; it was claimed that education would make members of a subordinate class more virtuous. Virtue is how a concept of function is given a moral sense: to become virtuous as being better at fulfilling a function.[11] For those working in industry, to be virtuous is to be industrious. Virtue is also tied to an increase in happiness. In Bell's case, the idea was not simply that the students will become useful to the company but that their own happiness will be realized by being employed in this way. Bell describes his monitorial school as a means for creating happy as well as useful subjects.

> By its economy of time, labour, and expense, it is admirably fitted to diffuse the blessings of religious knowledge among the great body of the rising generation. By its wonderful power of checking vice of every kind, and promoting good order and good conduct, it cannot fail to elevate the character and improve the morals of the lower orders of the people, and establish in them habits of sobriety and subordination conducive to their real happiness and best interests. By confining instruction in the elements of letters, and in that portion of religious knowledge, which is useful and necessary to the great body of the children of the poor, to a small part of the day (two half-hours may suffice), and devoting the rest of the time usually spent in school to handicrafts, to trades, to gardening, to works of husbandry, or other manual labour; it bids fair to produce that eminence in art and skill, and sleight, which early practice can best effect, and to form the youthful character to economy, diligence, and industry. (1808, 113)

The happiness of the children is explicitly associated with subordination and sobriety. We could return here to Darwin's descriptions of natural selection as a checking power. Here the school becomes the selector: what is selected is deemed virtuous and what is checked is a "vice of every kind." Virtues and vices become what enables or compromises the usefulness of a "race of people." In the previous chapter I also referred to Darwin's discussion of methodological selection as the selection of attributes of one species because they are useful *to* another. I suggested instrumentality could be defined as the redirection of *to*: becoming useful *to* others. We are learning how virtue as such becomes instrumental: what makes the child good is what would make the child useful *to* the company.

And so, if industry became virtue, idleness became vice. I have already noted, via Foucault, how idleness was understood as that which must be eliminated by the correct use of the body. It is important to recognize how idleness was transformed into a psychological and moral quality during this period. Richard Adelman suggests that for Adam Smith and Adam Ferguson, idleness was "shorthand for the cession of activity or for the suspension of those engagements that cause the species to progress so rapidly," but that in Jeremy Bentham, idleness becomes a "psychological category" (2011, 46).[12] I will explore in due course how idleness or ennui is understood by Bentham as a danger to health and happiness. But we can note how this use of use (and of nonuse) entangles biology with morality. If idleness or nonuse became understood as the cause of degeneracy, as I explored in chapter 2, then the biological fate of the species is made dependent on the moral redemption of the laboring classes. The laboring classes must be *for* what they are deemed *for*. The figure of the strong blacksmith's arm discussed in the previous chapter, however much a phantom limb, gave somatic expression to this principle.

Vices can thus be understood as that which would compromise the extraction of utility. And vice also became a means of locating pathology in different classes of people. Utilitarian thinker James Mill commented on the Bell-Lancaster controversy by referring to the differences between the classes of children they taught. He defends the achievements of Lancaster over Bell on the ground that Bell worked on a population that was easier to manage. Mill explains:

> What alone Dr. Bell claims, or is entitled to claim, in this business, is the school of Madras. With that his merit begins and ends. Now, undoubtedly, we shall be the last to speak of that merit lightly. A school had been appointed at that settlement for a most unjustly degraded and ill-used race of beings, the half cast children of Europeans, by the East India Company, which has acted with more of beneficent intention towards its subjects during the period of its sovereignty, than any other government during that period upon the face of the earth, but whose beneficent intentions, from uncontrollable causes, have almost always been defeated by its agents abroad. (1812, 69)

This reference to the beneficence of the East India Company is suggestive, and it allows us to witness how good use is defined against "degraded and ill-used." Empire is justified as making better use of a race of beings. That Mill understands Lancaster's work as more important than Bell's because of who he was working on does not mean he considers the laboring classes in London a superior class or even race (in fact, the laboring classes back home are defined by Mill and many others as a different race, just as different races were often defined as different classes). Rather Mill identifies the laboring classes as more willful and more difficult to teach (or to govern) than a race he describes as "mild and passive." Mill argues:

> Surely that must be a weak or an unthinking man who can suppose that what sufficed to maintain order and obedience among two hundred boys, and these the most mild and passive of the human race, subsisted, too, in the house, and totally dependent for every thing upon their governors and masters, would be all that is found necessary to maintain order, and the spirit of application, among a thousand boys gathered out of the streets of London, the most turbulent and intractable at their age, perhaps, of human beings, and who, spending their days and their nights with their (too often vicious) parents, have no dependence upon their master, except for their lessons. (70)

Racial and class ideologies worked together to denote population as posing different kinds of problems that needed to be resolved by the development of techniques of governance. It is thus impossible to separate the project of diffusing useful knowledge from the spread of ideas about "the other" as in need of redemption whether the other is defined as a different race or class.

Utility as such is given redemptive power. Joseph Lancaster opens his *Improvements in Education*, first published in 1803, with vivid descriptions of the conditions of the children of the poor.

> The condition of this class is deplorable indeed: reared up by parents who, from a variety of concurring circumstances, are become either indifferent to the best interests of their offspring, or through intemperate lives, are rendered unable to defray the expense of their instruction, these miserable and almost friendless objects are ushered upon the stage of life, inheriting those vices which idleness and the bad example of their parents' naturally produce. The consequence of this neglect of education, are ignorance and vice, and all those manifold evils resulting from every species of immorality, by which public hospitals and almshouses are filled with objects of disease and poverty, and society burthened with taxes for their support. In addition to these melancholy facts, it is to be feared that the laboring class in the community is becoming less industrious, less moral, and less careful to lay up the fruit of their earnings! ([1803] 1807, v)

Here being deprived of education is understood as preventing the laboring classes from acquiring the virtues they need to enable them to fulfill their function. Joseph Lancaster argued, "The rich having ample means of educating their offspring, it must be apparent that the laboring poor, *a class of citizens so evidently useful*, have a superior claim to public support" (vi, emphasis mine). Here an adjective becomes mobile, transferring a quality from one thing to another: the useful in useful knowledge is transferred to a class, the laboring class becoming self-evidently the useful class. The implication is that those who are useful should be publicly supported not because learning would be useful for the laboring population but because it would enable the laboring population to be useful.

We could summarize the proposition thus: it was *more* useful for *more* to be useful. This aim to increase public utility is understood as supporting the existing social as well as moral order: "The object is not, by more than Herculean labour, to produce either a new establishment, or assume an improper power in the old one, but *to cause the schools of which it consists to approximate nearer to public utility*; and that only, by mild, manly, and Christian conduct, on the part of the society" ([1803] 1807, 157, emphasis mine). Here the emphasis is not only on the increase in public utility enabled by the schools but on promoting the right kind of moral conduct. Indeed, Lancaster suggests that creating a useful class is necessary to stop children from following the paths toward vice laid out by their parents: "Their parents are of the lowest class, by conduct as well as poverty; and would sooner send them to a packthread ground, or other nursery for vice, where their minds are in danger of ruin, for the sake of trifling present gain, than to school, where their morals might be formed aright, and they trained to future usefulness, to themselves, and to the community" (137). Judgments made about the vices of the "lowest class" render the project of spreading useful knowledge not only a civilizing mission but one of saving or rescuing children. I will return to the violence that surrounds that judgment in my conclusion to this chapter.

Usefulness is treated here as future oriented, as what can be extracted from a body given the use of the right methods. And Lancaster refers to monitorial schools themselves as providing the necessary methods of extracting usefulness, contrasting the monitorial schools with existing provisions for the poor in London: "Let us turn from the disgusting scene— from these graves of genius, even in its cradle; and see what they would be under proper regulations, which, modified, and carried into effect by prudent hands, would soon direct the public attention to them, as institutions pregnant with real usefulness" (1803, 2–3). The reference here to "proper regulations" and "prudent hands" is a reference to the methods of the monitorial system, which are thus positioned as techniques of giving birth to a usefulness that is assumed to exist, to extend Lancaster's own analogy, like an unborn fetus within the body of a class.

A Useful Class

The monitorial system rested on a simple principle: that the best students would teach the other students, thus freeing up the time of the master. Bell explained, "It is the division of labour, which leaves to the master the simple and easy charge of directing, regulating, and controlling his intellectual and moral machine" (1808, 3). Delegation is central to how the machinery works: the redistribution of work to other parts of the body. In fact, the master is freed from being a teacher and thus is *freed to master*. The machinery is, however, about more than the freedom to master. The machinery works because of how becoming monitors affects the students in a moral sense by improving them. Bell notes that "unlike the mechanical powers, this intellectual and moral engine, the more work it has to perform, the greater is the facility and expedition with which it is performed, and the greater is the degree of perfection to which it is carried" (36–37). As students are given more work, including the work of teaching as well as learning, their own work is refined or perfected.

The refinement requires that work is distributed not equally but according to ability or level. Bell notes, "By these means, no class is ever retarded in its progress by idle or dull boys; and every boy in every class is fully and profitably employed; and, by thus finding his own level, his improvement is most effectually promoted, and rendered a maximum" (1808, 20). The techniques being defined here are about the production of an able body as the body whose progress must be enabled as well as the transformation of the idle child into a social problem; managing that child becomes about reducing their influence. Licia Carlson describes how custodial departments "developed routines, punishments and physical tasks to prevent idleness" (2010, 44).

The prevention or reduction of idleness is central to the moral machine of the monitorial school: a way of stopping some students from slowing other students down. We have already noted, via Foucault, how idleness became understood as that which must be eliminated by the correct use of the body. The engine of the school runs more smoothly the more it exercises the students at more or less the same time. *A class becomes the body from which uselessness must be eliminated.* Bell suggests that the monitorial system works by how it combines students together, even when they are differentiated from each other according to skill: "It is example, method, general law and equal justice, which take hold of children, by their love of imitation, and their sense of fitness and propriety, and obtain an immediate and willing conformity" (1808, 3–4). The school, in other words, follows from ordinary principles of learning: in particular from imitation as well as a social sense that Bell calls "their sense of fitness and propriety" but might also be simply described as an enlarged sense of sympathy with others. Bell summarizes the method as "conducting a school through the medium of the scholars themselves" (157). Through imitating those who precede them, children willingly conform.

Sympathy becomes part of the machinery, which is to say, sympathy is repurposed as a tool. Bell's description of the children as becoming the medium is evocative of the terms of Foucault's argument in *Discipline and Punish* (1977). I think there is also something else going on, which I would describe as the function of social sensibility. Bell notes, "At Madras, the most obstinate and hardened offender could not stand out for three days against an order to his schoolfellows not to speak to him or play with him" (1808, 13). The withdrawal of social support—and shame—works to bring students into line. Sympathy becomes not just an attunement to the feeling of others (fellow feeling) but an orientation toward ends that become shared. Bell in explaining his method thus gives stress to how students should interact with each other.

> Each boy in rotation, beginning with the head boy, or as many as may be thought to suffice, beginning at any part of the class, spells a word the most difficult in the lesson which has been read. When he mistakes a letter, the boy next in order, who corrects him, must only name the single letter, where the mistake was committed, when he takes his place; the same boy (the first) goes on spelling the rest of the word, subject to the same spelling correction as before, from the boys below him; and he must spell his word over and over again, if necessary, till he make no mistake: then all, who have risen above him, have each his own word in order, so that, in one round, as many words will be spelt, as there are scholars in the class, each spelling his own word. (73–74)

The process of learning how to spell a word becomes a shared process; a way of communicating down a line creates a line. Note how one student comes to correct the mistake introduced by another student. Errors become a collective responsibility to remedy. A rotation system is ironing out an error introduced into the machine, rather like the way an iron might smooth over a wrinkle. And indeed Bell's own model of the monitorial school uses the metaphor of the garden. Errors are eliminated rather like weeds.

> The same difference (it is the simile of a. [sic] classic and celebrated writer), there is between two pieces of ground alike by nature.—The one, rude and uncultivated, overgrown with weeds and thorns, is at once offensive to the spectator, unprofitable to the proprietor, and useless to the community.—The other, a garden richly laden with herbs and fruits, and adorned with plants and flowers, is at once pleasant to the eye, grateful to sense, profitable to the owner, and advantageous to the public. The same is the disparity between the mind, which, rude and uncultivated, is covered with ignorance, and overgrown with error, and that which is enriched with the fruits of useful knowledge, and adorned with the flowers of ornamental literature. And the same superiority the one individual has over the other, the same is the preeminence of the kingdom, where the inhabitants are well educated, over those who are left in a state of ignorance—a discrimination notoriously striking between a nation acquainted with letters, and one in a state of nature. (93)

This association of error with uselessness is important.[13] An error is that which has to be weeded out of the system. Weeds could be defined as "plants out of place," following on from Mary Douglas's reuse of an "old definition" of dirt as "matter out of place" ([1966] 1994, 35). A weed is that which is unwanted, neither useful nor beautiful. In chapter 1, I explored the unused path: a path that has become overgrown from not being used (figure 3.1). We can think of overgrowth as compromising of utility, that is, as negating the ability of the child to follow the straight and narrow path, the path that leads in the right direction toward a moral end. If the school is a garden of useful knowledge, children must cultivate their minds by weeding out of themselves that which would compromise their moral growth.

It is in the work of Joseph Lancaster, however, that we can establish the significance of the figure of the monitor to this transformation from an overgrown garden to one that is "enriched with the fruits of useful knowledge," to use Bell's terms. Even more than Bell, Lancaster focused on positive methods for directing the child toward useful ends. Indeed, we could recall Foucault's own designation of power as positive, as a yes

3.1. Compromising of
utility.

saying rather than a no saying: "power that exerts a positive influence on life that endeavours to administer, optimize, and multiply it" ([1976] 1990, 137). Power exerts a positive influence by *optimizing* as well as administrating life: power as the power to create more from life. Lancaster's pedagogy aims to extract more from the child by the creation of expectation. He notes, "'The hope of reward sweetens labour,' and the prospect of something to be attained in future, is very pleasant to the human mind: no man, or class of men are more useful to society, or rendered more happy by their labours, than those whose hopes depend solely on their own exertions" (1803, 18). Here a man or class of men becomes "more useful to society" by being rewarded for their own exertions. Lancaster suggests the "very nature of expectation" can be a "wire-drawing machine to human industry. In proportion as this sweetener of human toil is intermingled in our cup, so do we remit, or increase, our activity. Would the merchant trade, the mariner toil, or the husbandman plough, without the hope of profit, port, or harvest?" (18). Activity is increased by being made sweet; one thinks here of sweat and sweet intermingling in "our cup." It is significant that Lancaster evokes the laborer to demonstrate the work. What is sweet is mixed up with the laborer's work. And that mix is future oriented. Children are assumed to work harder by the promise of what is to come. Lancaster's model is predicated on the utility of what I called "the promise of happiness." It is assumed that through the promise of a sweetener, the child will become more active; the more active the child, the sweeter the outcome.

Positive affect becomes a pedagogic tool: the teacher aims for the children to associate what they want the children to do with a happier outcome. We can return to the law of exercise discussed in previous chapters and consider how this law translates into a technique. The psychologist Edward Thorndike (1911) refers in fact to two laws: the law of exercise and the law of effect. The law of exercise suggests that an association between a stimulus and a response is strengthened from repeated use. The law of effect suggests that if behavior produces a "satisfying response" in a situation, it is more likely to be repeated in a similar situation. Both laws make use of use insofar as they make use of repetition. Lancaster's pedagogy combined both laws. Lancaster uses the law of exercise in the method of simultaneous instruction: the children are required to repeat the same words at the same time. We thus learn that it is not just associations that are strengthened by repetition. A "we" can be what is strengthened by the very requirement to use the same words at the same time. To return to my discussion of the well-used path in chapter 1, we might note how it is not only that the more a path is traveled upon the clearer it becomes. A path can also become clearer by more traveling upon it; *more* can refer to how *many* travel upon the same path (figure 3.2).

Lancaster also uses the second law of effect. If the child gets the word right, the child is rewarded. The sweetening of an anticipated outcome is assumed to lead to that outcome. The monitorial system thus teaches us how and why positive affect was crucial to the techniques of social control, a way of directing the subject to useful ends by increasing rather than decreasing activity.[14] For Lancaster, lessons must also be short given that the child's attention is short: "By this system the attention is fixed; *there is no idleness*; the mind must be engaged in the business in hand; a lesson is to be said every ten minutes; the monitor's eye is on every child; the pupil's task is easy—the time allowed for learning it is short" (1824, 54). A child's activity is increased by reducing the time of lessons. The pedagogic aim was not only to increase the activity of the child but to *narrow* the range of that activity.[15] Lancaster recommended, for example, that only a few books be read in class: "The books made use

3.2. More can refer to how many.

of in this school, as reading lessons, are the Bible, Testament, Turner's Introduction to the Arts and Sciences, Trimmer's Introduction to the Knowledge of Nature and Reading the Scriptures, Martinet's Catechism of Nature, and Watts's Hymns for Children" ([1803] 1807, 163). The children are required to read the same books over and over again: the fewer books you read, the more you read each book. The more the same paths are used, the fewer paths are used.

When children are rewarded, they are directed down a narrower route. *Happiness is used as a technique to narrow the routes.* The rewards teach us about routes. In Lancaster's model, many of the rewards are about mobility: you go up the hierarchy of the class if you do well; you do not go up, or you go down, if you do not. Hierarchy itself becomes a sweetener. We can understand why Lancaster has been described as the "first bourgeois schoolmaster." As David Hogan explains, "The Lancastrian language of the 'school class' was the bourgeois language of the social class—a hierarchical but continuous structure of opportunity in which the rate of mobility was determined by meritocratic performance in competitive examinations" (1989, 389). Markets and merits were developed through a combination of affect and use: to move up the class was both a positive affect and an effect of correct use.

The monitor as a figure was crucially tied to this use of affect: to become a monitor was a happy outcome, a way of moving up a class in both an educational as well as social sense. I began my chapter with Lancaster's approach of directing a child away from mischief and toward what we call simply "useful ends." The monitor is made central to this redirection: "I have ever found *the surest way to cure a mischievous boy was to make him a monitor*" (Lancaster [1803] 1807, 32). The implication here is that liveliness can be directed toward useful ends not only or simply by the students monitoring themselves (like the prisoner who takes on the gaze of the prison guard) but by some of the students becoming monitors of the others: looking at others (rather than yourself) is *how* you take on the gaze of the master. The direction of the gaze is somewhat different than described by Foucault in his discussion of the Panopticon prison. The monitors do take on the gaze of master but they do so not by monitoring themselves but by monitoring others. The monitorial gaze is *other-directed* more than *self-directed*. The difference of the architecture of the school in comparison to the prison is that students are not separated or contained in singular cells. The master's gaze can thus be relayed through *sideways glances*, becoming distributed through the body of a class. While the monitor takes on the master's gaze in order to improve the work of the other students, the task remains that of *inspection* and is oriented toward helping the master carry out his work. The monitor is "inspecting the performance of each boy in his class, being responsible for any mistakes they commit and preparing them for the superintendent's inspection" (52).

We can consider the implication of the use of monitor as a *mediator*. The monitor as a member of the class who is also a teacher functions as a *go-between* between the teacher and the taught and, by implication, between the governor and the governed.[16] So if the panoptical gaze might be routed along what appears to function as a horizontal axis (between students who are positioned alongside each other), the horizontal is made vertical (some students take the place of the master). We need to remember that the monitorial system is also a reward system and that becoming a monitor was itself intended as a reward. Even if the monitorial method rests on creating a sense of solidarity, it depends on a division. To become a monitor is to be singled out, singling as rewarding, by acting as a surveyor of other members of your own class. To be rewarded is to identify or align oneself with the master in accomplishing his task of inspecting the performance of others. The monitor becomes a method: *it is by policing others that you police yourself.*

The figure of the monitor evokes that of the mimic explored by Homi K. Bhabha, who described the colonial project as requiring the colonized to become "mimic men," drawing on a reading of Thomas Babington Macaulay's (1832) "Minute for Education" (1994, 124–28). Macaulay argued that the aim of education in colonial India should be to create an elite class of persons who would be "Indian in blood and colour, but English in taste, in opinions, in morals, and in intellect" ([1832] 2003, 237). The monitor as mimic would also be required to be like the master, using his words, achieving his manner, but without becoming him (differences of "blood and colour" cannot be transcended). To borrow Bhabha's terms, the monitor would become "almost the same but not quite, almost the same but not white" (1994, 128). We can note here how mimicry exercises a gap between using and being at the same time it appears to close that gap. To become more alike is of course not to be. The requirement of the monitor to be like the master (mimicry as identification) was useful to the master as it extended his capacity to keep an eye on things. Identification with the master is enacted by becoming his "eyes and ears," such that the master's "eyes and ears" are freed up for other business.[17]

This is not to say the monitorial system is simply or only about identification with the master or that it is simply or only about surveillance. The idea is also that the monitor by teaching the other students had the lesson more firmly impressed upon his own mind: "The *repetition* of one word by the monitor, serves to rivet it firmly on the minds of each one of the class, and also on his own memory; thus *he* cannot possibly teach the class without improving *himself* at the same time" (Lancaster [1803] 1807, 47). We can think of the method being outlined here as commitment to memory; words leave an even firmer impression on the mind by being spoken by the monitor and then repeated by a whole class. We might pick up on the verb chosen by Lancaster for the effect of shared repetition: riveted. To be riveted implies to be commanded by attention and derives from the noun "rivet," which comes from the Old French *rivet*, a nail, clench, or fastener. If the word is committed to memory by being spoken by a monitor and then repeated by the class, perhaps what is being performed is a fastening—learning a lesson as becoming attached to the monitor. Each is improved by this binding of a singular subject to collective object. The control mechanism is here also a mutual improvement mechanism.

It is interesting how Lancaster's language is picked up by Bentham. I turn to Bentham's writings on education in more detail in the next section. But we can take note of what Bentham adds to Lancaster's description: "By teaching *others*, the scholar is, at the same time, teaching *himself*: imprinting, more and more deeply, into his own mind, whatsoever ideas he has received into it in the character of a *learner*: taking of them, at the same time, a somewhat new and more commanding view, tinged, as they are, with enlivening colour by the associated ideas of *reputation*, and of that *power*, which has been the fruit of it" (Bentham 1843c, 47). Bentham suggests that ideas become more firmly imprinted and enlivened when they enhance subjects' own ideas of themselves. Ideas become firmer the more they are associated with an increase in the sense of what subjects can do. The monitor-as-method could be understood as a form of discipline expressed by the maximization of capacities: "Before the effect of novelty is worn off, new habits are formed; and the happy children who are trained under the mild and generous influence of the British system of education, learn obedience with pleasure, and practice it with delight, without the influence of the rod or cane to bring them to order" (Lancaster 1812, 83). Perhaps the schoolroom could be understood as a transition from *discipline and punish* to *discipline and care*: to care for the children is to ensure their happiness in receiving instructions.

The rod can disappear as a tool of punishment. In *Willful Subjects* (2014), I describe how poisonous pedagogy became a positive pedagogy by the disappearance of the rod. We could certainly think of the monitorial system as positive pedagogy. But the difference is that the object is to create *a useful class*. The rod does in fact reappear in the monitorial schoolroom; the rod is used as a pointer, to direct children this way or that, or a rod is used to point to a tablet, removing the need for touch. Removing the need to touch was a result of the number of children in the room; space has to be tightly regulated so there was just such-and-such distance between bodies as well as between tables and walls. Everything is designed in the schoolroom to maximize how many children can be taught at the same time in the same room.[18] It is because of this density that high levels of control were necessary.[19] Spaces can be organized around what they are for. Spaces might have to be organized even more tightly the more are required to be accommodated. The use of a rod as a pointer reminds us that the object of the monitorial system was not a singular child but a class of children. It is the children of a subordinate class who are treated as a class. A useful child thus stands in for a useful class.

Utilitarianism as Technique

Bentham's writings on education draw extensively from the work of Bell and Lancaster. Before discussing Bentham's "Chrestomathia," it is worth considering the relation between Bentham's educational project and his wider utilitarian project. In the first instance, we can consider how educational techniques also functioned as political techniques, that is, were offering a means of governing a population. Foucault's *The Birth of Biopolitics* described utilitarianism as a "technology of government" (2008, 41). At one level this is, of course, a reference to utilitarianism as a calculating or counting system that renders the population as such into an object of government. But as Anne Brunon-Ernst has shown, utilitarianism also became a "technology of government," given how utilitarianism rendered conduct *as such* into a concern of government (2012b, 108).

Given that Bentham considered the aim of government as being to maximize happiness, it is not surprising that utilitarianism also functioned as a system for influencing conduct such that it became conducive to the achievement of that aim. Government is given a comparable task to that of the schoolmaster—finding the best means to direct individuals toward useful ends: "All the indirect expedients which can be usefully employed must, then, *have for their aim the direction and control of men's inclinations*, the putting in practice of the rules of a logic hitherto but little understood, the logic of the will—a logic which would often seem to be in conflict with that of the understanding" (Bentham [1802] 1914, 193). Indeed, Anne Brunon-Ernst has shown how for Bentham, individuals would be guided by an "invisible chain of direct legislation" (2012b, 121).[20] For our purposes, what is of special interest is Bentham's discussion of rewards, which he suggests should operate under the principle of utility.

> REWARD, in the most general and extensive sense ever given to the word, may be defined to be—a portion of the matter of good, which, in consideration of some service supposed or expected to be done, is bestowed on someone, in the intent that he may be benefited thereby. When employed under the direction of the principle of utility, it operates as a motive for the performance of actions useful to society, in the same manner as, under the same guidance, punishment operates in the prevention of actions to which we ascribe an injurious tendency. (1843c, 192)

This description of reward as a system teaches us how utilitarianism became an educational as well as political technique: you reward what is deemed useful to society while "actions to which we ascribe an injurious tendency" are punished. Bentham's opening sentence of *An Introduction to the Principles of Morals and Legislation* is well known: "Nature has placed mankind under the governance of two sovereign masters, pleasure and pain" ([1789] 2007, 1). From Bentham's description of rewards we learn how pleasure and pain can be used to govern as tools that are also *directives*: you would increase the pleasure or happiness attached to ends deemed "useful to society" and increase the pain or unhappiness attached to what is deemed injurious.

I want to take as an example Bentham's writings on the poor laws to consider what follows when pain and pleasure become governing tools. For Bentham, any relief or charity given to the poor must be painful rather than pleasant: he argues that relief must be unpleasant so that people would not claim it. (1843d, 401). Bentham justifies making it harder to receive relief on the grounds that most beggars are unhappy and wretched.

> Unfavourable influence on happiness, even in the instance of the begging tribe itself, taking the whole together.—There are many, it is true, who, for a time at least, would, unquestionably, be no inconsiderable sufferers by the proposed change. But the greater part would be gainers in point of happiness, at least in the long run: since—(it being a property of this as of other unlaborious professions to be overstocked)—for one prosperous and happy beggar, there are probably many unprosperous and miserable ones; wretches who, notwithstanding, keep lingering in their wretchedness; sometimes for want of power, sometimes for want of resolution, to emerge from it. (1843d, 401)

The implication of this argument is that poor laws should make the lives of those seeking relief more wretched in order to dissuade pauperism. Otherwise "under the existing poor laws, every man has a right to be maintained, in the character of a pauper, at the public charge: under which right he is in fact, with a very few exceptions, (amounting not to one perhaps in fifty), maintained in idleness" (401). We can recall here that for Bentham, all human beings tend toward what is easier as well as most pleasant. But the universality of his happiness principle does not mean the consequences are the same for all classes. Bentham's key premise was that relief maintained idleness, and thus encouraged pauperism, which was against the greatest happiness principle, which he sometimes articulated as "the greatest happiness of the greatest number."[21] If general happiness depends on the unemployed not being maintained in idleness, then relief must be made to cause unhappiness. What in previous work I described as a pedagogic technique, making the consequences one does not want unhappy (Ahmed 2010, 54–56), can thus also be understood as government policy: consequences are made unhappier in an effort to redirect subjects toward ends that are determined as beneficial by those who govern. Remember, deviation is hard. Deviation is made hard.

We can turn now to Bentham's own plan for a school organized around useful knowledge. Bentham in his writings on the Panopticon prison, upon which Foucault draws, had already discussed how the monitor is a method through what he calls the inspection principle. He notes, "The object of the inspection principle is directly the reverse: it is to make them not only *suspect*, but be *assured*, that whatever they do is known, even though that should not be the case. Detection is the object of the first: *prevention*, that of the latter. In the former case, the ruling person is a spy; *in the latter he is a monitor*" (1843b, 66, emphasis mine). The monitor's task is to give assurance, and is understood not to detect crime or deviation but to prevent it. It is clear how and why a discourse of utility slides into a discourse on happiness.[22] The monitor is given the positive task of maximizing the subject's happiness by directing the subject toward the right ends. In "Chrestomathia," Bentham refers to Aristotle's principle of *eudemonia*, linking his utilitarian approach to happiness as the end of government, with the more classical concern with happiness as the end of an individual: "Directly or indirectly, *well-being*, in some shape or another, or in several shapes, or all shapes taken together, is the subject of every thought, and the object of every action, on the part of every known *Being*, who is, at the same time, a sensitive and thinking Being" (1843c, 82).[23] For Bentham, *eudemonia* becomes an art, "which has for the object of its endeavours, to contribute in some way or other to the attainment of *well-being*" (82). We can see here that if use leads to usefulness, usefulness is defined as the attainment of well-being. Happiness becomes the end, thus associating usefulness with positive affect as well as positive value. Bentham states that "the name for the universally practiced art is the pursuit of happiness" (83).

The introduction to "Chrestomathia" was written by Southwood Smith, a friend of Bentham's who was also a medical doctor influenced by utilitarianism, and who was eventually given the task of dissecting Bentham's body after his death. I mention this detail as I will be returning to the question of useful death in my conclusion to this chapter. Smith notes that "Mr Bentham was one of the first to recognise the extraordinary improvement in the method of instruction developed by Mr Lancaster and modified and extended by Dr Bell" (1843, ii). Smith understands Bentham as refining their methods into a system that could be put to use by others: "It was necessary to bring out the principles of the new method more distinctly than had yet been done and to shape them into so many instruments, each capable of being applied, by ordinary hands, to its specific use: it was equally necessary to review the whole field of knowledge in order to ascertain to what branches of instruction these instruments might be applied with the greatest promise of success" (ii).

Indeed, Smith also rests his case about the use of use by differentiating useful knowledge from polite learning. He notes that "the perception, in the public mind, has become more clear and strong, of the folly of consuming more than three-fourths of the Invaluable time appropriated to education, 'in scraping together,' as Milton expresses it, 'so much miserable Greek and Latin,' by persons of the middle classes, to whom it is of no manner of use; to whose pursuits it bears no kind of relation; who, after all, acquire it so imperfectly, as to derive no pleasure from the future cultivation of it" (iii). Knowledge of classical literature, it is argued, would be "no manner of use" to classes for whom adulthood requires entering certain kinds of employment. Indeed, what is "of use" to the middle and working classes would be what is handy or near: knowledge that would be useful would relate to the tools used in employment but also the sensual and physical qualities of the world. Utility here becomes a style of empiricism, a concern with what's what—a way of pointing to things that are available within an immediate horizon. Indeed, Bentham associates empiricism, a concern with "things of all sorts," with what he calls parliamentary business. Bentham writes, "The classical scholar may be better qualified for decorating his speech with rhetorical flowers: but the chrestomathic scholar, after a familiar and thorough acquaintance has been contracted with things, with things of all sorts, will be, in a much more useful and efficient way, qualified for the general course of parliamentary business" (1843c, 17–18). I will return to what is meant by business in due course. What is also emerging here is a specific understanding of *pragmatics*: what is practical and efficient for a working life as an orientation toward objects. The history of the emergence of an idea of useful knowledge is thus also a history of useful objects (see chapter 1).

As I noted in the first section of this chapter, arguments about extending education had to be made in the context of considerable concern that useful knowledge would lead to insubordination. The principles of the Chrestomathic School are defended against certain concerns. One of these concerns is "uppishness," by which Bentham means the concern that learning will lead to students desiring more than is afforded by their station. Given his writings on the poor laws referred to earlier, his answer might seem somewhat surprising: "To the supposed inferiors, no branches of useful instruction will be laid open, which will not be equally open to the supposed superiors. If under the impulse of emulation or any other spring of action, they are driven to keep pace in improvement with those apprehended rivals, so much the better for themselves" (1843c, 20). It is clear from this description that Bentham differentiates upward mobility (for the middle classes) from downward mobility (for the upper classes). This is why Smith stresses in his introduction that creating a happier class of persons would not cause "injury whatever to any other class" (1843, iii).

"Chrestomathia" begins with the advantages of the system of useful knowledge that it introduces. The first advantage is defined negatively: the avoidance of ennui, that which is "felt by him whose mind unoccupied" (1843c, 8). Indeed, the most common word used by Bentham is "vacant," a mind that is not furnished by thought. In chapter I, I referred to an image of a toilet door with the sign "occupied." The sign can also say "vacant." Vacant can mean not in use, unoccupied, but it can also operate as an invitation: a vacant toilet is one that you can use because it is not being used by another (figure 3.3).

If idleness tends to be used to refer to a body that is not in motion, vacant is used for a mind that is waiting to be used. Such waiting is understood by Bentham not simply as potential but as negation, as a "state of uneasiness." Not to be in use is to be deprived of any sense of purpose. Bentham writes: "For the designation of the means of securing being and well-being, the words—calling, vocation, and occupation, were commonly employed by our forefathers, meaning always, on these occasions, profit-yielding occupation, as the words—business, the means of livelihood, are employed by us their successors. The word avocation, a most incompetent and equivocal term, has of late years been vulgarly, and we may almost say commonly, obtruded upon the words calling, vocation, employment. A vocation is a calling; an avocation is a calling off" (1843c, 8). Avocation, vacancy, and unemployment all become suspensions of

3.3. Vacancy as invitation.

activity: *a calling off*. Bentham thus associates moral health and activity with specific kinds of employment. So to be unemployed—in the specific sense of not to be in a profession or have a job—is to risk mental as well as physical degeneration. Indeed, it is given that this association between employment and happiness is so strong that Bentham can argue for making relief to the poor painful and unpleasant. This position, in other words, was not an exceptional moment of cruelty in an otherwise liberal archive but an expression of normative commitments. Reflecting on this association between happiness and employment has led me to conclude that my critique of happiness in *The Promise of Happiness* (2010) was, if anything, understated.

For Bentham, an unemployed or vacant mind can also be dangerous. In fact, to have a vacant mind is to be endangered by one's own self. Bentham notes, "Among unfurnished minds [like an empty house], from the excitements it affords to sensuality, idleness, and mischievousness, company, in portion to its abundance, is the great source of danger: hence, in the like proportion, will be the great source of security" (1843c, 13). Vacancy is thus associated with vice or weeds: "Weeds of all sorts, even the most poisonous, are the natural produce of the vacant mind" (10). As such, the task of the Chrestomathic School is to fill the mind with useful things, either figured as furniture, or as plants and flowers: "For the exclusion of these weeds, no species of husbandry is so effectual, as the filling of the soil with flowers, such as the particular nature of the soil is best adapted to produce. What those flowers are can only be known from experiment; and the greater the variety that can be introduced, the greater the chance that the experiment will be attended with success" (10). The day school will furnish the mind, thus improving the state of things: "The state of the house and family, whatever it may come to be, and the state of the shop, the counting-house, and the profession, whatever they may come to be, will, to a greater or lesser degree, be sure of being rendered better than they would have otherwise been" (12).

Bentham's text provides tables of how the Chrestomathic School will organize knowledge as stages. The students learn in the first stage by beginning with the most simple and concrete things. And Bentham is not referring here to an object or thing that is abstracted from ordinary life. He begins instead with the sensuous encounters we have with things. Bentham is intent on showing how lessons have already begun because we have such encounters that ignite curiosity and interest: "Every man, woman, and child, to whom there has been given the amusement of seeing a collection of birds and beasts, has received a lesson in Zoology—a lesson of the sort here proposed" (24). Bentham does elevate sensuous and immediate encounters with things by suggesting these encounters provide the basis of knowledge, although there is a clear hierarchy here that is temporalized into stages: from empirical encounters to more abstract speculation. Bentham notes, "To a certain extent, every labourer's man employed in the working of a mine, is a Mineralogist" (24). This is because "the acquaintance which the labourer in mines has with Mineralogy, is confined to the production of this own mine. The acquaintance which, in the proposed school, a scholar, at the first stage, will have with the same science, will be less particular, though more extensive; indeed, as extensive as it can be made" (24).

The tables that form the basis of the Chrestomathic School thus function as timetables: you start with the most immediate things, which in time leads to greater abstraction. The key premise is simple: the most generally useful branches are first administered; the least generally useful branches are last administered. Quite simply, what *is most useful is what is useful to most*. The most useful is also what "will be found the easiest and the pleasantest" (14). And what *is least useful is what is useful to the least*. The least useful, which would be last administered in the Chrestomathic

School (and which some pupils would not take because only some students stay till the end), would be the hardest and most unpleasant. The table of knowledge thus could be imagined almost like a social pyramid: the most at the bottom receive that which is useful to the most but not that which is useful to the least, while the least at the top receive that which is useful to the most as well as that which is useful to the least. In effect, the most get the least because the least get the most: they get what is taught first and last, what is easiest and more pleasant, as well as what is hardest and most difficult. And so it is thus: "In the last stage of all comes mathematical science by itself. Of this branch considered apart and contradistinguished from mechanics, *the usefulness will be found less extensive in respect to the number of persons to whom it can be of any use*" (14, emphasis mine). However, I would argue that this idea of a usefulness that is less extensive is how class becomes an ordering principle within the school itself: creating a few who have a different use for use; creating a few for whom use resides in more manners of things, including not only concrete and sensuous things but also numbers and other more abstract entities.

We can contrast Bentham's plans for his own Chrestomathic School with his writing on education in workhouses. For education in the workhouse, Bentham recommends the full employment of all parts of the body: "To answer in perfection the purposes of health and development of strength, a system of exercise taken together, should be *general* in respect of the parts concerned in it, *not local*: *it should find employ for every limb and every muscle*: it should not be confined to particular limbs, or particular motions of the limbs" (1843d, 396, latter emphasis mine). We can hear from this account the accuracy of Foucault's description of the correct use of the body; every limb must be employed for a body to be used correctly. But this requirement to be fully employed is implied to be specific to a situation. Bentham argues that education in the workhouses should be organized under the principle of utility, not usage: "In the choice of *subject-matters* of instruction, *utility—not usage—*should be the guide. . . . The utility in view ought to bear reference—in the first place to the situation of the individual, *during* the apprenticeship; in the next place, to his situation in the world at large, *after* the expiration of it" (397). The implication here is that utility for those in the workhouse is a system of reference; the skills that will be taught are those that will be useful with reference to a situation. This is another use of intended functionality: for some, what is taught can only be taught in accordance with what is intended for them (with what is deemed their function).

By implication, for others, usage and not utility would be a guide. If everything must be in use for something to be useful, not everybody is required to be useful. Idleness, even if understood by Bentham as a universal tendency (a tendency toward what is easy and pleasant), is not deemed universally compromising: for some, idleness would be permitted or might even become expressive of the relative freedom of a situation.

For the poor, then, Bentham is explicit: utility must be tightened as a system of reference; what is to be taught is to be taught with reference to a set of skills that is required for an occupation. In the Chrestomathic School, we have a *loosening of that referential system*. The school is being designed: "By the middle rank of life, for the use of which the proposed system of instruction is designed, useful and not merely ornamental instruction is required" (1843c, 17). As such, the aim is to create more things for which a person is fit: "The more things he is more or less acquainted with, the more things he is fit for, and the better chance he has acquired of meeting with some *occupation*, . . . according to his *condition*, and which shall be at once within his *power*, and suited to his *taste*" (16).

The diversity of career pathways open to the middle-class students could be thought of as the loosening of the relation between form and function. Pierre Bourdieu, in his monumental study *Distinction*, describes the formation of a middle-class disposition as an aesthetic disposition that privileges form over function (1986, 5–6). Function, in other words, becomes associated with a lack of refinement. Refinement here refers to how the system for utility *is loosened*, suggesting that for those who are not laborers, use can become more creative, more detached from the requirements of a system. Loosening and tightening thus become mechanisms for distributing utility unevenly across a social body. The lower a person is deemed to be, the tighter the relation between form and function; the higher, the looser. In chapter 2, I explored what I called class and gender fatalism with reference to the blacksmith's arm; the son of the blacksmith inherits the efforts of his father and is thus pointed in a certain direction. Fatalism becomes functionalism: the lower you are in a class hierarchy, the more you are supposed to be determined by function—*function as fate*.

The loosening of the relation between form and function can also be how class interests of those positioned higher in a hierarchy are disguised by operating under the sign of the universal. Marx's critique of Bentham's utilitarian ethics in a footnote in *Capital* exposes how the language of usefulness is useful to capitalism. Marx's critique begins by addressing the question of usefulness in relation to nature.

> To know what is useful for a dog, one must study dog-nature. This nature itself is not to be deduced from the principle of utility. Applying this to man, he who would criticize all human acts, movements, relations, etc., by the principle of utility, must first deal with human nature in general, and then with human nature as modified in each historical epoch. Bentham makes short work of it. With the driest naïveté he takes the modern shopkeeper, especially the English shopkeeper, as the normal man. Whatever is useful to this queer normal man, and to his world, is absolutely useful. This yard-measure, then, he applies to past, present, and future. ([1867] 1990, 668)

The figure of the shopkeeper becomes a norm and a yardstick, a way of measuring use. This is not to say that Bentham's point of view is the shopkeeper's: that figure is being employed to do certain work. What is useful to a shopkeeper is what enables the shopkeeper to be useful, that is, to perform a social function. Bentham often refers to "society" in measuring utility; we have already considered his argument that you should reward "the performance of actions useful to society" (1843a, 193). Society is a placeholder for those who count, those whose interests count. Those who count disappear from the equation. To measure usefulness is thus to universalize use: what is useful to him becomes what is absolutely useful. The universalizing of use is how a "to" in "useful to" is redirected and erased.

Uses of Death

Use became a technique by being made necessary for life. We can return to Pascal's story of the useless foot shared in my introduction to this book. The foot is willful when it does not recognize that it is a part of the body; the useless foot causes its own death by causing the death of the body of which it is part. Death can be used as a warning. An injunction to be useful, to become a subordinate member of a body, is often presented as a life project. The materials I have gathered in this chapter, in associating use with life, also make use of death.

The association of use and life can be fatal. I have noted how Bentham makes an association between happiness and employment. He also makes an even stronger association between unemployment and death. Bentham tells the story of the once industrious Mr. Beardmore, who sold his business for a good profit and then suffered a rapid decline until his early death (1843c, 9). Bentham quotes directly from Mr. Beardmore's obituary, which appeared in the *Gentleman's Magazine* of 1814.[24] While working, Mr. Beardmore was not just industrious; he was also happy and admired: "From inclination active, and from habit indefatigably industrious he had hitherto commanded such an exuberant flow of good spirits as made him the object of general remark among friends, whom his kindness and vivacity delighted. Early rising contributed much to the support of this happy and equable temperament. He preserved a memory richly stored with pleasant anecdotes, sprightly remarks, and useful information on a great variety of topics, derived not from books, but from living studies" (9). Mr. Beardmore is a model of life, of how being useful is to be living a full and happy life. When he sells his business, he loses not only his employment but also himself: "From the fatal hour in which he quitted business, however, he grew insensibly more and more the victim of listlessness and ennui. With high animal spirits; with a mind still active, and a body still robust; with confirmed health, independent property, an amiable wife, a plentiful table, and a social neighbourhood, Mr Beardmore was no longer 'at home' in his own house. The mainspring of action was now stopped" (9). Without employment, Mr. Beardmore is not even able to be at home. Bentham literally makes use of this story of demise and death to warn of the danger of falling out of use—to reuse one of the use expressions discussed in chapter 1—or losing a sense of dignity and purpose. To fall out of use is to fall out of life. To cease to use one's faculties is to cease to be.

The implication is that without employment of a particular kind, a "legitimate business," there is no activity: work becomes the only form of activity that keeps a person, at least one of a certain class, alive. Implicit in this approach to use is thus an approach to being. Our useful archive is thus full of dead bodies: literally, even, including the bodies of those who have contributed documents to the archive. Bentham's own body was dissected, under his strict instructions, three days after his death in 1832, with the intent of creating an auto-icon. Southwood Smith, a medical doctor and friend of Bentham's, who was influenced by Bentham's utilitarian philosophy, carried out that dissection. In his lecture given afterward, Smith rather morbidly addresses Bentham's dead body: "There lie before us the mortal remains of one of the most illustrious men of our country and our age" (1832, 2). He asks why that body is here, in "the school of science" and not the tomb. He answers his question by explaining the task: "If, by any appropriation of the dead, I can promote the happiness of the living, then it is my duty to conquer the reluctance I may feel to such a disposition of the dead, however well-founded or strong that reluctance may be" (71). Here, making use of a dead body for the purposes of dissection and display becomes another method for promoting happiness, however reluctantly, and indeed of fulfilling Bentham's own principle of the greatest happiness for the greatest number. Making use of a dead body becomes a moral task performed for the living, aiding them in the pursuit of knowledge. As a result, Bentham's own body becomes part of the archive.

Smith had in fact in 1828 published a pamphlet, *Use of the Dead to the Living*, and his lobbying led directly to the 1832 Anatomy Act, which aimed to end the practice of "grave robbing" and to secure legal access to dead bodies for the purpose of scientific research. We could describe his pamphlet as calling for useful death, a call that was premised on the value of the knowledge that could be obtained from the dissection of bodies. Smith wrote: "Disease, which it is the object of these arts to prevent and to cure, is denoted by disordered function: disordered function cannot be understood without a knowledge of healthy function; healthy function cannot be understood without a knowledge of structure; structure cannot be understood unless it be examined. The organs on which all the important functions of the human body depend are concealed from the view. There is no possibility of ascertaining their situation and connections, much less their nature and operation, without inspecting the interior of this curious and complicated machine" (1828, 3). A dead body would be useful as it would allow access to the functions of the body that are normally hidden from view.

Whose dead bodies come into view? We know, of course, that Bentham made his own dead body useful, or intended his own dead body to be useful. But this was an act of intention or will, enabling Bentham to make his own death a continuation of a life philosophy. His dead body was a gift. Usefulness for an English gentleman was offered as a grand gesture, as a way he could be committed to memory. Other deaths that haunt our useful archive could be described as stranger deaths; they are deaths of those who will remain anonymous. *That anonymity was there from the start.* We do not know how many of these bodies were used in the project of useful knowledge; we do not know who they were, those whose bodies were dissected on the grounds of being unclaimed. Smith's plan was that the bodies of those persons who die in all infirmaries and hospitals throughout the

kingdom, "unclaimed by immediate relatives," be "appropriated to the purpose of anatomy," as well as the bodies of those persons who die in all workhouses, poorhouses, houses of correction, and prisons. It was the poor, the
paupers, the incarcerated, as well as the unloved and unwanted, who were
deemed appropriable, could we even say usable, for science. Notably then
the disposability of some bodies renders them useful: the docility-utility
relation is central to what Achille Mbembe (2003) calls necropolitics. Some
bodies become disposable *because their utility can be extracted through death*.
Smith develops his case for useful death as follows:

> No one can object to such a disposal of the bodies of those who die in
> prisons; no one can reasonably object to such a disposal of the bodies
> of those who die in poorhouses. These persons are pensioners upon
> the public bounty: they owe the public a debt: they have been sup-
> ported by the public during life; if, therefore, after death they can be
> made useful to the public, it is a prejudice, not a reason—it is an act
> of injustice, not the observance of a duty, which would prevent them
> from becoming so. It is true that many of these persons are honest
> and respectable; and have been reduced to indigence by misfortune:
> were they all so it would not alter the state of the argument. Some
> concession and co-operation on the part of the public, for this great
> public object, is indispensable, without which nothing can be done:
> but if any concession be made, it can be made with respect to this
> class of persons better than any other, because it can be made with
> less violation of public feeling. Nor is any indignity either intended
> or offered to these persons. They are appropriated to this service not
> because they are poor, but because they are friendless: because, that
> is, no persons survive them who take such an interest in their fate as
> to be rendered unhappy by this disposal of their remains. That they are
> without friends is no good reason why their memory should be treated
> with indignity; but it is a good reason, it is the best possible reason
> why they should be selected for this public service. (1828, 51–52)

The poor become understood as the ones who owe society, named here as
the public, as if what they do have is a deprivation of others or as if they
are themselves a deprivation of others. For the poor to donate their own
dead bodies is understood not as a gift, which was reserved for gentlemen or men of science, but as a repaying of debt. The public matters as a
public bounty; the public becomes a purse that those in poorhouses are
draining. Deprivation here is understood not only in terms of the lack of

the means to support oneself but a deprivation of love: the poor become friendless as well as unhappy. It is the constitution of an unloved and unlovable class of persons that renders the use of their dead bodies something other than an indignity; it would indeed be an injustice for them not to make their death useful insofar as they are understood as having been supported in life. The narrative (still told, still familiar) makes poverty into vice, misfortune into guilt, inequality a natural expression of differences in moral worth. Indeed, Smith implies that the poor, the incarcerated, and the wretched would (as well as should) choose such a repayment as an alternative to donating their living bodies. In other words, he argues that the requirement to make a dead body useful is a better alternative than the requirement to making a living body useful.

> And, after all, the true question is, whether the surgeon shall be allowed to gain knowledge by operating on the bodies of the dead, or driven to obtain it by practising on the bodies of the living. If the dead bodies of the poor are not appropriated to this use, their living bodies must be—and will be. The rich will always have it in their power to select, for the performance of an operation[,] the surgeon who has signalized himself by success: but that surgeon, if he have not obtained the dexterity which ensures success, by dissecting and operating on the dead, must have acquired it by making experiments on the living bodies of the poor. There is no other means by which he can possibly have gained the necessary information. (52)

We can begin to understand how what seems to be a general or even universal requirement to be useful falls on some and not others; utility while presented as a universal value, or at least one that alludes in some way to the greatest number, is a system for extracting life even from the death of those deemed a lower class. It is not even a question that the poor could avoid this fate. If the greatest number matter, it is here not as a means of calculating worth but because of how their lives as well as deaths are rendered resources for the less, more or less.

But we need to go further to track the uses of death. It is not only that those who refuse to be properly employed are understood as consigning themselves to death. I want to turn one more time to the children taught by Bell and Lancaster. As I have noted, they both represent themselves as saving children from degradation, giving children a chance to get more from life although the monitorial system seems more predicated on getting more from children. Bell's pupils are regularly described as orphans, children whose immediate families were already dead. But were they? Bell's descriptions of the children are revealing: "The great object for which the Military Male Orphan Asylum had been founded, was to rescue the children of the soldiers from the degradation and depravity of that class to which their mothers mostly belonged" (cited in R. Southey 1844, 170). Many of the children Bell taught were not in fact orphans; some children were illegitimate, and many others had deceased fathers but living Indian mothers. Those Indian mothers are described as degraded. Many of the children in becoming orphans—that is, in receiving that designation—were taken from their Indian mothers. The project of educating the children so they would be of use to the company, which was represented as a benevolent project of saving the children from degradation and depravity, was also about cutting children off from their families and local culture. Satadru Sen has described this process as *orphaning*, a process through which children are severed from their kin, either literally or discursively (2012, 132).[25] Becoming useful to the company depended on death not as a biological fact but as a social act. The company itself becomes the family, the master the father, by treating the child's family as dead whether or not they were.

This use of death returns us to the political stakes in the category of the unused. In chapter 1, I considered how land can be declared or made unused to justify the appropriation of land. Judy Whitehead has tracked how the Lockean category of wasteland was used in the colonial project in India. As she describes, "The concept of wasteland began its career in India" as "a social category that applied both to the supposedly unproductive uses that lands were put to, to lands held in common, or to land left idle" (2010, 84). Idleness becomes here not only a theft of a potential value—unproductivity as disuse—but a negative quality that connects places and people. Whitehead suggests that this framing of land as wasteland extended to persons: "By metonymically signifying both landscapes and people, the category of wasteland gestured towards a multivocal array of policies that applied to both the uses of land and the users of land" (93). We could think too of how living beings were rendered appropriable by being framed not as desert but as deserted. Christopher J. Hawes offers an important record of the "making of the Eurasian community" in his book *Poor Relations* (1996). Hawes describes Bell's project of teaching Eurasian children as "the development of their moral character and utility to British society," which could only be "undertaken by Christian hands, away from their Hindu or Muslim mothers" (28). He adds, "To those involved in the process the raw materials taken into the orphanages seem unpromising" (28). Children become "raw materials," to be worked upon and transformed into cultured products by an act of separation from "their Hindu or Muslim mothers." Children are treated as if they can be emptied of culture and history, rendered vacant—from desert, wasteland, to deserted, abandoned.

We have another way of describing this desertion: theft. The language of happiness and utility masks the violence of that theft. Returning to Lancaster, we might note how he was often referred to as "the poor child's friend" (Taylor [1996], 2012). We can recall that Lancaster himself represented his schools as rescuing children from "the lowest class," as stopping children from being ruined by the vices they would otherwise have inherited. Can we make use of other terms to tell Lancaster's story? I have already noted that by the time of Lancaster's death, he had fallen into debt and disgrace.[26] It has also been reported that Lancaster was unduly violent toward the children who lived with him in his private household (Vogler 2015). Reading through the early minute books of the Royal Lancastrian Society, it is hard to get a sense of these other histories. As I noted in my introduction to this book, you mainly encounter in these materials an administrative history, a history of financial transactions; little information is given about the children themselves. We have lists of names of the boys being taught at the different schools. The few details given, however, are revealing. There are a number of references to the sorry and abject status of Irish boys. There are references throughout to how children were moved between private households; we hear of a duke who does not want the boys he was sent and returns them to Lancaster. This history of how children were circulated, used, and abused as objects is a history available only in glimpses at the edges of the archive. But glimpse it, we must and we can.

There are many histories of use to tell. I have told only some of them.

4

Use and the University

On February 9, 1825, the Scottish poet Thomas Campbell published a letter in *The Times* addressed to Sir Henry Brougham, a liberal member of the House of Commons, a Benthamite, and one of the founding members of the Society for the Diffusion of Useful Knowledge (SDUK). This letter was followed up by another piece published in the April edition of the *Monthly Review*. Both pieces of writing (Campbell 1825) called for the formation of a new English university, to be based in London, which was to offer a secular alternative to Oxford and Cambridge. That university, originally called University of London, now called University College London (UCL), was founded a year after the publication of Campbell's letter, almost to the day, on February 11, 1826, the same year that the SDUK was established. Campbell's letters could be considered the first attempt to give written expression to the utilitarian principles upon which the modern university was to be based, though his role in establishing the new university has been largely forgotten.

A painting by Henry Tonks, *The Four Founders of UCL* (1923), does place Campbell at the founding moment (figure 4.1). The UCL Art Museum describes the painting thus: "Kneeling at the right is the architect William Wilkins who presents his plans of the building to Jeremy Bentham, standing in the centre of the composition, and the poet Thomas Campbell who first conceived the idea of a London University. At the left stand

4.1. Henry Tonks, *The Four Founders of UCL*, painting, 1923. UCL Art Museum, University College London.

Lord Brougham, lawyer, politician and Benthamite, and behind him the diarist, former *Times* correspondent and retired barrister Henry Crabb Robinson who was instrumental in establishing the Flaxman Gallery."[1] The painting places Bentham himself as the recipient of the plan. Bentham did not play any such role in the setting up of this university (he was over eighty at the time), although he is often called UCL's "spiritual father," including by UCL.[2] Perhaps Bentham is placed by the artist at the scene *because he is expected to be there*. Of course, at another level, Bentham's body is there, even if he was not the recipient of the architect's plan. The auto-icon of Bentham's dead body referred to in the conclusion of chapter 3 remains on display at UCL in accordance with Bentham's own will (figure 4.2).

Bentham had instructed that "the whole figure may be seated in a chair usually occupied by me when living, in the attitude in which I am

4.2. Auto-icon of Bentham.

sitting engaged in thought" (cited in Starck 2006, 43), although Bentham's head is now located in UCL's Institute of Archaeology, and a wax head is in its place. We could consider Bentham's body as a phantom limb in a similar way to the blacksmith's arm. The investment in the distinction between mental and manual labor as a social distinction is evidenced by these contrasting figures—arm and head, body and mind, laborer and gentleman.

The story of the founding of UCL teaches us how the emergence of the modern university cannot be understood without reference to utilitarianism, how at least in England the very idea of a modern university was a utilitarian idea. Indeed, Robert J. C. Young (1992) has called London University "the Chrestomathic University." Recognizing this long history helps challenge any notion that utility arrives late to the university, as if utility is a foreign policy imposed on universities by governments. I have opened this chapter with the story of the founding of UCL for a reason. I wanted to show how an account of use and the university could be offered as an extension of the history of monitorial schools addressed in the previous chapter. Thomas Campbell himself makes direct reference to Andrew Bell and Joseph Lancaster in making a case for a new university organized around useful knowledge. An account of use and the university could also be offered as an extension of my discussion of using things from chapter 1: universities depend on paths and postboxes; they have routes and routines. The university could even be considered an object in use or a container technology. As Zoë Sofia has shown, a container is "not just about what holds or houses us, but what we put our stuff into" (2000, 185). An account of use and the university could also extend the discussion of ideas of use from chapter 2; the university could be understood as holding or housing ideas, which could be understood as "the stuff" of the university. I will indeed consider the housing of eugenics by London University in due course.

Houses are built over time and ideas can be shaped by where and how they are housed. When I visited the archives of London University held by UCL, which include the minute books, I was able to witness the history of decisions about how the university was to be built. The minutes from May 20, 1827, report, "It was resolved that each member of council should use his personal influence to induce such proprietors as he may select." A network of influence is how a university is funded, how a university is assembled as a body. On May 6, 1827, stones were brought to the Building Committee, Portland and Edinburgh Stones, in order to help make a decision about which stones to use. I think of stones there, on the table—part of the proceedings. These are different kinds of stones than Darwin's stones that I referred to in chapter 2; these stones have been cut, made to fit. The stones, however fitting, still have a story to tell. If bricks become walls, stones become steps. Jay Timothy Dolmage notes how steep steps are material but how they also create an idea of the university, reminding us "that access to the university is a movement upwards—only the truly 'fit' survive this climb" (2017, 44). Eugenics then might be understood not only as housed by the university but as shaping how it is built, stone by stone, step by step. A building can be built around an assumption of who it is for; those who fit become the "truly fit."

Accounting for use and the university is thus a way of bringing the arguments of each of my three preceding chapters together. While I will conclude with a discussion of how utility operates as policy within the university, it is important to my argument that I do not start there; to start there would not allow us to witness how use shapes what is already here, who is already here. In this chapter, I am drawing on data I have collected for two research projects—the first on diversity work in universities (2003–9) and the second on complaint within universities (2016–19)[3]—as well as material I have collected from being a diversity worker based at universities for over twenty years, in addition to my own involvement in a series of inquiries into sexual harassment and misconduct promoted by a collective complaint lodged by students. I bring the projects together in part because working on complaint returned me to diversity work. We become diversity workers when we try to challenge or dismantle the structures that are not built to accommodate us. Diversity work and complaint provide a lens with which to explain how institutions take shape. Once assembled, it can seem that institutions are as they are. You come to know how "being as they are" is work when your work is to change how things are.

Uses of Diversity

A history of the emergence of the modern secular university has much to teach us about how accessibility was a crucial value for the university even if that was not the term being used. In 1835, Thomas Spring Rice wrote as Chancellor of the Exchequer to obtain a Royal Charter for the University: "It should always be kept in mind that what is sought in the present occasion is an equality in all respects to the ancient universities, freed from those exclusions and religious distinctions which abridge the usefulness of Oxford and Cambridge" (cited in Meisel 2008, 127). If the word *equality* appears here as an aspiration for equal status to Oxbridge, that aspiration is directly tied to a concept of inclusion (freedom from exclusion), as well as being predicated on an extension of usefulness. Today, UCL references this history as its founding principles: "UCL was established in 1826 in order to open up education in England for the first time to students of any race, class or religion. By 1878, it had become the first English university to welcome female students on equal terms with men." The mission statement of UCL makes use of the term *diversity* as one term among others for describing itself: "a diverse intellectual community, engaged with the wider world and committed to changing it for the better; recognised for our radical and critical thinking and its widespread influence; with an outstanding ability to integrate our education, research, innovation and enterprise for the long-term benefit of humanity." A modified version of this core mission forms the first sentence of UCL's equality and diversity strategy.

The use of *diversity* as a description and strategy is not specific to UCL. Diversity is frequently used by universities as a way of describing their core educational and social missions. The word *diversity* may be used in mission statements such as the one I cited here, or in speeches made by vice chancellors, heads of departments, and managers, as well as in brochures and publicity materials produced by communications and marketing departments. We might call these uses of diversity "official diversity." I have in previous work offered an analysis of such official uses of diversity, though I have not foregrounded the significance of *use* to my analysis of what diversity is doing.

Diversity is in use within universities in both senses of being in use discussed in chapter 1: it is in circulation and has become a form of currency. Diversity is often used to signal a kind of commitment to something, including a commitment to change: change as diversification. So, for example, in the case of UCL's strategy, diversity and equality are used firstly as what it does and what it is good at: "UCL is regarded as a sector leader in the field of equalities and diversity." This claim is followed by a qualification: "and yet our staff and student data, and some lived experiences, tell a different story." Sometimes a qualification to an argument is how an argument can be made. The qualification makes clear that being regarded by a sector as a diversity leader does not mean that is how you are regarded by staff and students.

We can note here that despite the implication that diversity requires commitment and work, even for those who are leading the sector, diversity is widely understood as having lost its meaning. Perhaps diversity is used too easily or too much. One recent article asks: "How does a word become so muddled that it loses much of its meaning? How does it go from communicating something idealistic to something cynical and suspect? If that word is 'diversity,' the answer is: through a combination of overuse, imprecision, inertia and self-serving intentions."[4] In chapter 1, I discussed how words can become overused—worn out and worn down. Diversity might be one such word: used so much that it seems not to do very much at all.

One way of reflecting on what diversity is doing is to ask those appointed as diversity practitioners about how and why they use the term. In the UK, those who are employed as diversity workers are usually administrators. The hierarchy between academic/administrator is powerful.

The split between heads and hands described in chapter 2 becomes a division of labor within the university: many academics think of themselves as head workers and perceive administrators as hands and handy. Diversity and equality are also dismissed as being simply an administrative function: as about audit and accountability, as mechanisms that restrict academic freedom. This dismissal of diversity and equality often means in practice a dismissal of diversity workers. A practitioner explained: "It is another area of equality—an academic/non-academic divide. It's absolutely horrified me. I've never experienced anything like it. It is really surprising that it's just, well you know if you aren't an academic you don't get listened to." You do not get listened to; to be an administrator is to be looked over, assumed as beneath and below.

Diversity workers make do with what is available to them. The tools they use are tools that are already supplied by the institutions they are trying to transform. One of my first questions to diversity workers was about the word *diversity*, but it was also, I now realize, a question about use. I asked practitioners about whether they use that word or why they think that word is useful. Practitioners often made decisions about what words to use by considering whom they are addressing: different words work for different people; diversity works for some constituencies more than others. You might use the word *diversity* because of who you are speaking to; consciousness of use is also consciousness of audience, use as *to*. I think of the process as rather like trying on different clothes: you have to work out which words work for different audiences. We learn from trying words that do not fit. Not fitting is an experience of not getting through.

Most of the practitioners I spoke to use the language of diversity even when they are critical of how organizations use the word. Some practitioners suggested that they use the term *diversity* because diversity is the term that is in use. The appeal of the term *diversity* might point to a circularity or loop: we use *diversity* because it is being used; it is being used because we use it. It is important to note that this circularity is not specific to diversity but describes the slippery phenomenon of what we might call simply linguistic fashion: words come in and out of use by being used or not being used. Institutional knowledge can be defined as knowledge of fashion: knowing which words are most in use is about how one can be affectively aligned with others. One practitioner observed: "I would say that the term *diversity* is just used now because it's more popular. You know it's in the press so why would we have equal opportunities when we can just say it's diversity." We can "just say its diversity" if diversity is "just used now." Use becomes a reason for use, the circularity of a logic transformed into a tool.

The word *diversity* might be "just used now," because of its affective qualities as a happy or positive term. One practitioner stated: "Diversity obscures the issues. . . . diversity is like a big shiny red apple, it all looks wonderful but if you actually cut into that apple there's a rotten core in there and you know that it's actually all rotting away and it's not actually being addressed. It all looks wonderful but the inequalities aren't being addressed." Diversity might be a useful word because of what it does not address. If diversity creates the impression of addressing something without addressing anything, diversity is used as a way of managing impressions. Intended functionality can be used to refer not only to the intended function of an object (which can be used queerly in a way that disagrees with an intention as I noted in chapter 1) but also what is *stated* as the intended function of an action. There is a gap between what is given expression as intention and what is being done. Diversity workers often work in this gap, and might have to make use of it. By this I mean that they can use that organizations do not do what they say to challenge what they do.

While some practitioners do not use the word *diversity* because it is too positive, for other practitioners the positivity of diversity makes it useful. The term *diversity* is used because it is less threatening; diversity offers a route through people's defenses. Another practitioner noted: "I think it's really difficult: to use a term that's not acceptable is not to be able to do anything. In a way, you need to use a term that's not going to make people feel threatened if you're going to try and work with them." To use a term that is unacceptable to many is not to get very far. Another practitioner explained that she uses *diversity* because "it is not a scary word." You use a word because it is not charged; it does not threaten those to whom you are speaking. Diversity allows us to reconsider what it means for something to be *user friendly*. Diversity is a friendly word because of what it does not bring up. Of course there is a problem in a solution: diversity might be used more because it does not bring up what brings you to use it in the first place.

Diversity could be described as a buzz word: what we can hear might be the sound of it being used, or buzz as busy. I noted in chapter 3 how concepts become organizing of a field by the work that is done around them.

Working with diversity, I have come to understand how the story of how words are used more cannot be told without reference to the fate of other words. Part of the story of diversity's usage is also a story of recession: how other terms have lost their appeal, becoming old, tired, and dated. One practitioner explained:

> I think it [equity] became a tired term because it was thrown around a lot and I think . . . well, I don't know . . . because our title is equity and social justice, somebody the other day was saying to me, "Oh, there's equity fatigue, people are sick of the word *equity*." . . . Oh well, OK, we've gone through equal opportunity, affirmative action—they are sick of equity—now what do we call ourselves?! They are sick of it because we have to keep saying it because they are not doing it.

The tiredness or even sickness of the old terms is here a symptom of a certain institutional reluctance: you have to repeat the terms because they are not doing it; they are not doing it because you are repeating the terms. The implication of the arguments about equity fatigue is that in using less tired words, practitioners might themselves be energized or perceived as more energetic: "Those terms had got tired and I think that there's a bit of 'if one thing gets tired, looks like you've got tired as well.'" If you can become tired by your association with tired words, then the word *diversity* offers a way of appearing or even being less tired. As this practitioner went on to say, "You're put in a position where you have to say these things because nobody else will say them. People don't listen to you because you're the one who's saying it." You keep saying it because they are not saying it. The tiredness is part of the loop of repetition: you use the terms more because they are not working, and because you use them more they are not working. The implication of this argument is that certain words get heavy or acquire baggage from their use; they get weighed down by their associations. The more words circulate, the less they seem to do. We could say diversity does less because it is used more. It remains possible that diversity will also become tired through repetition. As one practitioner described it, "They're not tired of it yet; I think it's a term that they think, 'Oh yeah, diversity.' Diversity they can cope with." Coping with diversity might be conditional; they are not tired of it yet. This still implies that tiredness might happen somewhere down the line. Diversity does less because it is used more. Or diversity is used more because it does less. Perhaps both of these statements are true. If

4.3. Go that way!

you use diversity because it does less, doing less becomes as much as you can do.

Diversity is used not only as a word but also as an image. Images are instantly recognizable as images of diversity, those happy smiling colorful faces, because that is how they have been used. In her important book *Space Invaders*, Nirmal Puwar notes how "in policy terms, diversity has overwhelmingly come to mean the inclusion of different bodies" (2004,1). In practice, "different bodies" often means those who look different from white, or not looking white, or looking not white. In an interview I had with staff from a human resources department of an elite university, we discussed the findings of a research project that had been commissioned about how their university was perceived by external communities. The research found that the university was perceived as white as well as male dominated. The findings should not have been surprising: like many elite universities in the UK, the university was in fact white and male dominated, especially at senior levels. But the response was to treat the perception as wrong; the staff I interviewed described their project as being to modify the perception by *changing the image*. They intended to create a new brochure by using more colorful faces.

New here might have its uses: the investment in new can imply old patterns can simply be changed by a change of image. You can change the image but not change the organization. You can change the image in order not to change the organization. When we are talking about the uses of diversity as an image, we are talking about more than an image. Simply put: those who are *less* represented are used *more* to represent the organization. The further away you are from the norm, the more you have to appear. *Being used more* needs to be understood as political as well as emotional labor. I still remember when we began our research project on diversity, how the organization that funded us kept wanting to photograph us (for further discussion, see Ahmed 2012). We were the only research team that included people of color. By representing us, they could represent themselves as being more diverse than they were. Being a happy symbol of diversity can be hard work, especially if your experiences are not happy. The smile masks more than organizational failure; it masks your own experience of that failure. Heidi Mirza describes how her university kept using her smiling face: "Visual images of 'colourful' happy faces are used to show the university has embraced difference. My 'happy' face appeared on the front of the university website—even though every week I asked for it to be taken down, it still kept popping up" (2017, 44). Diversity work can also be the work you have to do *not* to appear smiling or even *not* to appear.

Institutional Mechanics

We can now make sense of how diversity often operates as a use instruction: a path or even an arrow, which tells you which way to go (figure 4.3). The ease with which diversity travels demonstrates the difficulty of getting through. One practitioner described her job as follows: "It is a banging your head against a brick wall job." I have drawn from her insight in describing diversity work as *wall work* (Ahmed 2012, 2017). You sense how repetition becomes a sore point: if you throw yourself against a wall, it is you that gets sore. And what happens to the wall? All you seem to have done is scratched the surface. And this is what diversity work can feel like: scratching the surface; scratching at the surface (figure 4.4).[5]

Scratching seems to convey the limits of what we have accomplished. But even if you just scratch the surface, you can still end up liable for damages. When we consider how diversity can be framed as damage, we need to remember that many diversity practitioners are appointed by universities to diversify them. And yet practitioners experience the institution as what is blocking their efforts. Let me share with you one example of a practitioner who developed a new policy on appointments.

> When I was first here there was a policy that you had to have three people on every panel who had been diversity trained. But then there was a decision early on when I was here, that it should be everybody, all panel members, at least internal people. They took that decision at

4.4. Scratching the surface.

the equality and diversity committee which several members of SMT were present at. But then the director of human resources found out about it and decided we didn't have the resources to support it; and it went to council with that taken out, and council were told that they were happy to have just three members, only a person on council who was an external member of the diversity committee went ballistic—and I am not kidding went ballistic—and said the minutes didn't reflect what had happened in the meeting because the minutes said the decision was different to what actually happened (and I didn't take the minutes, by the way). And so they had to take it through and reverse it. And the council decision was that all people should be trained. And despite that, I have then sat in meetings where they have just continued saying that it has to be just three people on the panel. And I said, "But no, council changed their view and I can give you the minutes," and they just look at me as if I am saying something really stupid; this went on for ages, even though the council minutes definitely said all panel members should be trained. And to be honest sometimes you just give up.

A decision made in the present about the future is overridden by the momentum of the past. The past becomes like that well-trodden path: what usually happens still happens, despite a change of policy, even through a change of policy. An old policy is another well-trodden path (figure 4.5).

4.5. An old policy.

Or perhaps we could say that the new policy is so light that it does not even scratch the surface: they keep saying it has to be just three people; they keep doing what they are saying. Each time they do what they did, the furrow left by following the same route becomes deeper. A policy that has been brought into existence by following the right procedures, by doing the right things in the right way, does not stop what usually happens from happening. The head of personnel did not need to take the decision out of the minutes for the decision not to bring something into effect. I have named this dynamic "nonperformativity": when naming something does not bring something into effect, or when something is named in order not to bring something into effect.

The wall refers to that which keeps standing. The wall is how things are stopped, which means that *what stops movement moves*. When the mechanisms for stopping something are mobile, to witness the movement can mean to miss the mechanism. I think this is very important as organizations are good at moving things around; movement can be used as a distraction from what is not being done. In our example, what stopped something from happening *could have been* the removal of the policy from

4.6. The postbox that is not in use might have another function.

the minutes; it *could have been* the failure to notice this removal, but it was not. It was the way in which those within the institution acted after the policy had been agreed. Agreeing to something can be another way of stopping something from happening.

A diversity policy can come into existence without coming into use. I noted in chapter 1 how a sign is often used to make a transition from something being in use to being out of use, like the sign on the post-box. From the point of view of the would-be poster of a letter, you need to know the postbox is not in use in order to know not to post a letter through a hole; otherwise your letter would just sit there: *not much use*. Maybe the diversity worker puts the policy in the postbox because she assumes the box is in use. An assumption can be what you receive from others. She is, after all, following the usual procedure; she is using the tools she is supposed to use in the way she is supposed to use them. The postbox that is not in use without any sign indicating that it is not in use might have another function: to stop something from going through the whole system (figure 4.6).

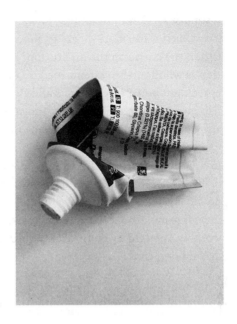

4.7. Sometimes you just give up.

Diversity work is often mechanical: you have to work out how you are stopped from getting a new policy through a system. The mechanical is also experiential; the wall is an *experience* of being stopped or gives expression to that experience. We can return here to my discussions of wear and tear in chapter 1. Marx argued that "wear and tear" can be a result of use or disuse; a machine might wear out after it has been used for such-and-such amount of time, or a sword might become rusty by being left in a scabbard. In this instance, the policy becomes rather like that rusty sword: from rusty to dusty. The policy becomes unusable by not being used.

Consider too how much energy the diversity worker expended bringing a policy into existence that does not come into use. Maybe she ends up being used up, rather like that tube of toothpaste: limp, spent, wasted. As she said, "Sometimes you just give up" (figure 4.7).

The story of how the wall keeps standing is thus the same story as the story of how the diversity worker is shattered. That the story is the same story needs to be understood as significant. To be used up or depleted is a feeling but also a structure; we could understand being used up as a *feeling of structure*. You are depleted by an encounter with a wall that is not even perceptible to others. We need to remember that many diversity workers are employed by institutions to diversify them, to bring, as it were, more diversity about. If you are employed by the institution to transform the institution, you might assume that the institution is willing to be transformed; in other words, you might assume an agreement between your ends and the institution's ends. To be stopped from achieving those ends by those who employed you is to become a means to ends that are not your own. Diversity workers too can be used to create the appearance of doing something or used to create an impression that diversity is being done. Diversity workers can end up being depleted not simply because of how much effort is required to do what they do but because of how much effort is expended in not bringing something about. Being used up is a measure of how diversity workers are used by institutions: used up as being used.

Thinking through how diversity policies are stopped even after they have been agreed has helped me think about what happens to complaints, to follow them around, to ask where they go and do not go. I have been learning about how complaints travel by talking to administrators, students, and academics about the process of making complaints within universities. Making a complaint also requires becoming an institutional mechanic: you have to work out how to get a complaint through the system. It is because of the difficulty of getting through that a complaint often ends up being about a system. This point might seem counterintuitive given that most organizations have complaint procedures. Surely to make a complaint is to follow a procedure for making a complaint? Listening to those who have made or tried to make formal complaints has taught me that the gap between what is supposed to happen and what does happen is densely populated.

Many universities in the UK include as part of their complaint policies a discussion of how they will record and monitor complaints. One university writes that complaints will "assist in identifying problems and trends across the University." They then write that complaints will "form the basis of positive publicity, in demonstrating that identified issues have been resolved." When complaints record a problem, they can be quickly folded into a solution: a record of how universities have resolved something—resolution, dissolution. Complaints can thus be used in a similar way to diversity: *a way of appearing to address a problem.*

A complaint procedure is often represented as flowchart: flow, flow, away we go, with paths and arrows, which give the would-be complainant a route through. I spoke to one administrator about her work in supporting students through the complaints process. She explained:

> So your first stage would require the complainant to try and resolve it informally, which is really difficult in some situations and which is where it might get stuck in a department. . . . And so it takes a really tenacious complaining student to say, no, I am being blocked. . . . If something bad has happened, and you are not feeling that way inclined, you can understand why a student would not have the tenacity to make sure that happens, and to advocate for themselves. They might go to the student union, and the student union is really bogged down . . . or they might go to the central complaints office and they get a very bureaucratic response back and get put off. So you can imagine that something on paper that looks very linear is actually very circular a lot of the time and I think that's the problem, students get discouraged and get demoralized and feel hard done by, and nothing's getting resolved and then they are in a murky place and they can't get out.

If a procedure exists in order to clear a path, that path can be blocked at any point. Blockages can occur through conversations; if those you speak to are bogged down, you can get bogged down. A conversation can be another wall; a complaint can feel like "talking to a wall." A complaint is not simply an outcome of a *no*; a complaint requires you to keep saying *no* along the way. This practitioner acknowledged that what is required to proceed with a complaint (confidence and tenacity) might be what is eroded by the very experiences that lead to complaint ("something bad has happened," "not feeling that way inclined").

Unsurprisingly, then, stopping is part of the life course or biography of a complaint. One problem identified in some of my interviews is the relative inaccessibility of policies and procedures. One student described: "It took us forever to try and find the complaints procedure PDF on the database. We knew it existed but it was like a mythical golden egg; we just couldn't find it. And when we did it was so big that even two PhD students spent weeks trying to get through the small print, to find out what the complaint process was." If you cannot find the policy, you cannot follow the path laid out as procedure. Remember: the less a path is used, the less a path is used, until you can hardly see the sign for the leaves. Or if you do find the policy, but it is hard to use, we might call the policy user unfriendly—you might be discouraged; you might try to find

4.8. If you can't find the policy, you can't follow the path.

an easier route, not complaining as easing a passage through an organization (figure 4.8).

A would-be complainer is one who has taken some steps in the direction of a formal complaint, perhaps by making an informal disclosure to a line manager, supervisor, or peer. Many complaints are stopped at this point through the use of warnings. In chapter 1, I referred to the overuse of exclamation points: when the signs used for emphasis are used too much, they no longer function to emphasize something (although by not functioning as emphasis, they might be doing something else). With small modifications, an exclamation point can offer a more precise instruction. When a singular exclamation point is black, and contained by a red triangle, it becomes a warning (figure 4.9).

A warning is an ominous sign, a sign of the danger-to-come. Warnings surround complaints as if to say to proceed is to endanger your own person. Warnings are typically stronger than advice about how to proceed; they are often issued in an emergency. When an emergency is implied, an instruction is given about how to treat a situation. Sometimes to be warned is

4.9. Stop! Danger ahead!

to be told there is no time to think about a course of action. This is not to say that the tone of a warning is always stern; intonation depends on use. Sometimes warnings are given calmly, spoken in the language of care, because, after all, to be given such an instruction is also to be told how a potential danger can be avoided. One student explained: "I ended up going back to the chair, and saying, look, this is harassment and I am going to file a complaint. And his response was essentially, 'Well we are just thinking about your career, how this will affect you in the future.'" The implication is that to proceed with a formal complaint is not to think about your career; being advised not to complain is offered as career advice. Your career is evoked as a companion who needs to be looked after. Maybe your career is a plant that needs watering so that it does not wither away; if your career would wither as a consequence of complaining, then a complaint is figured in advance as carelessness, as negligence, as not looking after yourself.

Warnings are useful because they articulate a *no* predicated not on some abstract rule but on the complainer's own health and safety. Another student noted: "I was repeatedly told that 'rocking the boat' or 'making waves' would affect my career in the future and that I would ruin the department for everyone else. I was told if I did put in a complaint, I would never be able to work in the university and that it was likely I wouldn't get a job elsewhere." Complaining is framed as self-damage as well as damage to others—ruining a department, no less. This student described how the pressure not to complain was exerted: "In just one day I was subjected to eight hours of grueling meetings and questioning, almost designed to break me and stop me from taking the complaint any further." You can stop people from doing something by making it harder for them to do something. Remember, deviation is hard. Deviation is made hard. Warnings can operate not simply as predictive utterances but also as threats. This student commented on how the head of her department made reference to her source of funding during one of these meetings. To be reminded of how she is dependent on the department for resources is to be told how they can make her topple over.

If warnings are used to discourage a certain course of action, they also function as positive directives: you might be encouraged not to make a complaint. Indeed, one academic described this approach as a default setting: "The default academia thing, the university thing: it will be fine; if we do wait, don't make a fuss." Not making a complaint becomes a form of civic virtue and even good citizenship; patience is tied to a positive outlook as if the best way to approach a wrong is to assume it will right itself. The flip side of a warning is a promise, an institutional version of what I called *the promise of happiness*, a promise that if you don't complain you will get further.

Complaints can also be stopped by the appearance of being heard. I spoke to one academic about how she came to a decision about whether to complain about the conduct of senior members of the university, including heads of departments and a pro vice chancellor around a table. She was the only woman at that table. She described how they were "talking about women's bodies, what they look like, what they do to them as men, what they would do to them. Very sexual. Very sexist jokes. Very sexually overt conversations and I was sitting there as if I was not there." It was a deeply distressing experience in part as she had assumed the organization to be as progressive as it said it was. She took the matter up by speaking to another pro vice chancellor and the director of human resources: "I had a hearing . . . but I think it was just to placate me." Being placated is another way a complaint is stopped; you might receive a nod, a yes, yes. Nods seem to surround complaints. One student described what happened when she talked to the head of her department: "He seemed to take it on board; he was listening, he was nodding. Ten days later I still had not heard anything. A space of limbo opened up." Thus far I have primarily used the category of "nonperformative" to refer to speech acts.

A body too can appear to act. A nod can operate in the realm of the non-performative; a nod can be made in order not to bring something about.

When these senior managers did not do anything—and not doing is an action, not simply inaction—she decided not to take the complaint any further. And she came to that decision in part because of what had happened at her previous institution; she had supported a number of students who had filed a complaint against a male lecturer for sexual misconduct and sexual harassment. She explained: "I think I just suddenly thought this is too much. And I had just come from an institution where I had spearheaded a group of students, making a complaint against a lecturer, we took it all the way to the top and the lecturer got off." He got off despite the evidence (in this case ten students provided firsthand testimony). It was this experience of not getting anywhere that led her to decide not to make a complaint about the conduct of these senior managers. We carry complaints with us, whether or not we make them; when a complaint is stopped, that stoppage can lead to yet more stoppages down the line.

Another academic described what followed when students lodged a complaint about the behavior of professors at research events. A meeting was set up: "They said they would have an open meeting but it was just about calming [the students] down." Venting is used as a technique of preventing something more explosive from happening: you let a complaint be expressed in order that it can be contained. Once the students have vented their frustrations, once they have gotten complaint out of their system, the complaint is out of the system. The mechanism is rather like a pressure relief valve, which lets off enough pressure so that it does not build up and cause an explosion.

Another method of stopping a complaint is to declare a complaint "not a complaint" because it does not fulfill the technical requirements for being a complaint. For example, a member of staff made a complaint about bullying from the head of her department. The experience of bullying had been devastating, and she suffered from depression as a result. It took her a long time to get to the point where she could write a complaint. She described what happened once she was able to file a complaint: "I basically did it when I was able to, because I was just really unwell for a significant period of time. And I put in the complaint and the response that I got was from the deputy VC. He said that he couldn't process my complaint because I had taken too long to lodge it." Some experiences are so devastating that it takes time to process them. And the length of time taken can be used to disqualify a complaint. The tightening of the complaint as genre—a complaint as the requirement to fill in a form in a certain way at a certain time—is how many struggles are not recorded.

If organizations can disqualify complaints because they take too long to make, they can also take too long to respond to complaints. One student described how the university took seven months to respond to her complaint, and then another seven months to respond to her response to their response to her complaint: "It is my theory they been putting in the long finger and pulling this out, dragging this out over unacceptable periods of time, to try and tire me out so that I will just give up." Sometimes it can seem exhaustion is not just the effect but the point of a complaint process. Exhaustion can be a management technique: you tire people out so they are too tired to address what makes them too tired.

In chapter 1, I discussed efficiency as the ratio of useful work relative to the output of energy. We can now consider how inefficiency can sometimes be useful as a technique for expending energy. I use the term *strategic inefficiency*, to point to how organizations have an interest in slowing or stopping complaints. We might think of inefficiency as annoying but indiscriminate, affecting everyone and everything. Listening to those who have complained has taught me that inefficiency can be discriminatory. An international student was waiting for her complaint to be processed while her visa was running out: "Ten days before my visa was about to run out I applied for a new visa. And they were like how can we give her a visa she is on probation. You have to have good standing to get a visa and they were like this complaint thing is open." For students and staff who are more precarious because of their residential, employment, or financial status, the longer a complaint is kept open the more you could lose. Those who have less need to complain are those who could most handle the consequences of complaint. We can establish a connection between the discriminatory effects of inefficiency and the efficiency with which organizations reproduce themselves as being for certain kinds of people: those whose papers are in the right place, those who are in the right place; those who are upright, able; well resourced, well connected.

You can lodge a complaint, it can even go through the whole system, and still nothing happens. Perhaps complaints end up in a filing cabinet: filing as filing away (figure 4.10). One student said of her complaint, "It just gets shoved in the box." Another student explained, "I feel like my complaint has gone into the complaint graveyard." When a complaint is filed away or binned or buried, those who complain can end up feeling filed away or binned or buried. We need to remember that a complaint

4.10. Filing as filing away.

is a record of what happens *to* a person. Complaints are personal. Complaints are also records of what happens in an institution. Complaints are institutional. The personal is institutional. One academic researcher shared her complaint file with me: "One of the things I talked about in those documents, I am very open, I was under such stress and trauma that my periods stopped. . . . That's the intimacy of some of the things that go into it, bodily functions like this." A body can stop functioning. A body can announce a complaint. That body is in a document. And that document is in a file. And that file is in a cabinet. To file a complaint can mean to become alienated from your own history, a history that is often difficult, painful, and traumatic.

The Institutional as Usual

We know about the institutional (as usual) from those who are trying to transform institutions. Diversity work generates data on institutions, snapshots of institutional life taken from the point of view of those trying not to reproduce that life.

Here is a snapshot. I am having an informal meeting with a diversity practitioner. She is talking to me about how she felt about her job, how she felt about the university that employed her. She speaks of how most of her time was spent preparing for committees, which usually meant writing documents: writing the agenda for the next committee, minutes of the last, new policies for consideration, often prompted by changes in legislation. There is a lot of paperwork—a lot of stuff—in diversity work. Diversity work is stuffy. I will turn to how diversity workers become stuff in due course. How institutions do committees varies. Once you have been somewhere for a certain length of time, as long as it takes not to be surprised by your surroundings, you have become *used to it*: business as usual. You know what usually happens; the usual is a field of expectation that derives its contours from past experience. The usual is the structural in temporal form. Some of this routine is about formal process: the motions you go through, how often committees feel like going through the motions; reviewing the minutes from that past meeting; chairs and secretaries with their specific tasks; any other business, always last. In committees, we know what usually happens: the institutional as usual.

Committees are also spaces: there are ways of talking, ways of being seated, ways of organizing the table and the chairs, ways of doing the work. When a room has been properly assembled, a meeting can progress. In our conversation, the diversity practitioner spoke of one time when she turned up for the equality and diversity committee for which she was the secretary. This committee is chaired by a senior member of the university, a white male professor. At the time all members of the senior management were white male professors: he is how the professor usually appears. In the previous section I noted how a new appointment policy does not stop what usually happens from happening. The usual can refer to whom as well as what: who usually happens (and who does not). You do not appear as a professor if you are not how a professor usually appears.

However he appears, the professor is there because he is the chair. When the diversity worker turned up, she found the room was already occupied. The chair was already there, as was another member of the committee, also a white male professor. They were lounging around, confident, taking up the time. They were talking about the breakfasts they used to have when they were students at Cambridge University; they were laughing; a shared memory of consuming. A memory can be consuming. A memory can occupy space. A casual conversation about a past experience of an elite institution can fill the space—the space becomes elite, for a select few, how a few are selected; a sense of ownership spills out and over, our space, our diversity, our university, ours. She said they did not stop talking to each other when she, the person who had sent them the papers that were on the table, entered the room; they just kept talking to each other as if she were not there. Perhaps for them she was not there. This practitioner said to me about her experience of turning up at a diversity committee, only to find it was already occupied, and her words have stayed with me because they got through to me: "I realized how far away they were from my world." We learn: a committee set up to transform a world can be how a world is reassembled. We also learn: those of us who arrive in institutions that were not intended for us bring with us worlds that would not otherwise be here.

A background can be what is shared. What is behind you can be what enables you to enter the room, to occupy a space. We could think of this history as a history of wearing. We can return to my metaphor of the institution as a well-worn garment introduced in chapter 1: an institution acquires the shape of those who have shaped it. An institution is easier to wear if you have the same shape as the shape of those who came before. A history of use can be inherited as ease. As I noted in *Queer Phenomenology*, the word *inheritance* can mean to receive as well as to possess (2006, 125). An inheritance not only can be *what* you receive but can be a matter of *how* you are received. An inheritance can be an easing of being, an enabling—how spaces are shaped by those who came before.

We can think back to the sign *occupied*. We can think of all the different ways in which the university is occupied (figure 4.11). This occupation leaves traces on walls; portraits of past leaders can surround you; and a background can be what you have to confront. You do not need to know the histories to encounter what they have left behind; use leaves traces in places. Perhaps you can feel alienated because you are surrounded by what does not accommodate you. Alienation can be revelation. My first post was in women's studies. I had an impression of this organization as a friendly and feminist space. But then I became head of the department. Well, if women's studies was a feminist bubble, becoming head of the department meant that bubble burst. I began to attend faculty meetings. I remember going to one meeting at the top room. I remember going into that room and seeing all the paintings of white men. They were modern in style but traditional in content. I remember women coming around in uniforms serving tea and cakes. But the thing I really remember:

4.11. The university is occupied.

the secretary and the chair of the board engaging in sexual innuendo throughout the meeting. I remember people laughing. I remember feeling shocked in part by how it seemed to be business as usual. Sexual jokes, sexual banter, portraits of white men, former leaders, reminding you of who led the university to be where it is, and then there were the women serving coffee: yes, my feminist bubble had burst. All these different elements combine—thick, becoming wall.

Portraits, names, the walls can be busy. Busy can be business. The University College London received funds from Francis Galton to found a program in national eugenics. The university has mostly removed the word *eugenics* from his legacy, that word too associated with what is damaged, but it has kept his name. You can take out the word but keep the thing. That Galton's name remains in use does matter: a donation preserved as a sign in a landscape. There is a Galton professorship, a Galton lecture theater; UCL houses the Galton collection. The history of eugenics can be given a home; use leaves traces in places. To be at UCL is to confront this history. In 2016 a panel took place at UCL titled "Why Isn't My Professor Black?," with Black British scholars William Ackah, Nathaniel Adam Tobias Coleman, Deborah Gabriel, Lisa Amanda Palmer, Nathan Richards, and Shirley Anne Tate.[6] Why isn't my professor black? What a

4.12. The more he is cited, the more he is cited.

good question—what a necessary and important question! At the end of the panel, a member of the audience asked another necessary and urgent question about UCL's continued use of Francis Galton's name. The president and provost of UCL answered, "My only defense is I inherited him." Use inheritance becomes use as inheritance.

In my defense, I inherited him: we can think too of the use of a name as how a history is kept alive. Citation too is another way a history is kept alive—citation as a reference system. You are asked to follow the well-trodden paths of citation, to cite properly as to cite those deemed to have already the most influence. The more a path is used, the more a path is used. The more he is cited, the more he is cited (figure 4.12).

A path is kept clear through work; occupation depends on erasure. Such-and-such white man might become an originator of a concept, an idea as becoming seminal, by removing traces of those who were here before. When use leaves traces in places, occupation can involve the removal of traces. You can inherit a removal. Sometimes occupation is achieved by how work is discarded. Eve Tuck describes settler reading practices: "The reading is like panning for gold," which works by "sorting it by what is useful and what can be discarded" (2018, 15). Settler readers, she suggests, "read like settlers," reading for "particular content which can be removed for future use" (15). Other times occupation is achieved by not even having to regard work by those who are deemed "the others" at all. To be trained within a discipline is to learn to follow a citational path: certain work does not have to be regarded because it does not come into view if you follow a path, which means work can be discarded without deliberation.

Good habits in citation are about extending a line: you have to show how much you know of a field by citing those deemed to have shaped that field. To extend a line is to reproduce an inheritance. Diversity work is also about generating understanding of how reproduction works, how the reproduction of the same old bodies, doing the same old things, is a result of *work* rather than being something that "just happens." The university is shaped by a history of appointments. When I visited the UCL archives, I did not find what I hoped to find: some interesting uses of use in the letter books and minutes from the period during which London University came into existence. But I found something else: a repetition of a form that I was used to, so used to that I often do not notice it.[7] The secretary wrote letters in response to those who expressed interest in teaching at the new university. Once you had read one of these letters, it seemed you had read them all: they were standardized; each letter might as well as have been a copy of another letter. A standard is what you create when you use the same form. I began to skim over these letters, as if I had read each one before. But then one letter jumped out: it was quite different; it was exceptional. It was a letter sent in response to Professor Johann Friedrich Meckel in 1827. Meckel was a German scientist who adopted Lamarck's evolutionary beliefs. He was a star professor at the time, though his work is not well known today. Meckel's name survives, as far as I can tell, because of the use of his name to name things: his name was given to a condition (Meckel's diverticulum), a syndrome (the Meckel syndrome), bone structure (Meckel's cartilage), as well as a protein (mecklin). One thinks here of naming as another way some are preserved in the archive, how some are committed to memory.

What struck me about the letter sent to Meckel is how the standards are suspended for the star professor; the letter is long and gushing, personal and keen. The suspension of the usual procedure: I began to see how suspension is crucial to the reproduction of the same thing—a suspension of the usual is usual. I know of many cases where the usual procedures are bypassed to enable the recruitment of such-and-such star professor, even though this bypassing is a bypassing of equal opportunity procedures that are supposed to be compulsory. I remember one time when a head of my department reported happily how we were joining with another department to enable such-and-such star professor to teach at the college. As usual the star professor was a white man. He is how a professor usually appears. I remember intervening grumpily, with another question that was really an exclamation: What about the equal opportunity procedures? What about equal opportunity procedures! He looked at me blankly, and went on, as if I had not said anything, as if I was interrupting the proceedings. Other feminists in the room shared my grimace, but we knew that nothing we could say or do would stop the process, because it was perceived to be of general benefit for the university to hire the star professor. To put an end to the process would be understood as depriving the organization of what is assumed (who is assumed) to benefit the most.

We can return to the example of the diversity policy that did not come into use. That policy was a new policy about how academic appointments are made. We can begin to appreciate another difficulty here: diversity workers often try to develop new procedures to stop the reproduction of the same thing, but procedures are what are suspended to enable that very reproduction.[8] One early career academic who described to me in acute detail the intense and everyday misogyny and racism in her department also speculated on how her department came to be that way. And she referred to how the human resources guidelines were often bypassed to enable such-and-such white man to be hired or promoted.

> We have the HR guidelines; I have been on the promotion committee for about 5 years and I saw it in action. Even though we had an HR representative right there and we had these guidelines and people would be saying, "Oh yeah, but he's a great guy, you know, I like to have a beer with him, he really should, he really does deserve reader, let's go for it." . . . The same thing with the short-listing and interview panels that I was involved in. So someone would say that women's presentation was outstanding but really he's the guy you'd want to have a pint with, so let's make the figures fit. So they'll wiggle the numbers around so even if he just gets one point more, he gets the higher score.

This criterion for appointability—hiring someone you would want to have a pint with—cannot be made official; it would contradict equal opportunity commitments. The procedures are not so much suspended (the right form is still being filled in) but adapted or corrupted: if he does not get the highest score, you wiggle the numbers, making the figures fit. The figures are made to fit when a person is deemed to fit. Think back to the snapshot of what happens in a diversity committee: how casual modes of conversing can be how spaces become occupied. So fitting becomes a matter of *fitting in*; you are more likely to be appointed if you fit in with those who are already assembled: *being like as being with*.

We can return here to my discussion of the laws of use and disuse in chapter 2. An institution is an environment. Environments are dynamic; it is because environments change that uses change. An institution, however, also functions as a container technology, a way of holding things or holding onto things. You reproduce something by *stabilizing the requirements for what you need to survive or thrive in an environment*. These requirements do not have to be made explicit; once a requirement has been stabilized, it does not need to be made explicit. Indeed, once these requirements are stabilized, they are reproduced unless a conscious willed effort is made to stop them from being reproduced. Institutions work hard not to enable a diversification that might otherwise happen because of the dynamic nature of life. In stabilizing the requirements for what you need to survive or thrive, institutions could be described as *antilife*.

We could return here to Darwin's use of the architect metaphor, in which natural selection is compared to the building of a house from uncut stones: the stones that are used are those that happen to fit. An institution too is built. It might appear as if the moment of use is hap: that this person or that person just happens to fit the requirements the way the stone just happens to be the same size as the hole in a wall. But once a building has been built, once it has taken form, more or less, some more than others, will fit the requirements. Fitting is still dependent on work: social reproduction works by tending to disappear as work. We are describing how a body seems somehow already attuned to a bourgeois set of requirements. An expectation is also about cutting, creating a shape that needs to be filled. Hap can then be used ideologically: *as if they are here because they just happened to fit, rather than they fit because of how the structure was built*. The institutional as usual refers not only to who is usual, who usually turns up or who usually appears, as well as to what is usual, the kinds of posts to be filled, but to a combining of a who and a what; many elements combine to enable a vacancy, a hole in a wall, to be shaped in order that some fit and for some to be shaped in order that they fit what needs to be filled.

A structure could thus be defined as the removal of hap from use in the determination of the requirements. In Lamarck's model, use becomes inheritance; when use becomes habitual, use shapes form, lessening the effort required to do something within an environment. When you fit, and fitting here is formal, a question of form, *you inherit the lessening of effort*. A path in the sense of a career path, a route through an organization as well as a life, is not simply made more usable by being used. Some have more paths laid out more clearly in front of them because they already fit the requirements. It is not just the constancy of use that eases a passage. Use is eased for those who inherit the right form, whereby rightness means the degree of a fit with an expectation. *For as before* acquires another resonance here: when a world is built *for* some, they come *before* others.

Misfit Genres

People do come to inhabit organizations that are not intended for them; you can make the cut without fitting. If you arrive with dubious origins, you are not expected to be here, so in getting here you have already disagreed with an expectation of who you are and what you can do; then an institution can feel like the wrong shape. When that well-worn garment does not fit, you do not fit. You become, to use again Rosemarie Garland-Thomson's (2011) important term, a *misfit*. Fitting becomes work for those who do not fit—you have to push, push, push; and sometimes no amount of pushing will get you in.

A complaint might be what is necessary because you do not fit, giving expression to how you are *not* attuned to the requirements of an organization: *a complaint as a misfit genre*. Sometimes you have to complain in order to be able to enter the room. An academic described how she has to keep pointing out that rooms are inaccessible because they keep booking rooms that are inaccessible: "I worry about drawing attention to myself. But this is what happens when you hire a person in a wheelchair. There have been major access issues at the university." She spoke of "the drain, the exhaustion, the sense of why should I have to be the one who speaks out." You have to speak out because others do not; and because you speak out, others can justify their own silence. They hear you, so it becomes about you; "major access issues" become your issues. I noted earlier how a diversity worker has to keep saying it because others are not doing it. Sometimes you have to keep saying it because they keep doing it. Some have to complain about the structures that enable and ease the progression of others.

What gives some a route through can be what slows or stops others. Routes become routines. And you can be a misfit given what has become routine. An organization that organizes long meetings without any breaks assumes a body that can be seated without breaks. If you arrive and cannot maintain this position, you do not meet the requirements. If you lay down during the meeting, you would throw the meeting into crisis. A social justice project might require throwing meetings into crisis.

Perhaps because organizations are trying to avoid such crises, misfits often end up on the same committees (otherwise known as the diversity committee). We might end up on the diversity committee because of whom we are not: not white, not cis, not able-bodied, not man, not straight. The more nots you are, the more committees you end up on! We can be misfits on these committees. A woman of color academic explained: "I was on the equality and diversity group in the university. And as soon as I started mentioning things to do with race they changed the portfolio of who could be on the committee and I was dropped." I noted earlier that diversity might be used more because it does less. The word *race* might be used less because it does more. Any use of the word *race* is thus an overuse. She added: "Whenever you raise something, the response is that you are not one of them." Not one of them: using words like *race* seems to *amplify* what makes you not fit, *picking up* what you are not. Perhaps a *not* is heard as shouting, as insistence, a stress point, a sore point, an exclamation point. Perhaps when a not is heard this way, you are being given a warning (figure 4.13).

Earlier I introduced the figure of a would-be complainer as the one who has indicated to herself or to others that she is considering filing a complaint. We are learning: you can become a complainer without giving any such indication. It is hard to do certain kinds of institutional work without being heard as a complainer. A figure too can be a file; the complainer is a rather stuffed file. If you then make a complaint, you are picking up an already stuffed file. As Leila Whitley and Tiffany Page have observed: "When a woman files an objection to sexual harassment she becomes in the language of the institution *a woman who complains*, and by extension a *complainer*" (2015, 43). Another academic described how becoming a complainer can take you away from your work: "If you

4.13. A complaint: when a not becomes an exclamation point!

have a situation and you make a complaint, then you are the woman who complains, the lesbian who complains, and it gets in the way of being in the role: being a good colleague, a good mentor, a great teacher, a supervisor. And you can feel the change in your voice and the dynamic in meetings. And you don't like to hear yourself talking like that but you end up being in that situation, again. And you think, 'It's me,' and you think, 'No it's not; it's systematic,' and you think, 'It's me.'" That conversation you have with yourself—it's me, it's the system, it's me, it's the system—takes time. And it can feel like everything is just spinning around. Spinning, spilling: maybe you reach a point, a breaking point, when it spills out.

You might fly off the handle (figure 4.14). To fly off the handle can mean to snap or to lose your temper. If the handle breaks, you become the one who cannot handle things. She further noted: "And then of course you get witch-hunted, you get scapegoated, you become the troublesome uppity woman; you become the woman who does not fit; you become everything the bully accuses you off, because nobody is listening to you. And you hear yourself starting to take that, not petulant tone [bangs table], come on. You can hear them saying, 'Oh, there you go.'" A diversity practitioner had said something very similar to me: that she only had to open

4.14. You might fly off the handle.

her mouth in meetings to witness eyes rolling as if to say, "Oh, here she goes." Both times we laughed: it can be relief to have an experience put into words. It was from experiences like this that I developed an equation: rolling eyes = feminist pedagogy. Complaints too are surrounded by rolling eyes. The word *complaint* derives from old French, *complaindre*, to lament, a lament, an expression of sorrow and grief; *lament*, from Latin, *lamentum*, "wailing, moaning; weeping." Complaint catches how those who challenge power become sites of negation: you become a container of negative affect, one that is leaky: speaking out as spilling over.

If a structure can be exhausting, it can be exhausting to point it out. An academic told me how she set up a writing group in her department and the meetings became dominated by senior men: "What I found in each of the meetings were senior men who were bullying everyone in the room." The bullying took that form of constant belittling of the work of more junior academics as well as postgraduate students: "The first session someone was being just really abusive about someone's PhD, saying it was rubbish." Racist comments were made: "I'm from London and London is just ripe for ethnic cleansing." She described how people laughed, how the laughter filled the room. She commented on these comments: "These were the sorts of things being aired." These were the sorts of things: sentences as sentencing; violence thrown out as how some are thrown out. Even the air can be occupied.

She decided to make a complaint because she "wanted it recorded," and because "the culture was being reproduced for new PhD students." A complaint becomes a recording device; you have to record what you do not want to reproduce. She gathered statements from approximately twenty people in her department. A complaint can be a feminist collective. A meeting was set up in response to her complaint. At that meeting she was described by the head of human resources as "having a chip on her shoulder"; a grievance was heard as a grudge. Perhaps it is not surprising that if you keep chipping away at the old block, they quickly find that chip on your shoulder. She added: "They treated the submission as an act of arrogance on my part." It was as if she put a complaint forward as a way of putting herself forward; a complaint was treated as self-promotional. Her complaint went nowhere. When those who try to stop a culture from being reproduced are stopped, a culture is being reproduced.

A complaint becomes necessary because of what has already been reproduced. A complaint is not a starting point; to make a complaint, informally or formally, is to complain *about* something that *precedes* the complaint. Complaints have what we might call a backward temporality: they take us back. And what precedes a complaint can be what stops you from getting through. One student gave an account of turning up at a postgraduate retreat. She had been away from the department for some time, and she sensed something had shifted.

> It was the cultural shift I recognized as I came through the doors. There was a lot of touching going on: shoulder rubs and knee pats. It was the dialogue. They were making jokes, jokes that were horrific; they were doing it in a very small space in front of staff, and nobody was saying anything. And it felt like my reaction to it was out of kilter with everyone else. It felt really disconnected, the way I felt about the way they were behaving and the way everybody else was laughing. They were talking about "milking bitches." I still can't quite get to the bottom of where the jokes were coming from. Nobody was saying anything about it: people were just laughing along.

You can open the door and be hit by it: a change in atmosphere, intrusions into personal space, words out and about. The sexist expression "milking bitches" seemed to have a history. Each time the expression is used, that *history is thrown out like a line*, a line you have to follow if you are to get anywhere. When laughter fills the room, like water in a cup, laughter as a holding something, it can feel like there is no room left. To experience such jokes as offensive is to become alienated not only from the jokes but from the laughter that surrounds them, propping them up, giving them somewhere to go. As she further described the situation:

> You start to stand out in that way; you are just not playing along. He was doing things I think to try and provoke me to react to him. I think he was doing it under the guise of humor. But he specifically went for me, verbally, at a table where everyone was eating lunch. It was a large table with numerous amounts of people around it, including staff. . . . I was having quite a personal conversation with someone . . . and he literally leaned across the table or physically came forward—he was slightly ajar to me, he was really close—and he said, "Oh my god, I can see you ovulating."

A refusal not to go along with something can be how you appear. Just by not laughing, not going along with something, she came to "stand out." I think this is very important: a complaint can be registered before anything is even said, expressed by how a body is not attuned to an environment. And because she did not find the jokes funny, because she was not condoning the behavior, because she was not happy with what was going on, he came after her. Her personal space invaded, words flung out, flung at, she was reduced to a body, pulled back, woman as ovaries; she was not allowed to do her own thing, to converse with others, to be occupied as a student.

Spaces can be occupied by how bodies can take up spaces *as if those spaces belong to them.* A sign can tell us that the room is occupied, as we learned from that toilet door. Spaces can be occupied without the use of signs. Universities too can be occupied, but sometimes the signs used by universities do not tell us that they are, or even how they are. In fact, the sign might be telling us the university is vacant or has a vacancy, not in use as ready for you to enter (figure 4.15).

A policy too can be a sign, a use instruction, a signaling of a direction. And a policy might be telling us that the university is open—that harassment will not be tolerated. A policy can be about what ought not to exist. The idea that something should not exist, or even that something does not exist because it should not exist, might be how something stays in use. I have observed that a policy can come into existence without coming into use. *Policies that are not in use can still be used as evidence of what*

4.15. Vacant, a vacancy, open.

does not exist. Norms too can operate all the more forcefully by not appearing to exist. This student described what followed her experience.

> I think the staff member knew I was deeply upset by it. I pretty much left the table. And he (the staff member) followed me out and started a conversation, and this is when probably in hindsight it started to get difficult, in that staff member started to lean on me; immediately he said to me, "Oh, you know what he's like, he's got a really strange sense of humor, he didn't mean anything by it," and the implication was I was being a bit oversensitive and that I couldn't take a joke, and that I need to sort of forget about it and move on.

She ended up leaving the table. Note that there was an effort to stop the student from complaining about the situation within the situation. She was told not to say anything, not to be oversensitive, not to do anything, not to cause trouble. This is how banter is used: to justify use as if words can be stripped from a history. A use is sustained by a fantasy that a use can be suspended. If norms operate all the more powerfully by not appearing to exist, you end up under obligation not to notice their existence, that is, not to experience norms *as* norms, not to experience some forms of expression as demeaning, not to experience harassment as harassment. Shirley Anne Tate has described how racial harassment is treated as "just" a style of communication that "you should just get used to" (2017, 55). So it is not simply that banter is used as if words can be stripped of their histories. *Those to whom harassment is directed are asked or required to strip words of their histories.* And so, those who experience harassment as harassment are understood as bringing the problem into existence.

Even to describe something as harassment requires persistence. If you do persist with it, you are harassed all the more: in this example the staff member, by trying to persuade the student not to complain, leaned on her. He positioned himself *with* the harasser, treating the verbal onslaught as joke, something she should take and keep taking. This response to harassment is harassment; this is the institutional response. The harasser physically came forward; the staff member leaned on her. Harassment can be the effort to stop you identifying harassment as harrassment, which means that the one who identifies harassment as harassment is harassed all the more.

This powerful testimony teaches us how a complaint is right in the middle of something, in the thick of it. And I have only shared a fragment of her story. She did go on to make a formal complaint. And she did not just leave the table; she left the academy. She left in part because of what she learned *about* the institution from how it responded *to* her complaint. The university came down on her by treating the complaint as a problem: a wall can be what comes up, what comes down. She described this process: "I lost my rose-tinted glasses, the way I saw those spaces being a place of excellence. I thought they were welcoming of difference. I had worked really hard to get to that space. When you come from the kind of background I have—no one had been to university to do a degree." I have noted how diversity can be a way of not addressing something. Diversity can also be used as an address: "welcoming of difference." Diversity might be represented as an open door. Students from diverse backgrounds are welcome, come in, come in: diversity as a tagline, tag along, tagged on.

Come in, come in: I think back to our postbox. There could be another sign on that postbox: "birds welcome" (figure 4.16). The sign "birds welcome" would be a nonperformative if the postbox was still in use because the birds would be dislodged by the letters, the nest destroyed before it could be created. I suggested in chapter 1 that use is a restriction of possibility that is material. You can do some things with paper because of the material qualities of paper. We are now learning *how restrictions can become material through use.* The letters in the box, the words that are thrown out:

4.16. A sign as a nonperformative.

they become materials, they pile up; they stop others from making use of something. What is material to some—leaving you with no room, no room to breathe, to nest, to be—can be what does not matter to others because it does not get in the way of their occupation of space; it might even enable that occupation. And so, you can stop others from using a space by how a space is being used, by what a space is being used for: *for as door*.

Behind Closed Doors

Doors: they keep coming up. If walls came up a lot in my research into diversity (Ahmed 2012, 2017), doors have come up a lot in my research into complaint. As I noted in chapter 1, doors are not just physical things that swing on hinges; they are also mechanisms that enable an opening and a closing. One woman of color academic described her department as *a revolving door* (figure 4.17): women and minorities arrive only to head right back out again—whoosh, whoosh. You can be kept out by what you find out when you get in.

A door can be what stops you from getting out.

4.17. You might have
to get out.

I am speaking to an academic about the first complaint she made when
she was a postgraduate student. One of her lecturers on her course had
been making her feel uncomfortable: "And then one afternoon, I went
into his office to talk to him about something—it was an office a bit like
this but without any glass, with a door that opened inwards and opened
on a latch—and he pushed me up against the back of a door and tried to
kiss me and I pushed him away, it was an instinctive pushed him away,
and tried to get out of the room and it was a horrible moment because I
realized I couldn't actually; it was very difficult to operate the latch."

We are back to the door, the back of the door: a door without glass,
solid, that cannot be seen through; a door as what you are pushed against;
the latch that will not open, getting stuck, trying to get out; the work you
have to do to get out. She did get out of his room, but it was hard. Behind
closed doors: harassment happens there, out of view, in secret. You can
be locked in, or locked out. That door is a teacher: it teaches us the significance of a complaint about harassment being lodged in the same institution where the harassment happened.

4.18. The same door.

A door was shut on her. The same door is shut on a complaint—the same door (figure 4.18). She submitted an informal complaint, a letter, detailing the assault. Where does her complaint go? Her letter ends up with the dean. And what did he do? She explained, "The dean basically told me I should sit down and have a cup of tea with this guy to sort it out." So often a response to a complaint about harassment is *to minimize harassment*, as if what occurred is just a minor squabble between two parties, something that can sorted out by a cup of tea, that English signifier of reconciliation. A complaint would become a failure, your failure, to resolve a situation amicably.

She did not proceed to a formal complaint. *Her complaint was stopped; he was not.* Now I say her complaint was stopped rather than she was stopped because she did go on to have a career; she is now a professor. But this experience of being assaulted and harassed when she was a student stayed with her. She explained: "I thought I got a first because of academic merit, but then after this happened I remember thinking, 'But hang on, maybe not, maybe this was some sort of ruse to try and keep me in the institution so he could keep the contact going.' . . . It starts undermining your own sense of your academic merit, the quality of your work and all that kind of stuff." Being harassed by a lecturer damages your sense of self-worth, intellectual worth, leading you to question yourself, doubt yourself. Her complaint was stopped, she was not, but she carries that history with her. Her complaint was stopped; he was not. What happened to him? She told us: "He was a known harasser; there were lots of stories told about him. I had a friend who was very vulnerable; he took advantage of that. She ended up taking her own life." She ended up taking her own life: so much more pain, so much more damage at the edges of one woman's story of damage. He went on; he was allowed to go on, when her complaint—and for all we know there were others too; we do not know how many said no—did not stop him. He has since retired, much respected by his peers, no blemish on his record.

No blemish on his record, no blemish on the institutional record: the damage carried by those who did complain or would complain if they could complain, carried around like baggage, slow, heavy, down. To hear a complaint is to hear from those weighed down by a history that has not left a trace in the official records. Damage to a person is deflected by being treated as potential damage to the institution (reputational damage) and damage to a person if a person is identified by a complaint. That damage is often evoked through or as concern, as *concern for consequence*, for how much he or they have to lose: careers, status, standing, and so on. Organizations become aligned with those who abuse power because they *share an interest in stopping what is recorded by a complaint from getting out.* One student said, "It is like you are complaining to your abuser." The institution in protecting abusers takes their place. We can use the term *institutional abuse* to describe this taking place. And I would add here when that protection fails, when an abuse of power is exposed (usually after much activism and work usually undertaken by students), the figure of the abuser is transformed into that of the stranger or foreigner, as being inexpressive rather than expressive of the values of an organization.

The figure of the abuser as a stranger is useful to organizations. The location of danger in an outsider is how an organization can appear as safe and protective even when abuses of power have taken place. The figure of the abuser is also useful to those who abuse power: abuses can slide by undetected if those who abuse power do not appear as abusers usually appear. An abuse becomes an aberration rather than an expression of a system. But an abuse can usually happen because of ties that already exist, because of intimacies and connections, which means that those who abuse the power given to them by organizations might not appear as abusive because an abuser is assumed as a stranger. To challenge the exteriority of the figure of the abuser requires giving up any moral confidence that we can clearly differentiate an abuse from use. It is worth recalling here that *abuse* is a use word. It has two distinct but related meanings whether used as a noun or a verb. Abuse can refer to the improper use of something or abuse can refer to violent, cruel, or ill treatment. The first sense makes clear that abuse derives from use. The second shows how use can be at stake in the determination of situations of violence and cruelty. A person or a thing when misused is being abused, whether the intent or the effect is cruel and violent.

In my opening of this book, I referred to how instrumentality and affection can be part of the same story (a useful pot, a useless foot). Indeed, instrumentality often works through affection. Many who abuse the power they receive by virtue of position can do so because of how they are then received: with affection. To recognize an abuse is made hard because of that affection. Those who abuse the power given to them by organizations often create a portrait of themselves as being in need: they might create the impression of being a victim of a hostile organization, as in need of protection, or present themselves as suffering, and in need of love and affection.

Perhaps we can then consider how sympathy as such becomes distributed, or, to use the terms introduced in chapter 3, how sympathy becomes machinery. Many of those I have spoken to about complaint described meetings with heads of department or deans where there is a sustained attempt to stop them from making a complaint. I have given examples of such meetings. We could interpret these meetings as evidence of top-down bullying from management but that would capture only some of what is going on. Heads of department are often operating not only as managers but also as colleagues and sometimes even as close personal friends of those whose conduct is under question.

When a student made a complaint after being sexually assaulted by a lecturer—he had forced himself on her in his office after locking the door—she was called to a meeting with three professors and a dean. She described the meeting for us: "One of the professors said laughing, for instance, 'Ah, X, he is always like this, isn't he? Always very seductive and funny. . . . He has been always like this since we were studying together. . . . He also touches me when talking, so what?' . . . while the other was saying, 'Ah, I know him for so many years, it must be some misunderstanding, for sure,' while the other was just smiling and nodding, before even having heard what I had to say."

A history can be casually evoked (studying together; I have known him for years) and a complaint about assault dismissed as misunderstanding, smiling, nodding: it is right, he is right, you are wrong; he is being wronged. If sympathy is part of the machinery, then a machine can lean; it can be built out of past leanings; friendly like. A complaint can be stopped because of what is shared, who is shared: friendships, loyalties, personal, professional; affection becoming cement in a wall, a bond, a bind, be kind, he is one of a kind, one of our kind. Closing the door is also about closing ranks; when you are shown the back of a door, their backs have become doors. As another student described it, "They have each other's backs."

Complaints thus teach us about the *continuity* of abuses of power with the use patterns of an institution. And by use pattern I am precisely *not* referring to official policies. I am referring instead to how universities are occupied, how a network can come alive to stop complaints from getting through rather like how electricity travels through wire: hiring as wiring (figure 4.19).

How data is transmitted through organizations—the speed with which some information travels—has something to do how they are built to meet some people's requirements. Paths into the organization become paths through an organization, a history kept alive as a communication network. When a circuit is broken, its conductive elements no longer form a complete path. A complaint becomes a crisis for an organization when it threatens to break a circuit; a complaint is treated as an error message, a beep, beep, that could stop what travels (who travels) along a path. A complaint can then function like a switch, an alarm, or an alert that triggers a reaction; when a network comes alive, it is in order to protect those who are the most networked, which is to say, a network is how a complaint is stopped: you can hear the buzz of electricity or the phone lines becoming busy. When I say a network comes alive, I am not suggesting this activity is coordinated by one person or a group of people who are meeting in secret, although secret meetings probably do happen. Meetings do not need to happen; what does not get out is built in.

The more a path is used, the more a path is used. *The more they are connected the more they are connected.* The more they are connected, the

4.19. Hiring as wiring.

more others are invested in that connection. In the previous section, I described how spaces can be occupied through conduct: action as bonding, as binding. We can now think of conduct in terms of the transmission not only of values but of information, energy, and resources. The body of a professor becomes a *conductor*; information, energy, and resources travel through that body; you have to go through the professor to get anywhere. We could understand this process as *institutional funneling*; how paths become narrower and narrower at the exit points. Uses of use, a restriction of possibility that has become material, uses of use, a narrowing of the routes; the more a path is used, the less paths there are to use; more going through less.

More going through less: a complaint is then treatable as a loose connection, as what could potentially stop not just a professor but could stop more, more and more, from receiving something through him. One student described how her complaint was framed by her peers: "We were accused of having caused the disruption in their studies. They valued their desire to have him as a professor over those who were suffering psychologically because of his harassment. We needed to be in 'solidarity' with those whose education was now being disrupted, not the other way around." A complaint is framed as a failure to share a connection, a lack of solidarity with others, who are cut off from a source of information and energy. We could also rethink the feminist killjoy as a loose connection, a faulty wire: she deprives others of what follows a shared connection, causing damage by virtue of not being properly attached.

To complain about harassment is to be judged as cutting yourself off from a collective. And then you are cut off from a collective. The implication is that if you do not get used to it, you end up out of it. If the choice is get used to it or get out of it, some cannot afford to get out of it. You might fear that the more you do not get used to it—the more you comment, question, challenge, or resist—the more damage you will suffer. Getting used to it can become a method of survival: to stay put, you end up having to work on yourself rather than on the situation.

There is so much work, painful work, surrounding complaints. And so much of that work is the work of clearing. It is not just that some have paths cleared for them. The clearing of a path does involve, has involved, the clearing of complaints: clearing as clearing up. When an MA student made a complaint about the conduct of the most senior member of the department, she was told by the convener of the program: "Be careful; he is an important man." He is an important man: a warning can take the form of a statement about whom or what is important. Importance is thus not only a judgment; it is a direction. You are warned against complaining about him *because of what he is deemed to be worth.* Despite the warning, the student went ahead with a complaint. In her terms, she "sacrificed the references." In reference to the prospect of doing a PhD, she said, "That door is closed."

That door is closed: references too can function as doors, mechanisms that enable an opening or closing (figure 4.20). References are how it is made possible for some to progress, others not. Reference systems also create paper trails, letters sent out; they are how some are enabled by their connections, how some gather speed and velocity, more and more, faster and faster: "he is an important man." References can be withheld or they can offer faint praise: when praise is faint, a no is being expressed; a no can be how someone has nowhere to go. Many do not make complaints because they feel they cannot afford to lose the references, to lose the connections.

Note also that punishment for complaint can entail the withdrawal of support; to withdraw support is enough to stop someone from going somewhere. Power manifests as the withdrawal of support for those who show how power manifests. In *Willful Subjects* (2014) I explored how force goes with and not just against the will: you can make it costly for others not to be willing what you will them to will. The costs of complaint can be raised without the need to use threats or reprimands. The power *to* enable

4.20. References can function as doors.

the progression of others, which is also the power to stop or to slow a progression, is how power *over* others is acquired. The more power is distributed the more power is concentrated. Power becomes handy. A complaint teaches us how power can be achieved without force through what might seem a light touch. The mere lifting of a supportive hand can function as the heaviest of weights. To lift a hand can be enough to close a door.

We can return to how diversity is often figured as an open door. For those who embody diversity, whose entry is understood as dependent on a door being opened, whose entry is understood as debt, the door can be shut at any point. Doors can be shut because of how you have to enter. Doors can be shut after you enter. A black woman academic describes how she was racially harassed and bullied by a white woman colleague:

> I think what she wanted to do was to maintain her position as the director, and I was supposed to be some pleb; you know what I mean, she had to be the boss, and I had to be the servant type of thing, that was how

her particular version of white supremacy worked, so not just belittling my academic credentials and academic capabilities but also belittling me in front of the students; belittling me in front of administrators.

How do you know it's about race? That's a question we often get asked. Racism is how we know it's about race; that wall, whiteness, or let's call it what it is, as she has, white supremacy, we come to know intimately as it is what keeps coming up. She adds: "I had put down that I would like to work towards becoming a professor and she just laughed in my face." That laugher can be the sound of another door slammed. To have got there, a black woman in a white institution, a lecturer, a senior lecturer, on her way to becoming a professor—she is now a professor—is to be understood as getting above her station, above herself; ahead of herself. To belittle someone, to make them little, functions as a command: be little! And that command is being sent not only to her, but to those who are deemed to share the status of being subordinate, students and administrators. Racial harassment can be the effort to restore a hierarchy: how someone is being told you are not where you should be or you are above where you should be, or you are where I should be or even you have taken my place. Some of us in becoming professors become trespassers; you are being told you need permission to enter by being told you do not have permission.

Backs can be doors. Doors can be walls. How support is given to some colleagues is how others are stopped from being colleagues. When another white colleague became head of department, that colleague says: "I want you to reconcile with her because after all she is my friend and colleague and all she ever did was write you some long emails." Reconciliation: we are back to that cup of tea. The damage caused by racial harassment is minimized. And that damage is then transferred from the person harassed to the harasser. Racism becomes damage to a friend, damage to a white friend; racism as damage to whiteness. An expression of desire for reconciliation might appear to be a friendly gesture. There is nothing friendly about this gesture. If she does not return the desire for reconciliation, if she is not willing to smooth things over, moving on, getting along, getting on, she becomes mean; the one who has not only broken a connection but refused to repair it. The situation becomes too hard to handle and eventually she leaves: "there are very few people left who work on race." She goes and the work goes with her.

Whiteness is reproduced as sympathy. And yes, that sympathy is part of the machinery. We learn from how affection is built into the university;

how horizontal relation between colleagues can be a means by which vertical lines are reestablished; how some are deemed to come first, to have priority over others, to be higher, more important, more; how others are deemed to come after, lower, less important, less. In chapter 3 I noted with reference to the role of utilitarianism in empire, how the colonized other is treated as *stuffing*. When we are considering how universities remain occupied, we are pointing not only to how restrictions become material through use but to how histories are material. Diversity can be how some of us end up as stuffing. A woman of colour described how her research expertise was used to secure funding for a project on diversity. When the project was funded, she is shut out. She describes: "If you are a mascot you are silent, everything you amount to is nothing, you are stuffing, if that, a skeleton with stuffing. I was kept out of the frame of the management structure; I had no control over how the money was spent, who was being employed, who was being invited to the advisory board. I was effectively silenced." You are stuffing; a skeleton with stuffing. You are supposed to be silent; you are supposed to symbolize diversity, or perhaps you provide the raw materials that white academia converts into theory. What happens when the stuffing speaks? What happens when those who embody diversity theorize for ourselves? She told me what happens. She documented seventy-two instances of racial and sexual harassment directed toward her because she refused to be silent. Harassment can be the effort to silence those who refuse to comply, to try to stop somebody from speaking: to shut her up as to shut her out. To refuse to be silent is to make a complaint.

Sometimes in order to survive institutions we need to transform them. But we still have to survive the institutions we are trying to transform. I am listening to an indigenous woman academic. She told me how she could hardly manage to get to campus after a sustained campaign of bullying and harassment from white faculty, including a concerted effort by a senior white man to sabotage her tenure case as well as the tenure cases of other indigenous academics. She made a formal grievance that did not get anywhere: "I had to send an email to her with the subject line in all capital letters with an exclamation point, my final email to her after seven months. THIS IS A GRIEVANCE! THIS IS A GRIEVANCE! And her obligation under the university rules and the process is that she has to put it forward. She did not. She did not put it forward." We are back to the clunk, clunk of institutional machinery; we learn how institutions work from how complaints are stopped. When you are harassed and bullied, when doors are closed, nay slammed in your face, making it hard to get anywhere, it can be history you are up against; thrown up against. When complaints take us back, they can take us back even further, further still, to histories that are still: "There is a genealogy of experience, a genealogy of consciousness in my body that is now at this stage traumatized beyond the capacity to go to the university. . . . So there's a legacy, a genealogy and I haven't really opened that door too widely as I have been so focused on my experience in the last seven years."

To be traumatized is to hold a history in a body. You can be easily shattered. There is only so much you can take on because there is only so much you can take in. We can inherit closed doors, a trauma can be inherited by being made inaccessible, all that happened that was too hard, too painful to reveal. Decolonial feminist work, black feminist work; feminist of colour work is often about opening those doors; the door to what came before; colonial legacies, genealogies; harassment as the hardening of *that* history, a colonial as well as patriarchal history, of who is deemed entitled to what, of who is deemed entitled to whom.

A complaint can be necessary: what you have to do to go on. But you still have to work out what you can take on. She went on by taking them on:

> I took everything off my door, my posters, my activism; my pamphlets. I smudged everything all around the building. I knew I was going to war; I did a war ritual in our tradition. I pulled down the curtain. I pulled on a mask, my people we have a mask . . . and I never opened my door for a year. I just let it be a crack. And only my students could come in. I would not let a single person come in to my office who I had not already invited there for a whole year.

Closing a door can sometimes be a survival strategy; she closes the door to the institution by withdrawing herself, her commitments, from it. She still does her work; she still teaches her students. She makes use of the institution's door by using it to shut out what she can, who she can. And she takes herself off the door; she depersonalizes it. And she pulls down the blinds and she pulls on a mask, the mask of her people, connecting her fight to the battles that came before, because, quite frankly, for her, this is a war.

Our battles are not the same battles. But there are many battles happening behind closed doors. I have shared some of them; sharing with you stories that have been shared with me. Behind closed doors: that is where complaints are often found, so that is where you might find us too, and what we bring with us, who we bring with us, the worlds that would not be here if some of us were not here; the data we hold, our bodies, our memories; perhaps the more we have to spill, the tighter their hold. I will return to spillages as queer use in my conclusion.

Utility and Policy

A history of a university is a history of what and who has been selected as well as what and who has not been. I have tried to show how selection goes all the way down, brick by brick, paper by paper, person by person. Once selections are made, they recede, becoming part of the background. We need to confront what is behind us. Institutions are built from small acts of use, from uses of use, from how building blocks put together, over time, become walls, walls that enable some bodies to enter, stay put, progress, others not. You come up against how use thickens like cement to form a wall when you try to transform organizations so they are more accommodating or when you enter organizations that are not built for you or when you make a complaint about an abuse of power.

I consider in this concluding section the question of how utility becomes a policy, a policy that builds upon what is already built. In debates about the role of universities, and in particular about the value of the humanities, the word *utility* often comes up. That word, however, is given a rather restricted genealogy, as if the requirement to be useful is a relatively recent requirement that has been imposed on universities by governments.[9] So, for example, Steven C. Ward describes the Dearing Report published by the National Committee of Inquiry into Higher Education (NCIHE) in 1997 as a "transitional document" that contained "neoliberal notions of the economic and utilitarian purposes of higher education" (2012, 26). Wendy Brown describes neoliberalism "not simply as economic policy, but as a governing rationality that disseminates market values and metrics to every sphere of life" (2015, 176). One of the four key ways that neoliberalism as a governing rationality impacts on higher education is the revaluing of "knowledge, thought and training" in terms of their "capital enhancement" (177).

We do need strong critiques of neoliberalism as a governing rationality.[10] Writing about the history of use, however, has led me to consider how much of what is named as neoliberal could be understood with reference to a longer history of utilitarianism, not only as a body of thought but as a set of practices or techniques for selection. In other words, the requirement on universities to be useful, to select what would be most beneficial (mostly defined in financial terms, though not always and not only[11]), builds upon longer histories of selection that have already shaped the body of the university, a body that combines stones, paper, and flesh, in the project of elevating or cultivating a mind.

We can think about selection as central to the emergence of a public; what is selected is often defined in terms of the public good. Jeremy Bentham in writing about the importance of publicity (an idea picked up by Jürgen Habermas in his account of the emergence of the public sphere) used the metaphor of a gymnasium: "The whole kingdom, the great globe itself, will become a gymnasium, in which every man exercises himself before the eyes of every other man. Each gesture, every turn of limb or feature, in those whose motions have a visible impact on the general happiness, will be noticed and marked down" (1834, 101). When happiness is the end, use becomes the means: to exercise one's limbs defined here as gesture and motion is to have a "visible impact" on the happiness of others. The point of exercising one's limbs would be to impact upon general happiness; to make use of is also to notice and to mark down.

Bentham is describing an ideal. It is rather terrifying. Perhaps Bentham's ideal has become our real. Simply put, the modern university has become rather like Bentham's fantasy of a world gymnasium. Many techniques of governance take the form of recording use. In the UK, the framework introduced for measuring the quality of research, the Research Excellence Framework (REF), requires recording use.[12] Citation indexes, for example, are used as evidence that your work is used. It is worth noting that these assessment exercises work through peer review. And peer review could be understood through the lens of "monitor as method" (discussed in chapter 3), in which colleagues are judged by other colleagues, to become a reviewer is an esteem indicator, and to be judged well by being reviewed is directly linked to rewards. The most recent exercise in 2014 introduced "impact" as a key criteria for assessing research excellence. Impact was described as "effect on, change or benefit to the economy, society, culture, public policy or services, health, the environment or quality of life, beyond academia." We can hear echoes of Bentham's model of a public that can monitor its motions. The idea that knowledge should be useful or even of general benefit was how the modern university was brought into existence; this is not a new idea. How do you give evidence of impact? In one workshop I attended, we were advised to solicit letters from external bodies that could be used as evidence of the impact of our own work. To show how you contribute to general happiness requires that you create evidence of that contribution: creating trails so you can tell tales.

Use becomes usable as evidence. And when citation becomes an index, other things follow: the more he is cited, the more evidence of impact; the more value to an organization, the more time he is given to do his work; the more he writes, the more he is cited; and so on, and so it goes on. When we are talking about being given time for the motions that can "have an impact on general happiness," we are talking about others doing other kinds of work; she does more of the housework, the administrative work, the pastoral work, work that is less valued, diversity work. I am using a gendered pronoun here for a reason, to point to how different forms of labor tend to fall on different bodies. There is more at stake in this tending. Sexism and racism in the academy are about whose path is cleared, the path that leads up, up, and up, higher still; they are about whose load is lightened, who becomes usable as a means to lighten that load, a lightening, that is assumed to be of general benefit: a higher score, we all get more.

If you cannot show how you contribute to general happiness, you become a drain, taking energy and resources away from something else. In order to avoid becoming a drain, selection becomes a necessary, even moral, activity. In chapter 2, I discussed how Darwin adopted the language of selection from animal breeding: methodical selection becomes natural selection. We can think of all selection as methodical, how from a diverse range of possibilities some possibilities are selected, that is, given the support necessary to be actualized, or how from a diverse population some bodies are selected, that is, given the support necessary to proceed. Selection can be self-selection, when you select what you do "do" from what could do, depending on what can be used as evidence of your contribution. Or selection can be made by others who might want you to do what would contribute most to your own progression. You can end up willingly not doing what cannot be used as evidence of your contribution.

We learn then that in order to secure a future, you might have to give up on certain possibilities in the present. To be selected might require not going in a certain direction. I have heard again and again from students, and from colleagues, how they were directed away from certain kinds of work, away from certain stances, away from words even: do not do a feminist project, that will not get you very far; do not do race, race is too narrow; race and gender are often framed as too narrow; the universal is given width, breadth, as well as speed, faster, lighter. We can, and we do, refuse those instructions. But we do need to listen to them, to learn from what they are asking. It is not just that you are directed away from what compromises your own happiness (your own career, your own trajectory) but from what would compromise general happiness.

To open up other directions, we might need to question selections, to question how those who are selected are selected. Universities already have in place a system for justifying selections when they are required to do so. A justification of a selection is necessary when diversity workers turn selection into a crisis, when universities are questioned about their procedures. Meritocracy is a term that is much used by universities because it helps justify their own selections—past, present, and future. Meritocracy is the fantasy that those who are selected are the best. A fantasy can be a system. When diversity workers question who is here, or who is promoted, they are questioning the system. Meritocracy is useful as an answer to a question about the system because it allows the system to recede from view. An answer can be a recovery: how you recover or cover over what has come into view by coming into a question. A system is about the assistance given to individuals, as I have already noted; to fit the requirements is to have a path cleared. When a system disappears from view, the assistance given by that system also disappears. The selected can then reappear as unassisted by the system. This is how diversity often comes up: diversity as how some receive an assistance that they would not have to receive if they were the best; how the best would not be selected; diversity as the lowering of standards, as if diversity and merit are two different tracks, two different ways of entering the organization.[13] The use of meritocracy teaches us how those who are selected define the best around themselves.

Selection is used by organizations as a way of controlling or directing human traffic. It is not simply that what is selected is the most beneficial but that selection is beneficial. Central to the use of selection by organizations is the maintenance of precarity: to be selected or not can determine whether you have a future with an organization. Sometimes the basis upon which decisions are being made is unclear; unclear decisions are a way of managing crisis such that to be employed is to be in a state of alert. You do not know when you could be managed out of existence. Being on a state of alert is not about being on an equal footing: some more than others will be dependent on being selected; selection becomes *more* important the *less* you are resourced, the closer you are to an edge, the higher the stakes; something that would be small to others (not getting funding for this or for that) would be enough to topple you over the edge.

Not to be selected is not to benefit from selection. It is made harder to proceed. We are back to one of my starting points: the less a path is used, the harder it is to follow. Not to be selected can mean not to be supported; it can mean a project ceases to be possible. Something ceases to be if it ceases to be possible. What is not selected is sometimes discarded: the paper that ends up in the waste bin, the paper that did not get anywhere. What is discarded is usually assigned useless. This assignment could also be considered *institutional death*. Something can be someone: you can reach a dead end; you can become institutionally dead. You do not have a route or career pathway in front of you because of what is behind you. This cessation is not the end of the story; institutional death is not the end of a story. An institutional death can be the start of another biography of use; leaving can be the beginning of another life. I will return to this point in my conclusion.

In order to have an institutional life, you might have to work to avoid institutional death. I want to suggest that "join or die" becomes an imperative, or even a choice, a fantasy choice. Join or die is another version of get used to it or get out of it. *Join* is a nice word. It sounds good, not scary: to join as to join in; to join as being part of something, as having a share in the happiness of others; to join as to be joined up with others. Being seen as choosing not to die, choosing not to have your projects cease to be (the double negative), and choosing your projects (turned into a positive) can mean you sign up to so much when you join up, including the presentation of the institutionally dead as a shared enemy, those to whom you must refuse proximity or allegiance.

The imperative to join up in order to survive within an institution can be experienced as a crisis for feminists and diversity workers. We are, after all, trying to transform the institutions that employ us. Even the projects that have transformation as their end need to be supported. A project too can be a path. We might use the more used path because, frankly, a project needs to be resourced. We might translate the work we do into the terms that are more likely to be picked up. We can be carried forward by what we pick up. We use the more used terms. The more we use the more used terms, the more we are aligned; we are going the same way others are going. If you tried to deviate, to change direction, you would get in the way of other people's motions. If we proceed on a path in order to disrupt it, we can end up not disrupting it in order to proceed.

I think of this problem as a paradox as well as a pain. It is a problem that we need to keep at the front of our work not because we can resolve it but because we cannot. It is a problem I learned about from talking to diversity workers; one practitioner spoke to me about not using terms that were, in her words, "more confrontational," to enable her to have more conversations with more staff across the university. She senses she could travel further by what she was not willing to confront. As I noted earlier, if *diversity* is used more because it does less, "doing less" becomes as much as we can do. We might use the word *diversity* because it is light; we might not use the word *racism* to avoid a fight; we might try not to rock the boat because we do not have a secure footing, although of course sometimes rocking is a motion that seems to have nothing to do with what it is we are doing.

There are risks in doing what is required to proceed. I think we know this. If our feminist projects are resourced by an institution, it might become harder to confront certain problems as institutional problems, to speak out about the role of the institution in enabling racial or sexual harassment, for example. Sometimes, perhaps especially when we are trying to address the role of the institution in enabling abuse and violence, we have to refuse to do what is necessary to proceed. If you refuse to do what is necessary to proceed, it can feel as if you have committed yourself to a path that leads eventually, in one way or another, to your own cessation. You can end up feeling that you have made yourself history.

How do we counter what has become as hard as concrete? We need activism here. We need dismantling projects here. These are the projects I turn to in my conclusion to this book. Even when we do what is necessary to proceed, we can still fight to change what is necessary. To build an alternative university requires crafting different routes from what is behind us: the fainter trails, the less used paths. I think crafting is a good word for this work: it takes willed work not to reproduce an inheritance, not to create the same old shape. We need to do this work collectively if we are to widen the routes; otherwise, deviation might simply mean cessation, institutional death, reaching the end of a line, not having enough support to keep going. If we are to do this work, feminism is necessary as a support system: we have to find ways of not getting used to it without getting out of it, even if sometimes, for our own survival, our feminist survival, we need to get out of it. Not getting used to it: this is probably one of the best descriptions I can offer of what it means to be a diversity worker today.

Conclusion

....

Queer Use

What better way to bring out the queerness of use than by attending to uses of queer? Queer: a word with a history. Queer: a word that has been flung like a stone, picked up and hurled at us; a word we can claim for us. Queer: odd, strange, unseemly, disturbed, disturbing. Queer: a feeling, a sick feeling; feeling queer as feeling nauseous.

In older uses of queer—queer to describe anything that is noticeable because it is odd—queer and fragility were often companions. In one of George Eliot's essays, "Three Months in Weimar," the narrator describes the sound of an old piano thus: "its tones, now so queer and feeble, like those of an invalided old woman whose voice could once make a heart beat with fond passion" (1884, 91–92). Feeble, frail, invalid, incapacitate, falter, weak, tearful, worn; tear; wear; queer too, queer is there, too. These proximities tell a story. A queer life might be how we get in touch with things at the very point at which they, or we, are worn or worn down—those moments when we break or break down, when we shatter under the weight of history. The sounds of an old piano evoking the sound of an invalided old woman: could this evocation vibrate with affection? Could a queer heart beat with passion for what is wavering and quavering?

That some of us can live our lives by assuming that word *queer*, by even saying "yes" to that word, shows how a past use is not exhaustive

of a word or a thing however exhausted a word or thing. As Judith Butler notes in *Excitable Speech*, "An aesthetic enactment of an injurious
word may both *use* the word and *mention* it, that is, make use of it to
produce certain effects but also at the same time make reference to that
very use, calling attention to it as a citation, situating that use within a
citational legacy, making that use into an explicit discursive item to be
reflected on rather than a taken for granted operation of ordinary language" (1997, 99). We can disrupt the meaning of an insult by making
its usage audible as a history that does not decide, once and for all, what
a word can do. To queer use is to make use audible, to listen to use, to
bring to the front what ordinarily recedes into the background. If queer
use has been a point I have made, providing me with a conclusion, queer
use also describes my method: to queer use as to front up to use; to make
use strange.

Queer use as reuse. Sometimes words are reused as if they can be cut
off from their history—when an insult is thrown out, for instance, and
reaches its target but is defended as just banter, as something you can,
should, make light of. I discussed such uses of banter in chapter 4. If we
reuse the word *queer*, we hold onto the weight, the baggage. A queer bag,
even: I think of my own queer bag discussed in chapter 1, a bag that is
worn from being worn (figure C.1).

You hold onto something because of how you have been shaped by
something. Eve Kosofsky Sedgwick suggests that what makes queer a
"politically potent term" is how it cleaves to "the childhood scene of
shame" (1993, 4). Queer acquires force and vitality precisely because
we refuse to use the word to make light of a history. To recycle or reuse
a word is to reorient one's relation to a scene that holds its place, as
memory, as container, however leaky. In concluding this book, my aim
is to bring out the implications of the queerness of use. Considering
the queerness of use is an opportunity to reflect on the ethical and political lessons I have learned from attending to the uses of use. There
are risks in taking up "queer use" in the way I am doing. I know I could
be asking "queer use" to do too much work; that I could be sliding over
too many histories. A risk is also a potential: queer use provides me
with a way of making connections between histories that might otherwise be assumed to be apart. This is how I understand it: queer use is
just a start.

C.1. Worn from being worn.

Refusing Instructions

I have been using *queer use* to refer to how things can be used in ways other than for which they were intended or by those other than for whom they were intended. I did not realize when I first used queer use in this way that it had been used like this before: queer use as reused. In fact you can find many newspaper articles from the late nineteenth century that use queer use in exactly this way—articles that refer to the queer uses of cups, bicycles, cigars, and cloisters. One article that appeared in the *Los Angeles Herald* on August 28, 1899, is titled "Queer Use for Cloisters." It stated: "The cloisters of the Church of St. Ethelreda, Ely palace, Holborn, London, are now being used for a purpose very different from that for which they were originally intended. Father Jarvis . . . has placed them at the disposal of any cyclist who may wish to store his machine while attending divine services."[1] One wonders whether cloisters could be used to store more than "his machines." Queer use is used here in a similar way to how I have been using it: queer use as when you use something for a purpose that is "very different" from that which was "originally intended." This use of queer use to describe how cloisters can become a shelter for bicycles returns us to Stephen Gould and Richard Lewontin's reflection on spandrels discussed in chapter 2. They borrow the term from architecture to suggest that some biological structures may not have been brought into existence because there was a use for them (I have called this *for is before*). Indeed, queer use has arguably become a design principle in architecture in the concern to create more flexible spaces. Jonathan Hill cites the work of Adrian Forty: "Against the presumption that all parts of a building should be destined for specific uses, a recognition that not all uses could be foreseen at the moment of design made 'flexibility' a desirable architectural property" (2003, 29). Buildings can be built with queer uses in mind, which is to say, with a commitment to a principle that not all uses could or even should be foreseen.[2] However buildings are built, a use for something can become possible *given* what has been built: queer use as coming after.

We can pick up the connection between what is queer and what is given. Queer uses would be about releasing a potentiality that already resides in things *given* how they have taken shape. Queer use could be what we are doing when we release that potential. Queer use has also been used to refer to how those who identify as queer make use of spaces. George Chauncey argues that there is "no queer space; there are only spaces used by queers or put to queer use. . . . Nothing illustrates this general principle more clearly than the tactics developed by gay men and lesbians to put the spaces of the dominant culture to queer uses" (1996, 224). The implication here is that uses are queer because spaces are not: queerness as what is injected into spaces by queer users. Perhaps queerness becomes catchy; queer users might leave traces of ourselves behind. When queers use spaces, spaces might become queer.

That becoming can happen; queerness can be infectious. But it does not always happen. I think back to the postbox that became a nest. We could think of those birds as queer guests, taking up residence in a room that is not built for them. To be a guest is to be welcomed. You can be welcomed without being able to take up residence. We are back to the sign *birds welcome* (figure C.2).

Maybe the door of the family too can appear open. Perhaps you are the queer aunties; come in, come in! You enter only to realize that the space is already occupied. Heterosexuality can indeed become an occupation, filling the room, water in a cup, full, fuller still, no room, no room; greetings, statements, heterosexuality given casually for children as projections of the future: he will be one for the girls, she will be one for the boys, and even my dog, Poppy, has been given such an assignment (if only Poppy could meet Tommy; they could be boyfriend and girlfriend).

C.2. Come in, come in!

When you inhabit such a world, you can feel like you are watching your-self disappear: watching your own life unravel, thread by thread. No one has willed or intended your disappearance. They are kind; they are wel-coming. But just slowly, just slowly, as talk of family, of heterosexuality as the future, of lives that you do not live, just slowly, just slowly, you disappear. As soon as you leave, you might have to get yourself quickly to the local gay bar so you can breathe! Sometimes to survive a restriction, we refuse an instruction. Creating our own dwellings becomes necessary given how queerness can be squeezed out of spaces.

Perhaps the potential to queer use might reside somewhere between our bodies and our worlds. Queer use might require a certain willingness to be perverse, to deviate from the straight path, the right path. The word *perversion* can refer not only to deviations from what is true or right but to *the improper use of something*. Perhaps the child who turns the key into a toy is not a pervert; the child is expected to play with things, although the child in being given freedom from intention can also become a container of freedom. But a boy who plays with the wrong toy—a toy vacuum, for

C.3. The same door.

instance, that is intended for a girl—might be understood as perverted
or at least as on the way to perversion. Correcting the boy's use of the toy
is about correcting more than behavior in relation to a toy; it is about correcting how the boy is boy. In chapter 1, I discussed how gender can tell
you not only what to do but what facilities to use. We are familiar with
the signs on the door—man, woman—that function as use instructions:
you are to use one door or the other door. And we are constantly being
reassigned gender through doors as well as other technological methods
for directing human traffic, that is, for telling us which way to go when
we have to go. And we are supposed to be as constant as that assignment.
And so: if you are assigned girl, if girl is your original assignment, you are
supposed to follow that path, which means using *the same door* that you
used before (figure c.3).

A transfeminist project shows how original assignments are themselves constructions. As Emi Koyama notes, "While the concept of gender as a social construct has proven to be a powerful tool in dismantling
traditional attitudes toward women's capabilities, it left room for one to
justify certain discriminatory policies or structures as having a biological basis" (2003, 249). Biology is used as a tool because biology is often
assumed to be about what is fixed or immutable. The very idea of two

distinct sexes is transformed into an architectural principle by the use of doors.[3] If we think of biological sex as a door, we learn how biology can function as technology, to return to my discussion in chapter 2. This intimacy of biology and technology helps us to explore the queerness of biology and to consider what Sarah Franklin has called *transbiology*. Franklin introduces the cyborg embryo picking up on Donna Haraway's (1991) creative reuse of the figure of the cyborg as well as her use of the concept of "*trans-*" to describe how new hybrid entities "blast widely understood notions of natural limit" (Haraway, 1997, cited in Franklin 2006, 170). The cyborg embryo is born and made, biological and technological. The cyborg embryo is a product of what Franklin calls the IVF/Stem Cell interface: stem cell research is dependent upon "surplus" or "spare" embryos generated by assisted conception technologies. Interestingly, Franklin's discussion of transbiology refers a number of times to doors. She describes how human stem cell derivation laboratories are built adjacent to assisted conception units and how the laboratories and clinics make use of doors to allow the passing through of biological materials—eggs and embryos—between them: "Like the cyborg embryo, transbiology is a mix of control and rogue, or trickster, elements. The hoods are noisy breathers, the eggs are dirty, and *the door is queer*" (2006, 175, emphasis mine).[4] The door is there because it offers the most convenient way to pass materials through; if paths can be created as an effect of use, so too can doors. The door is queer because it is not meant to be there; the lab is supposed to be a clean, controlled, and sealed environment.

We can pick up on the significance of the queer door. An opening created for convenience can have a queer potential: it can mean lessening control of what or who can pass through. The biological would then be about the potential of transfers and transits of many queer kinds. It might seem that doors function to contain us; to be told to use the same door is to be told who we are and what we can be. Perhaps use instructions are only necessary because they can be refused. Indeed, one might think of how the postbox can become a nest only by creating a queer door: the birds turn an opening into a door, that is, a way of entering the box. A queer door can be the effect of unexpected arrivals: openings intended for some things to pass through can end up providing an access point for others.

By considering the uses of use, I have been able to show how the potential for movement can be eliminated or almost eliminated before that potential can be realized in this or that instance. In chapter 1, I suggest that use can lessen the queerness of use; when things are used repeatedly in a certain way it becomes harder for things to be used in other ways. Those for whom use is harder are trying to use things in other ways. Timing matters. If use instructions are made because they can be refused, use instructions are made even more forcefully when they are refused. Some forms of use are corrected, punished; *do not use that* is saying, in truth, *do not be that*. Those who refuse the instructions know how they work.

Use instructions can be not only about how to use things properly, how to take care of things or yourself, but how you are directed along a path; that well-used path. An instruction can be a direction. A path can be a line on the ground, a line, a lead. A path can also be a route through life. Heterosexuality can function as a path, one that is kept clear not only by the frequency of use, and as I have shown a frequency can be an invitation, but also by an elaborate support system (figure C.4). A straight path is also the path you follow if you are living your life in the right way; you have to reach certain points in order for a life to count as a good life. The straightening of a path could also be understood as the elimination of hap: to be straight in a moral sense is to be upright and purposeful; it is not to be distracted by what happens or by what you encounter along the way. No wonder: to deviate from a straight path can be hard. *Deviation is made hard*: so much violence is abbreviated in this sentence.

To leave a straight path is to encounter things that are in the way; it is to be slowed down by what you need to progress. When you cannot pass *through*, you cannot pass *over* something. A perversion can be how we encounter things. The figure of the pervert comes up as the one whose misuse of things is a form of self-revelation. The pervert makes improper use of his or her own body. Intended functionality can also be how we relate to bodies: as if each organ had a purpose, shaped by what it was for. This idea of a proper use of organs was central to many of the educational books written for children during the nineteenth century. The ninth volume of *The American Phrenological Journal and Miscellany*, for example, begins with a statement on happiness: "Happiness is the one constitutional function of human nature, *the only legitimate product of every organ of the body*" (Fowler 1847, 9, emphasis mine). This statement is then given as an instruction to a child: to use their organs properly. The author explains:

Every organ and faculty which God has given to us, is good in itself, and was given us for a good and definite purpose; it is only the perversion, of an organ that produces bad effects in society. *By the perversion*

C.4. Heterosexuality: a path that is kept clear.

of an organ I mean the improper use of it; for example, our hands were given to assist us in doing a great many things necessary for our support and happiness; our feet were given us to enable us to walk; but if we strike each other with our hands, or kick animals, or each other, with our feet, we pervert the use of these instruments given us for our own good. (165, emphasis mine)

The instruction to use organs properly assumes that organs have a proper use, a use that is associated with health and happiness.[5] Let me advance a speculative thesis: compulsory heterosexuality too can operate as a form of intended functionality; we are allowed to play with our organs, to roam over each other's bodies as well as our own, but eventually we must use them for what they are for. Compulsory heterosexuality can provide a series of assumptions of how bodies are *supposed to function*, as a thesis of what bodies are for (and who they are for). In the writings of sexologist Havelock Ellis, for instance, the bodies of each sex are presented as directed toward the other. For instance, he describes vaginal fluid as "facilitating the entrance of the male organ" (1940, 17). Heterosexuality becomes a built-in design, which is to say, as that which is facilitated by the body. We might consider how reproduction quickly becomes the point, *repro-normativity*, a norm and an end: as what you are supposed to reach, the point of sex; the point, even, of life itself.

A pervert gets lost on the way. Or if you get lost, perhaps you are perverting the way. For Freud, there is perversion when there is a delay or departure from the point that is sexual union. For example, a perversion might involve lingering over intermediate relations to the sexual object, "which should normally be traversed rapidly on the path towards the final sexual aim" (Freud 1977, 62). Insofar as a point deviates from this straight line toward heterosexual union, we are making a perverse point. This point makes the line itself rather perverse. For Freud, "every external or internal factor that hinders or postpones the attainment of the normal sexual aim . . . will evidently lend support to the tendency to linger over the preparatory activities" (1977, 68). Even to linger can be to go astray. A delay is when you take up time that could have been used to get to the point. Queer use: we linger; we do not get to the point.

Queer use can be about lingering over things, attending to their qualities. To use things properly often means to paper over them. Paper as papering over: one thinks of paper. In *Queer Phenomenology* (2006), I called into a question a fantasy of a "paperless philosophy" as part of a critique of how philosophy might be oriented toward a certain kind of body, one for whom materiality would be an unnecessary distraction, one who has time freed for contemplation by how others do the paperwork, the domestic work, care work, diversity work.

Paper matters. Paper can also be queer; paper can be used queerly. Maryanne Dever suggests that for those who work in archives, "it is the lure of paper that attracts us" (2015, 66). It can be paper that allows us to pick things up, to find traces of histories that would otherwise elude us. I am reminded of Homi K. Bhabha's discussion of the Bible in his classic essay "Signs Taken for Wonders." Bhabha cites the *Missionary Register*, which reads: "Still [every Indian] would gladly receive a Bible. And why? That he may store it up as a curiosity, sell it for a few pice, or use it for waste paper. Such it is well known has been the common fate of those Bibles distributed in this place. Some are seen laid up as curiosities, by those who cannot read them: some have been bartered in the markets; and others have been thrown into the snuff-shops, and used as wrapping paper" (Church Missionary Society 1817, 186). The Bible in not being properly read is willfully destroyed. The Bible becomes a curiosity, reused or usable for other purposes: wrapping paper, waste paper.

The missionaries narrate the fate of the Bible in the colonies as being a result of the inability of the natives to be able to digest it: "It is true, that such of the Natives as can read, have leisure enough to read the whole Bible; but they are so indolent, so fond of eating and sleeping, or so lost in their vicious pursuits, that unless something at once *brief, simple*, and *powerful* be presented, it will not be likely to be read by them, and, if read, it will not be likely to arrest their torpid and sensual minds" (Church Missionary Society 1817, 186). If racism is used as an explanation of the failure of digestion, rendering the racial other a queer subject ("vicious pursuits," "torpid and sensual minds"), racism is used because of the failure of the colonial mission to transform the minds of the colonized into willing vessels. If not being willing to receive the will of the colonizer is to queer use or even to become queer through misuse (perversion as self-revelation), to queer use is to live in proximity to violence.

The demand to use something properly is a demand to revere what has been given by the colonizer. Empire-as-gift comes with use instructions. In chapter 3, I explore such a use of use: becoming a monitor as a commitment to memory, learning to use words in the right way, obedience as sympathy. Disobedience can be a matter of not being affected in the right way. The word *disobedience* brings to mind certain kinds of political action: the conscious and willed refusal to obey an instruction. Perhaps disobedience can be willful, *not being willing to receive an influence*, whether or not it is willed. Disobedience can start small, with not being impressed, or even not being *that* impressed: not finding the objects endowed with value to be impressive.

A failure to use something properly can be a refusal to use something properly. By speaking of the refusal to use something properly, I am not simply speaking of use in the present tense; recall that the settler colonial project was to empty the minds of the colonized as well as to empty the lands. A refusal to use something properly, to be impressed by the colonizer's words and things, depends on other prior refusals: a refusal to empty oneself of a history, a refusal to forget one's language and family, a refusal to give up land or an attachment to land, a refusal to exercise the terms that lead to one's own erasure or, to use Audra Simpson's (2014) powerful words, "a refusal to disappear." A refusal can be an inheritance.

You might have to refuse to ingest what would lead to your disappearance: the words, the ways; the worlds. Queer use can also be about not ingesting something; spitting it out; putting it about. If queer use is not ingesting something, not taking it in, queer use can also be about how you attend to something. To queer use can be to linger on the material qualities of that which you are supposed to pass over; it is to *recover* a potential from materials that have been left behind, all the things you can do with paper if you do not follow the instructions.

All the things you can do: when use becomes proper, queer use becomes misuse. Perhaps queer use is always a potential because use cannot be properly proper. A queer archive might come into existence because of a gap between what is and what is in use. I have noted throughout this book how use is assumed as necessary for being, to use something as to keep something alive, which is how use also becomes a moral duty, as if by not using something you would stop it from being. I have also pointed to a gap between what is and what is in use: a part of a body that is no longer useful may still exist; a policy might exist but not be in use; and, even, something might come into use without having existed (that phantom arm that keeps coming up). Perhaps use instructions are so insistent because of this gap, because you can use it *and* lose it, because the possibility of losing it cannot be eliminated. We might have to *mind the gap*, as diversity workers, so we do not end up exhausting ourselves by bringing things into existence that do not come into use. But we can also *queer the gap*: by finding in the paths assumed to lead to cessation a chance of being in another way.

Queer Vandalism

When we recover a potential from materials, when we refuse to use things properly, we are often understood not only as causing damage but as *intending what we cause*. Queer use could thus also be interpreted as vandalism: the willful destruction of the venerable and beautiful.[6]

Sometimes the nuclear family is held up as the source of the venerable and beautiful. In *The Promise of Happiness* (2010), I explored how the image of family is maintained by polishing its reflection: a labor of keeping up appearances, smiling as a way of covering over what does not correspond to happiness. We can think of this polishing as straightening; the removal of damage, the stains, and the scratches can mean the removal of traces of a queer existence. When queer desires are deemed damaging, it can be assumed we desire to cause damage as if we are trying to ruin a picture or as if we are demeaning something by not elevating it. Not following a family line is understood as breaking that line: queer as snap, snap, as if you are cutting up the family with a pair of scissors by arranging your life in a different way. *Not following something as destroying something*: no wonder they find us to be destructive. We can turn a finding into a will; we might be willing to destroy the nuclear family and marriage if that is what it takes to live our lives in queer ways.

For some, extending marriage to gays and lesbians would be enough to destroy marriage; gay marriage as queer vandalism. I think this position is far too optimistic: queers need to do more than marry each other to destroy the institution of marriage. In aiming for more, queer politics might recover the militancy of second wave feminist approaches to the nuclear family as an institution we should aim to destroy. One thinks especially here of Shulamith Firestone's *Dialectic of Sex* (1970), with its organizing assumption that institutions such as the family, which promise happiness by narrowing down what counts as a good life, should be dismantled. Given how the family is occupied, we might need to become squatters: to squat the family, to enter the building and do something else, to loiter, to linger, to go astray.

We might use the word *family* to describe our queer gatherings: queer use as reuse. I think of Susan Stryker's description of what was opened up for the "queer family we were building," when her partner gave birth to their child. She describes: "We joke about pioneering on a reverse frontier: venturing into the heart of civilization itself to reclaim biological reproduction from heterosexism and free it for our own uses." She adds: "We're fierce; in a world of 'traditional family values,' we need to be" (1994, 247). When things are used by those for whom they were not intended, the effect can be queer. We can laugh at the effect. Joking about queer effects is not unrelated to rage against the machinery of the family, which as Stryker shows renders some offspring into deviants and monsters. And that rage itself can be transformative: "through the operation of rage, the stigma itself becomes the source of transformative power" (1994, 249). It takes work to reclaim biological reproduction "for our own uses" just as it takes work to reoccupy the family, to make the familiar strange. And it takes work to rearrange our bodies, to rearrange ourselves. Stryker offers her own rearrangement by refiguring transgender embodiment as an affinity to monsters, to those who have been deemed monstrous, speaking back to Frankenstein in words sharpened by rage. Queer use: when we aim to shatter what has provided a container.

To open institutions up that have functioned as containers you have to throw usage into a crisis; you have to stop what usually happens from happening; and a "what" can be a "who," to stop "who" from happening.

C.5. Willing to cause
an obstruction.

We might occupy a building or a street with the intent to disrupt ordinary usage, to get in the way of how that space is usually used (for what and by whom). Political protest often requires becoming an inconvenience. We might have to park our bodies in front of that door (figure C.5). In protesting, we are willing to cause an obstruction. Of course, sometimes you can cause an obstruction by virtue of existing or by questioning the virtue of an existence. But we learn from how much of our political work requires disrupting usage. Usage can be how something recedes, an injustice, violence. To make violence seeable, sometimes you have to create a scene: to stop business as usual, to stop the flow of traffic, to make it impossible to open or close that door, to pass through or pass by.

Sometimes we need to disrupt usage to bring attention to a cause. At other times, that you disrupt usage teaches us about a cause. When you make use of an unoccupied building, for instance, you become a squatter. You might not necessarily aim to cause disruption; you might squat because you need to have access to shelter. But in doing what is necessary, you are refusing an instruction, a use instruction, which tells you not to enter unless you have legitimate access. To occupy an empty house without permission from an owner is to make an assertion: that ownership of a house does not justify the house being vacant. Ownership is not only the right to use something but the right not to use it. The future is owner occupied. It causes disruption not to render vacancy right or a right.

A squat can be part of a political protest. You might enter a building that is unoccupied in order to bring attention to a cause. In 2017 the feminist direct action group Sisters Uncut occupied Holloway Prison "to demand that the empty space be used to support local domestic violence survivors."[7] You have to occupy a building to demand that a building is used to support those who are not supported. We can learn from how survival and protest can be part of the same project. If you have to occupy a building in order to survive, in order to have somewhere to go to escape from violence that usually happens at home, domestic violence, that occupation is a political project; you counter the violence of a system by revealing the violence of a system.

Occupying empty buildings can also be about trying to fill those vacant spaces in a different way. It can be about how space is thrown into relief by not being occupied by, say, a white bourgeois family: this is what the bedroom is for, this is what the kitchen is for, each room to be used for bodies doing things in the right combination with other bodies. To squat, to make use of a space without owning a space, is to throw open the question of what space is for, to be released from the obligation to fill all the rooms in a certain way. Maybe queers become squatters of the family; we might not have a key to the door, but we can force it open by how we combine our forces. Queer use: in reusing old words for how we assemble we widen their range of uses. As Erika Doucette and Marty Huber note, "The range of uses for squatted buildings is often much wider than simply providing a place to live. These projects link ideals with material realities and utopias, as a crucial point for many queer-feminist living projects is finding ways to combine affordable and politically responsible forms of living/housing" (2008). A widening of use is necessary given the restriction of use. Experimentation with living and housing is a project of queering use, changing how we occupy spaces: a "who" change as a "what" change.

Queer use offers us another way of talking about diversity work: the work you have to do to open institutions to those for whom they were not intended. Even to try to open a container can be deemed damaging, ruining the value of something, given how often the value of things tends to depend on their restriction. I think of how when more of us become professors, we are used as evidence of the lessening of the worth of being professors. And opening up institutions is not a task that can be achieved by a singular action precisely *given* how institutions are closed—and often remain closed through the very appearance of being open. *What's the Use?* has provided an explanation of how it is through small acts of use that possibilities become restricted, how histories becomes concrete, hard as walls. My task has thus been to keep thickening my account of use, more and more, heavier and harder—to show how histories can occupy buildings, can stop spaces from being usable even after they have been declared vacant or open for business.

We know about closures from trying to open things. When you become a diversity worker, you learn how those who try to stop something from happening are themselves stopped. This is why I describe diversity workers as institutional plumbers; you have to work out how things are blocked because they are blocked. We might from this description assume that diversity workers are appointed to unblock the system. But blockages can be how the system is working. The system is working by stopping those who are trying to transform the system. This means that *to transform a system we have to stop it from working.* When you stop the machine from working, you have damaged the machine. Plumbers might need to become vandals, or we might have to pass as plumbers (fixing the leaks) to become vandals (making leaks bigger). We might have to throw a wrench in the works or become, to use Sarah Franklin's (2015) terms, "wenches in the works," to throw our bodies into the system, to try to stop the same old bodies, doing the same old things. The "wench in the works" has a queer kinship with the feminist killjoy—a kinship of figures can be a kinship of persons—as *nonreproductive agents*, as those who are trying to stop what usually happens from happening. A nonreproductive agent aims not to reproduce a line, not to follow in the footsteps of those who have gone before.

So much is reproduced by the requirement to follow. In chapter 4, I describe how you are required to follow the well-trodden paths of citation, to cite properly as to cite those deemed to have already the most influence. In order to craft new knowledge, we might have to cite differently: citation as how we can refuse to be erased. We can consider the work of indigenous and black feminist scholars such as Zoe Todd (2016) and

Alexis Pauline Gumbs (2016), who have showed how we can craft different knowledges by not following old citational paths. In *Living a Feminist Life* (2017), I had a rather blunt citation policy, which was not to cite any white men. In this book, I have not been able to have such a policy: following use has meant engaging with the history of utilitarianism, which is a history of books written mainly by white men. Even if I have been critical of this history, use *as* reuse, I have kept it alive. A reuse is still a use, damn it! If I have used their names, I am not writing to them, or for them. I write to, for, those who are missing, whose names are not known, whose names cannot be used: those who are faint, becoming faint, fainter still.[8]

An occupation can be secured as a requirement to follow a line, to use the well-trodden path. To speak of whiteness in the academy or of colonialism as the context in which Enlightenment philosophy happened is to bring up the scandal of the vandal. Decolonizing the curriculum as a project has been framed as an act of vandalism, a willful destruction of our universals: knocking off the heads of statues, snapping at the thrones of the philosopher kings. In chapter 4, I refer to one way that eugenics is given an institutional home by the naming of buildings, lecture theaters, and professorships after eugenicists such as Francis Galton at UCL. I noted how the use of Galton's name was justified at a panel, "Why Isn't My Professor Black?," as an inheritance. There has since been a wider and meaningful discussion of the role of Galton's legacy at UCL. This questioning of a legacy was represented to the wider public as the Galton Must Fall Campaign.[9] While we might support such a campaign if it did indeed exist, there was no such campaign; it was in fact invented to discredit the questioning of a legacy as "cultural vandalism." When it was pointed out that such a campaign did not exist, the newspaper made some small amendments clarifying that such a campaign "has yet to materialise." What is clarifying is how discrediting works. To discredit the questioning of a legacy is to discredit the questioner. Even posing a question or making a history questionable is framed as vandalism.

A judgment can be turned into a project. If questioning what is received as inheritance is understood as damaging institutions, we might need to damage institutions. A complaint too is often treated as (potential) damage to the organization. In chapter 4, I introduced some data from my study of complaint. This study was inspired by my own experiences of working on multiple inquiries into sexual harassment and sexual misconduct, which is to say my project was inspired by students. After three years of trying to get through, of coming up against wall after wall,

c.6. Becoming a leak.

I eventually resigned. I resigned because I had had enough, and because I did not want to stay silent about what had been going on. Resignation is another way of saying *no* to the system; you withdraw your labor, your body, yourself. The word *resignation* can seem to suggest giving up, reconciling yourself to your fate, to resign yourself to something. I hear the word *resignation* and I hear a long, drawn-out sigh rather like saying, perhaps, *what's the use?* But resignation can also be how you refuse to resign yourself to a situation. Perhaps you are giving up on something, a belief that you can do the work *here*, but you are holding onto something, a belief in doing the work. What appears to be giving up can be a refusal to give in.

I resigned in part because of the silence about what was going on. To get information out, sometimes you need to get out. There is no point in being silent about resigning if you are resigning to protest silence. When I shared my reasons for resigning, I became the cause of damage. To speak out is to become a leaky pipe: drip, drip (figure c.6).

Organizations will try to contain that damage; public relations works as a form of damage limitation, repairing an injury to the organization's reputation. Indeed this is how diversity often takes institutional form: damage limitation. Happy shiny policies will be put in place, holes filled without reference to what went on before. Organizations often use paper to paper over the cracks, the leaks. Or they send out paper in order to create a trail, paper that can be used as evidence of what has been done. Creating evidence of doing something is not the same thing as doing something.

But there is hope here; they cannot mop up all of our mess. One spillage can lead to more coming out: can lead, does lead. Just loosen the screw a little bit, a tiny little bit, and you might cause an explosion. We need more explosions.

Queer use might describe this potential for an explosion, how small deviations, a loosening of a requirement, the creation of an exit point, opening a door to allow something to escape, can lead to more and more coming out. Of course, this is why professional norms are so often about "keeping a lid on it." Institutional loyalty is performed as silence in case of institutional damage. In his 1993 Reith lecture, Edward Said argued that professionalism endangers the academic profession: "The danger comes from an attitude that I shall be calling professionalism; that is, thinking of your work as an intellectual as something you do for a living, between the hours of nine and five with one eye on the clock, and another cocked at what is considered to be proper, professional behaviour—not rocking the boat, not straying outside the accepted paradigms or limits, making yourself marketable and above all presentable, hence uncontroversial and unpolitical and 'objective.'"[10]

Norms of conduct—being professional—are tied to protecting the organization from damage. Silence becomes a form of institutional loyalty. Being unprofessional, rocking that boat, not accepting the limits of what you can do, or what you can say, is risky; you risk your own chances of progressing. Rocking the boat is riskier the more precarious you are; if you are already near the edge, and you rock the boat, you might fear you will topple right over. But the more secure you are, the more you have to conserve. We are returning to what I described as a paradox in my conclusion of chapter 4: that if you proceed on a path in order to disrupt it, you can end up not disrupting it in order to proceed. The more we are resourced by an organization, the more its losses become our own losses. When I spoke out about sexual harassment at my institution, I was told I had caused not only damage to the organization but damage to feminism. Perhaps we are learning the requirements of professional feminism. Perhaps in order to become a professional feminist, you need not to rock the boat; you need to polish the furniture, to stop information getting out, to protect the organization's reputation. Of course, we all have to work out what to do in conditions that are not of our making. Our decisions are compromised, necessarily so. But when silence about violence becomes a way of holding onto feminist resources, we have a problem.

We might need to become unprofessional feminists and let it out. A leak can be a lead. A leak can be a feminist lead. Even complaints that do

C.7. Hard to find, harder to follow.

not seem to get anywhere can lead us to each other. I have been learning how those who make complaints end up finding out about others who made complaints before them; complaint becomes a kind of intergenerational intimacy. One student who made a complaint about sexual harassment noted: "The scale of the response was so extreme in a way compared to what we were complaining about. Now on reflection I guess it was because there were hundreds of complaints they had suppressed that they did not want to have a lid lifted on it." There is so much more to come out because of how much has been contained.

It might seem that complaints that do not get anywhere disappear without a trace like that unused path, hard to find, harder to follow (figure C.7).

In making a complaint, we keep a history alive; we do not let go. Feminist memory can become a counterinstitutional project; we have to find ways of creating paths for others to follow, to leave traces in places. Another student spoke to me about making an informal complaint about white supremacy in her classroom: using that kind of term for what is *here*, at the university, can get you in serious trouble; she knew that but she was willing to do that. She became, in her terms, "an indigenous feminist monster," and she ended up completing her PhD off campus. She said that "an unexpected little gift" was how other students could come to her: "They know you are out there and they can reach out to you." You hold on by passing a refusal on. A complaint in taking you back can point forward, to those who come after, who can receive something from you because of what you tried to do, even though you did not get through, even though all you seemed to do was scratch the surface. Even what or who has been binned can acquire a new life. The complaints in the graveyard can come back to haunt institutions. It is a promise.

When we are stopped from getting *through*, we have to find other methods for getting information *out*. We might have to make other uses of paper, queer uses—leaflets or letters or posts that can be shared because they cannot be traced back to a source, a tale without a trail. We might whisper, speaking quietly to create a line of connection, so that information can be passed down. Vandalism becomes a tactic when we have to cut a message off from a body. We have to invent new methods for getting stuff out not just because we have exhausted usual procedures— such as complaint procedures—or because we are exhausted by them, though many of us have and are. We have to invent new methods because we have learned that working "in house" too often ends up being a restoration project, polishing the furniture so it appears less damaged—a labor I have called, with reference to the uses of diversity, "institutional polishing" (Ahmed 2012, 2017). In house, the master's house—we can remember Audre Lorde: "The master's tools will never dismantle the master's house" (1984, 110–13). Of course, we have limited options, and we use the tools available to us. Sometimes we do what is required: we might even be willing to reflect the good image the organization has of itself back to itself. But we have to be careful not to lose ourselves in that reflection. We do not want to polish away the scratches; they are testimony.

Yes, those scratches: we are back to those scratches (figure C.8). We can reach each other through what appears as damage, mere scratch and scribble. Complaints become writing on the wall: we were here; we did not get used it.

c.8. Writing on the wall.

Survival and Creativity

The riskier it is to speak out, the more inventive we have to become. The requirement to be inventive is not just a matter of communication. Audre Lorde in her poem "A Litany for Survival" evokes "those of us" who "love in doorways coming and going in the hours between dawns" (1978, 31). You might have to use the less-used paths, turn a doorway into a meeting place: a shadowy place can be a safer place to meet. You stop and loiter at the very threshold you are supposed to pass through quickly. You might have to try to slide by undetected because being seen is dangerous when you are seen as dangerous. Queer use can be a matter of survival, becoming fainter as your best chance of being at all.

Becoming fainter: a queer archive too is made up of fainter trails, "an archive of the ephemeral," as José Esteban Muñoz (1996) described so perfectly, an archive that is possible because queers are attuned to the fleeting, to the flickering, to the significance of what arrives only to disappear again (see also Halberstam 2006, 161). There can be queer possibilities not only in use—in how materials can be picked up when we refuse an instruction—but in being not of use. Perhaps these possibilities are closer together than they seem: queer use as finding a use for what has been designated not much use, finding that a potential has not been exhausted. Elizabeth Freeman suggests that a queer method attends to what has been deemed useless: "The point may be to trail behind actually existing social possibilities: to be interested in the tail end of things, to be willing to be bathed in the fading light of whatever has been declared useless" (2010, xiii). In queering the archive, we have affection for what has been discarded; we find uses for what has been declared useless.

Ironically, or perhaps not, it was a much-used book that gave me a glimpse of a queer use for what is not much use. I noted in chapter 2 how there is a discussion in *The Origin of the Species* of vestigial organs, as parts that are no longer useful but linger, however dwindled, such as the small eye of the blind mole; these parts are sometimes called leftovers. Vestigiality is the retention of structures or attributes of ancestral species that have lost their functionality: another version of the strange temporality of use. Let me quote again from Darwin: "Rudimentary parts, as it is generally admitted, are apt to be highly variable. . . . *Their variability seems to result from their uselessness*, and consequently from natural selection having had no power to check deviations in their structure" ([1859] 2009, 118–19, emphasis mine).

Darwin here is considering uselessness not as injurious but as indifference: what is useless neither helps nor hinders an organism. But we know how compulsory heterosexuality can make variations that seem indifferent to fate, fatal. And we know how deviants are punished, how deviation as such is understood as harm. And we know how uselessness has been a deadly assignment, a history of who and what is discarded: how the fragments are swept up and away. We can find other ways of telling the history of use and uselessness, hearing the queer potential in a sentence from a much-used book. That potential: not being selected is not to be checked; not being selected is to have more room to roam, to vary, to deviate; to proliferate. If queer use can be about survival, following the less well-used path in order not to be detected, queer use can also be about creativity, the variations that are possible when you are not selected and rewarded for going the right way.

Not being selected also means not being supported. And so, we have to create our own support systems, queer handles—how we hold on, how a life can go on—when we are shattered, because we are shattered. No wonder then: the stories of the exhaustion of inhabiting worlds that do not accommodate us, the stories of the weary and the worn, the teary and the torn are the same stories as the stories of inventiveness, of creating something, of making something. Some of this inventiveness can be understood as description; there is nothing mere about description. A world has too often been described from the point of view of those who are accommodated. A world might seem open if it was open to you. When we describe the world from the point of view of those not accommodated, a different world appears.[11] If you do not have a key—and as I explored in chapter 1, a body can be a key—a door is a wall. We have to share accounts of how doors are closed, for whom doors are closed.

When doors are closed to some people, they are also closed to our stories, which include our stories about closed doors. When a door is closed, you have to find other ways to get information out. You might have to make use of the resources available to you in order to create new resources. Barbara Smith describes why the Kitchen Table Press, dedicated to publishing the work of women of color, took its name: "We chose our name because the kitchen was the centre of the home, the place where women in particular work and communicate with each other" (1989, 11). She describes the commitment of this press: "Our work is both cultural and political, connected to the struggles of freedom of all of our peoples. We hope to serve as a communication network for Women of Colour in the U.S. and elsewhere" (12). You turn a kitchen table into a publishing house; the places where many of us gather, work, meet, and greet become communication networks, vehicles for sending information out, for getting out, for reaching each other.

The Kitchen Table Press closed soon after Audre Lorde's death. There are many more stories to be told about the life legacies of collectives that do not seem to last, at least in the form they assume at a given point in time. I think too of the UK-based organization OWAAD (Organization of Women of Asian and African Descent), which was established in 1978 and closed in 1982. A four-year institutional life can be a lifelong legacy. The 1985 book *Heart of the Race: Black Women's Lives in Britain*, written by Beverley Bryan and Stella Dadzie, who were founding members of OWAAD, and Suzanne Scafe, who was also a member, was recently republished. This book is a founding text in Black British feminism. The new edition includes an interview with Heidi Mirza and the authors. Heidi Mirza questions the narrative that OWAAD failed because it did not last: "Why should it last forever? These things don't. The whole point of organising: it doesn't last forever" (2018, 262). In addressing the reasons OWAAD did not last, Bryan, Dadzie, and Scafe have much to teach us about lives and legacies. We learn that for OWAAD to have lasted longer, it would have had to make different decisions; it would have had to change the direction of the organization in order to secure funding. Sometimes to secure a future for an organization requires funding. Sometimes securing funding requires giving up on a project. Sometimes to keep hold of a project, you must give up on a future for an organization. If an institutional death is sometimes necessary for a political life, an institutional life can sometimes require a political death. A cessation can be a continuation by other means. A legacy can be what is enabled for those who are part of an organization at the very moment it ceases to be; not lasting can be how a lifeline is thrown out, how you can reach others by what you refuse to give up. And so we learn: less lasting does not mean less important or even less widely received. What is fainter might survive in another sense: in the hearts and minds of those who tell the tale, a tale as another queer trail.

Perhaps what we create is fragile because we need it to survive. Attending to the uses of use has led me to reflect more about what is necessary, on *need* as politics. When a world has been assembled around your needs—when you are given what you need to live, to move on, to get on—need does not need to matter. If you have to work to have what you need, need matters. For Audre Lorde (1984), poetry is not a luxury but as necessary as bread. And Lorde often writes of bread—bread as what we make, kneading, as what we break, needing, to live our lives fully. Judith Butler reminds us that "for those who are still looking to become possible, possibility is a necessity" (2004, 31). I think of how a still lingers, how possibility is something we have to fight for still because of what is still. Use can be how a possibility has been restricted. Complaints are often what you have to make for something to be possible. Complaints too are necessary.

I think of Alexis Pauline Gumbs writing in response to the devastation of Hurricane Harvey—of the survival of indigenous, immigrant, queer, black, people of color, poor loved ones—writing of how their survival is **necessary**, emphasizing the word in bold.[12] I retain her emphasis; we can share an emphasis. I think of exclamation points, which began as an example of overuse but then became something we do, or even are: in making a complaint we are heard as shouting; in being we are heard as insistent. Necessary is bold as well as insistent; it requires being bold for some not to do what they are told. Necessary is a claim; *it is what some have to do to be.* The work we have to do to be could be understood as building work. If I have considered queer use as how we dismantle a world that has been built to accommodate only some, we can also think of queer use as a building project. We might aim not to build more secure institutions, using the well-used paths, but to build from the needs of those who are not enabled by following those routes. Such spaces might be understood as shelters: places to go for nourishment so that we can return to do the hard work of dismantling what has become built into a system.

For those who have to fight for what they need to survive, use itself becomes useful. Distance from use, rather like distance from necessity, often depends on the labor of others who will attend to one's needs. In chapters 2 and 3, I explored how elites distanced themselves from utility. The scholar sets himself apart from the administrator, the artist from the craftsperson. That some are required to be useful is how others are freed from that requirement. We can refuse any such distance or any such freedom predicated on having access to the labor of others who will attend to our needs. We can also value the labor of *that* attending. Those who do the housework, who have to take care of bodies and things, know stuff; to know is to know about needs. You come to know things from working intimately with them, working out how far to go before they too say no.

The project of queering use does not aim to create distance from use but to inhabit use all the more. We might respond to the problem of instrumentalism not by rejecting the idea of useful knowledge but by calling for knowledge that is useful to others, with this "to" being an opening, an invitation, a connection. We can follow those who came before us. bell hooks offers a powerful critique of how theory can be used "as an instrument of domination" (1994, 65), used to enforce rather than loosen hierarchies. hooks does not end there, with the sharp edge of a critique. She also suggests theory "may also contain important insights, thoughts, visions, that could if used differently serve a healing liberatory function" (65). For a past use not to be exhaustive, we have work to do, the work of enabling a tool to be used for other purposes. Marilyn Strathern reflects on the problematic of the requirement to produce "useful knowledge."[13] She notes the existence of an "evidence based era of policy," which is "articulated in an extreme form in the view that knowledge that cannot be communicated is useless knowledge" (2005, 75). But she also acknowledges that "there is nothing that cannot be useful if by that we mean putting knowledge to human ends" (73). Her attempt to value a different kind of intellectual work rests on an idea of cultivating capacities, which "need 'using' in the sense of exercising—use that is not pre-empted by possible usefulness" (103). Our task in challenging instrumental rationality is to make use of other uses of use.

And we might challenge how functionalism becomes fatalism, how for some *for* is treated as *before*, becoming an end before you even begin. But in challenging how the requirement to be useful can be imposed on us, we open up a conversation about usefulness and how it might matter. I think again of Audre Lorde, who especially in her later work often spoke of her desire to be useful to others. She spoke even of her desire for her own death to be a useful death (1988, 53). She writes of how she thought about death, about how to die (as well as how to live): "rather than just fall into death any old way, by default, according to somebody else's rules" (53). Not falling into death, not going the same way others are going, as things have gone before, requires asking questions. Usefulness here is about asking questions about how to do something, how to be something. She notes that you have no choice; mortality is the condition of having to die. But mortality acquires a different meaning for those whose existence is not supported: "We all have to die at least once. Making that death useful would be winning for me. I wasn't supposed to exist anyway, not in any meaningful way in this fucked-up whiteboys' world" (53). Usefulness might matter more for those who were not "supposed to exist." Usefulness then becomes a political address, a way of facing outward, toward others. Audre Lorde teaches us that we need to keep the question of use alive not because use does not matter but because it does. What's the use? I noted in my introduction how this question can sound like exasperation, giving up on the point of something. I considered how for Virginia Woolf that question, however difficult, throws everything into question. To make use a question is to inherit a feminist and queer project of living differently. Asking the point *of* use might be an address *to*. To be useful can be a way of addressing a world: a multiple plural *to*; *to* that faces many directions; *to* that can animate a life, too.

Animation: queer use as the work you have to do to be. The more you are blocked, the more you have to try to find a way through. The less support you have, the more support you need. We might become each other's resources; we prop each other up because we understand how diminishing it can be to have to fight for an existence, to have to fight, even, to enter a room. Perhaps the harder it is to be, the more use you have for use. We can return to Rosemarie Garland-Thomson's approach to misfits. Garland-Thomson uses the analogy of a square peg and a round hole: no amount of pushing will get that peg into the hole. Her conclusion is not that the peg needs to be modified in order that it can fit. Rather she suggests that "one of the fundamental premises of disability politics is that social justice and equal access should be achieved by changing the shape of the world, not changing the shape of our bodies" (2011, 597).

We need to change the shape of the world. Garland-Thomson also suggests we need to think about the world from the point of view of those whose shape has not allowed them to fit. In other words, she argues *for* misfitting: "Let me linger on a final reason why disability misfits should be in the world" (604). Lingering itself, I have suggested, can be a form of queer attention. Her reasons are as follows:

> The moral understandings, subjugated knowledge, or ethical fitting that can emerge from what might be called socially conscious, or even theoretically mediated, misfitting can yield innovative perspectives and skills in adapting to changing and challenging environments. Acquiring or being born with the traits we call disabilities fosters an adaptability and resourcefulness that often is underdeveloped in those whose bodies fit smoothly into the prevailing, sustaining environment. This epistemic status fosters a resourcefulness that can extend to the nondisabled and not yet disabled as they relate to and live with people with disabilities. For example, people born without arms all learn to use their toes to accomplish tasks that those of us with arms never are able to do. Blind people learn to navigate through the world without the aid of light, a skill useful when sources of artificial light that seeing people depend upon fail. Deaf people develop modes of communication that are silent. Such misfitting can be generative rather than necessarily catastrophic for human beings. (604)

Garland-Thomson offers a powerful critique of how worlds are built to enable some to fit, and not others. She is also suggesting here, with reference to the creativity of use, that the experience of not being accommodated, while painful, difficult, and exhausting—even catastrophic—is not only that. You acquire resources and skills in negotiating a world that is not built for you, making use of what you have because you do not have what it is assumed you need. In making use of what you have but what is not usually used to accomplish something—making use of your toes to do what hands usually do—you build something, create something, that would not otherwise be here. When we cannot make use of some things, we might find uses for other things. What is usually understood as a limit or a restriction can be an opening. If a restriction of possibility can be an opening, then being used up, being depleted, shattered, does not end there.

Misfitting can be understood as generative precisely given it involves friction; when bodies do not fit seamlessly into space, things happen.

Aimi Hamraie introduces the concept of "crip technoscience" to investigate the "critical design work of how misfit disabled users, for whom estrangement is already a pervasive experience, draw on the sensibilities of friction and disorientation to enact design politics" (2017, 103). Crip and queer meet at an odd angle. When you draw upon what does not fit, what is slant-wise or bent, you draw a different world. We can think of the disability design work of Liz Jackson, who describes how "our lives are spent cultivating an intuitive creativity, because we navigate a world that isn't built for our bodies."[14] Indeed, Jackson also notes how often the creativity of disabled designers is written out of the history of design, how too often disabled people are assumed to be the recipients of, rather than agents in, the design process. Jackson calls disabled designers the "original life hackers." When you have to modify things to make them usable, you are creating out of necessity. The expression "life hacker" also conveys how creativity can be a disruption in the order of things and can be intended as such. A hacker is also a vandal; you have to break into a system when you do not have legitimate access to that system. A break can be how you leak information out as well as how you expose the failure of that system.

Sometimes we do not have to break in; doors can be opened to those who have previously been refused entry. What happens then? Who do you become then? Reina Gossett, Eric A. Stanley, and Johanna Burton explore how trans people are now "offered many 'doors,'" that is, "entrances to visibility, to resources, to recognition, and to understanding" (2017, xxiii). They show how some doors can be traps that require accommodation to existing norms. Given doors can be traps, they suggest we can find *trapdoors*: "those clever contraptions that are not entrances or exits but secret passages that take you someplace else, often someplace as yet unknown" (xxiii). Secret passages, backdoors, trapdoors: they can also be what you find because of what you refuse. We have to navigate a world, the openings as well as the closings, making use of what we find along the way.

Sometimes you have to wiggle to make room. I think back to discussions of queer biology, how odd and curious life can be: those inversions, beaks that end up the wrong way up, what is cobbled together out of necessity from parts at hand. Can this be a kind of queer inheritance: how we inherit from past struggles to exist; small modifications, the widening of a passageway or an opening just enough to enable more to get by or to get through; a sociability as worn as wisdom, secret passages, meeting places, passing information down a line, about where to go, what to do?

How odd that from necessity we might become alive to possibility—how odd, how queer. When we consider use not only as the potential to increase capacity but as contact and friction, wear and tear, bodies come to matter in different ways. Queer use can be offered as an ethics of finitude, an appreciation of the wrinkle or the scratch, expressions of time on the surfaces of bodies and things, loving what does not, and will not, last. *What's the Use?* has been full of old and worn things, broken things, from Silas's much-loved pot, to cups that have flown off their handles (we too can fly off our handles), to used-up tubes of toothpaste, to that sense we might have of being used and used up, of having nothing left to give. A queer affinity can be an affinity with the broken or broken down, to what spills from a container, what shatters under the weight of history. Alison Piepmeier titles an essay "What a Shattered Coffee Mug Says about Life."[15] She writes: "Last week, I was having my second cup of coffee, using my beloved Princess Leia coffee cup. As I added to my ice coffee, I slipped. Princess Leia fell. The cup broke into pieces." When Piepmeier slips, the coffee cup slips. When it shatters, she is shattered. When it is in pieces, she is in pieces. Piepmeier shares with us this shattering story while she is losing her life, while she is dying. She tells us why the coffee cup matters to her. Her brother gave her that cup; a story of how we acquire something can be a story of how we love something. Once we love something, it can become part of a daily routine: "As I got older, the Princess Leia cup entered my life in more complicated ways. Her image became more and more central to my life. I drank from her every day. She became the image of my body. She was my picture on Facebook, in Gmail, and on my blog. Princess Leia became part of my regular morning life." Alison loved Princess Leia: "This Princess Leia, though, wasn't cartoonish. She was confident. She was fearless. She had character." I think of that bond, that fragile bond between Alison and Princess Leila, between Alison and her cup, between Alison and Carrie Fisher, fragility as fierce: "Her face is fierce. . . . There Princess Leia was, in my hands, broken but defiant."

Broken but defiant; we can shatter when things shatter. But this shattering can be fierce as well as fragile: how things can hold more than coffee, how they can hold an idea of who we are, of who we can become. Alison's daughter, Maybelle, witnesses her mother's grief at having broken Princess Leia, as she witnesses her mother's illness; her daughter understands "that things are changing." Alison's brother finds an online description of kintsugi. In the Japanese art of repairing broken pottery, kintsugi, a break is understood as part of the life of a thing; the break is repaired to show the break rather than to hide the break.[16] Her cup is repaired not to restore it to how it was before but "to recognize the beauty of the effort to mend what is broken, however imperfectly, however incompletely." The effort to mend, the striving, the work: "to see compassion in the work of both potter and physician." I am so moved by this beautiful piece of writing, to think about what it means to hold on not by trying to restore something to what it was before it was broken but to keep "the broken pieces together."

The broken can be queer kin. To offer a queer way of working is not to start anew, with the light, the bright, the white, the upright; it is to start with the weighty, the heavy, the weary, and the worn. When a history makes it hard to be, you feel that history as weight. In the first chapter of this book, I mentioned how there can be a certain point when something is used too much, a tipping point. A snap can be a tipping point: those moments when you cannot take it anymore, and you can no longer put up with what you previously endured. Something breaks, shatters. If sometimes we try to get used to what makes it hard, a snap can be how you give yourself a chance at being: snapping as how you do *not* get used to it. We reach a breaking point. We can aim to reach such a point, to take a break, to snap, so that we no longer bear the weight of a history. Our heavy histories are also snappy, rioting, gathering, passing *no* around. Consider the Stonewall uprising. I think of Sylvia Rivera, who, as a trans woman of color, tends not to be remembered in how those events are remembered. In an interview, she describes for us what happened on that day.[17] It was a day like other days for those who gathered at the bar—gays, dykes, drag queens: a racially diverse army of the willingly perverse, an army that is used to living with police violence, an army for whom such violence is usual. Rivera says: "This is what we learned to live with at that time. We had to live with it." But something happens on that day: "We had to live with it until that day. And then, I don't know if it was the customers or it was the police. It just [*snaps fingers*], everything clicked." The snapping of fingers, that sound, snap, snap, allows Rivera to convey the sensation of things falling into place, when suddenly—or it seems sudden but really it took a long time—a collective comes out with a "no," a collective that is fragile, fabulous, full, furious: "Everybody just like, Why the fuck are we doin' all this for? . . . Oh, it was so exciting. It was like, Wow, we're doing it. We're doing it. We're fucking their nerves."

A snap can be catchy, igniting a crowd—all those years of frustration, pain; all that is wearing, coming out, getting out; claiming the freedom to be what they have tried to stop you from being. To make snap part of how we tell the story of political movements is to show how exhaustion and rebellion can come from the same place. Even when snap comes from sap—from being tired out, depleted—snap can reboot; snap can boost. It can be electric, snap, snap, sizzle; so much comes out when you tip something over. Not getting used to it can be a queer aspiration, a queering of aspiration; it might be what we have to do collectively to breathe.

In not getting used to it, bodies become expressive. The word *express* comes from press. It implies something that is squeezed out. To say snap is expressive is to say what is shared is what is no longer contained. A hand clenches, refusing to be handy; an arm strikes. A queer use of the body allows bodies to do the talking. I think too of snapping fingers as part of this signaling of a refusal to get used to something. Marlon Riggs explores finger snapping as an expression of political resistance perhaps akin to the clenched fist for African American gay men. In Riggs's documentary, *Tongues Untied*, finger snapping offers a collective way of speaking: it is how tongues are released from bondage.[18] Finger snapping can say: don't mess with us. Finger snapping offers a way of speaking back and speaking to, a language of the body that gives room to be in a body that is not given room. Riggs's message is defiant: "Our notice is served. Our silence has ended. Snap!" ([1991] 1999, 311).

We have behind us many snappy messages of defiance. Here is another: we are here, we are queer; *get used to it*. To reverse an instruction is to refuse an instruction. Sometimes we have to become creative because of a restriction or to fight a restriction. We queer the places where we have been, a tail, a trail. We might think of desire lines, those lines on the ground left behind by users who have not followed official paths.[19] Desire lines are created only by use and can be thought of as the promise of queer use: trails that remind us where we have been, trails that tell us where to go to find each other.

I want to end this book by returning one last time to an image (figure c.9). This image of a postbox is a queer teacher. It teaches us that it is possible for those deemed strangers or foreigners to take up residence in spaces that have been assumed as belonging to others, as being for others to use. The postbox could have remained in use: the nest destroyed be-

C.9. A queer teacher.

fore it was completed, the birds displaced. A history of use is a history of such displacements, many violent—displacements that are often unrecognized because of how things remain occupied. It is because of this occupation, this settling of history, this weight, that queering use requires bringing things down. This is why it is not enough to affirm the queerness of use. To bring out the queerness of use requires more than an act of affirmation: it requires a world dismantling effort.[20] In order for queer use to be possible, in order to recover a potential that has not simply been lost but stolen, there is work to do. To queer use is work: it is hard and painstaking work; it is collective and creative work; it is diversity work.

Queer use is the work we have to do to queer use.

This image has something else to teach us. Creating a shelter and disrupting usage can refer to the same action:

A doorway becomes a meeting place.

A kitchen table becomes a publishing house.

A postbox becomes a nest.

Notes

....

Introduction

1 I did not realize until I decided to write on use that I would be writing a trilogy. Writing one book led to the next; they were not planned together. During my research into use I waited for a while to see if another word/concept would pop out from my materials. But there was no such pop, which is why I am confidently describing the books as a trilogy.

2 I explain in the last section of this introduction the inadequacy of this "in and out" as a description of how I ended up working.

3 See James R. Hagerty, "Marian Diamond Studied the Secrets of Boosting Brain Power," *Wall Street Journal*, August 4, 2017.

4 "Embracing the Future," *The Economist*, February 25, 2012.

5 I wrote about Silas's pot in *Willful Subjects* (2014) in a discussion of breaking things and also in *Living a Feminist Life* (2017) in a discussion of fragility.

6 The fields that are most specifically organized around the categories of use and function are design and architecture. It is not possible for me to review all the relevant works. But I have found the following helpful: for architecture, Hill 2003; Grabow and Spreckelmeyer 2015; and for design and use, Risatti 2007; Houkes and Vermaas 2010. I discuss how early works in psychology made use of use in chapter 1 and in biology in chapter 2.

7 A contemporary theorist who has singled out use as a core concept is Giorgio Agamben. In *The Highest Poverty*, Agamben argues that the task to think life "as a common use" would "demand the elaboration of a theory of use—of which Western philosophy lacks even the most elementary principles" (2013,

xii). Agamben provides what he defines as lacking over a body of work, including, most recently, *The Use of Bodies* (2015), in which his primary concern is to return to Aristotle's use of use (*chresti*). By a close and careful reading of Aristotle, Agamben shows how use does not differentiate an object from a subject and can be distinguished from an instrumentalism that creates an external good (the use of a chair for sitting is understood as different from the use of a loom to create wool). The problem is the implication that "today" use has lost meaning other than the instrumental creation of an external good. The premise of my own work is that there are many uses of use in contemporary culture and thought. The narrowness of Agamben's archive has consequences, in my view, for the scope of his argument.

8 The word *utility* comes to the English language via Old French (*utilite*, "usefulness") but has the same Latin root as the verb *use* (*uti*, make use of).

9 The literature on utilitarianism as moral philosophy is vast. Although I do not engage in a sustained way with this body of literature in *What's the Use?*, choosing instead to approach utilitarianism through education, I have learned from reading it. For a useful collection on utilitarianism as moral philosophy, see Eggleston and Miller (2014).

10 Interestingly, although the archives of happiness and use overlap, following use allowed me to track an association I did not make in *The Promise of Happiness* (2010), an association I would describe as fatal, between unemployment (understood not simply as activity but as a specific kind of activity) and unhappiness.

11 In chapter 2, for example, I could have written more about how use becomes understood as key to the acquisition of biological form from classical philosophy onward, but I wanted to ground my discussion in work written in the nineteenth century. I do smuggle in reference to Lucretius because his hap-filled model of use is so striking. I also note in chapter 2 how Lamarck and Darwin's uses of use relate back to Aristotle.

12 All three books have in fact made use of historical materials relating to the education of children, although in the first two books my examples were texts by philosophers on education. In *The Promise of Happiness* (2010), I explored the role of happiness (and unhappiness) in Jean-Jacques Rousseau's influential text *Émile* ([1762] 1993) In *Willful Subjects* (2014), I analyzed the shift from what Alice Miller (1987) called "poisonous pedagogy," educational techniques that rested on breaking the child's will, to more positive methods that focused on encouraging the child to will in the right way. *What's the Use?* also considers the development of positive methods that are about directing the child toward useful ends. But here it is not so much the singular child that is the object but a class of children; the difference in object is a difference in class. See chapter 3.

13 There is a long tradition of affirming useless knowledge, sometimes predicated on valuing contemplation and the life of the mind and at other times predicated on valuing speculation and experimentation. For examples,

see Russell [1935] 2004; Flexner [1939] 2007; Graber 1995; Manning 2017. I understand, appreciate, and respect this gesture of affirming useless knowledge. But my own research led me in a different direction in part because of how it showed how often class privilege has rested on the gesture of distancing oneself from utility. See the concluding section of chapter 4 for further discussion.

14 It is interesting that I was just thinking about the expression "what's the use?" and its intonation when I found the quote from *The Years*. I had not searched for Woolf on use, or for feminist killjoys. It was one of the first uses of "what's the use?" that I found by a simple search for the expression. A feminist killjoy will find feminist killjoys!

15 It is important that I have conducted empirical research alongside writing this trilogy. I began researching diversity in higher education by talking to diversity practitioners about their work in 2003. In fact, it was the uses of "happy diversity" that sparked my interest in writing about happiness. The research into diversity was difficult: we ended up being judged as failing to deliver what we promised because we did not tell a happy story about diversity. So rather than write a book based on the data, I decided to write *The Promise of Happiness* (2010). The idea to write on will and willfulness came from writing on happiness; it was in the materials. But during my research on will and willfulness, I decided to return to the diversity data. I wrote *On Being Included: Racism and Diversity in Institutional Life* (2012) before I returned to finish *Willful Subjects* (2014). I use some material from my diversity project in the fourth chapter of that book, "Willfulness as a Style of Politics," and some of my ideas about will and willfulness made their way into my analysis of institutions and diversity. The idea for writing on use came from my research into will and willfulness: it was in the materials (the quotes from *Silas Marner* and *Pensées*, to be exact). But as I have already mentioned, because of experiences I had at work, I stopped in the middle of the research to write *Living a Feminist Life* (2017) and to begin a new empirical project on complaint. So I have worked between my three word projects and my two empirical projects in a rather haphazard way: going from one to the other, stopping and starting. They have informed and shaped each other. The fourth chapter of *What's the Use?* is where I show that shape.

16 I already had decided to use this sentence from Steedman in my introduction before I bought my own copy of *Dust*. It was a used copy—as I noted earlier, I have been trying to use used copies. A previous reader had underlined that very sentence. Use can be a connection between those who do not meet.

17 In chapter 3 I do in fact share details that I learned from reading through the minute books—in particular about the treatment of the boys taught at the schools. If you read the minute books closely enough, you can find glimpses of other kinds of transactions right in the middle of the financial transactions.

1. Using Things

1 Thank you to Sarah Franklin for this point. Please note that when I say "a kind of transfer," I do not mean that something such as an affect is being transferred (it is misleading to describe affect as being transferred as if affect exists apart from a process of being affected). Rather, I am suggesting that how each surface affects the other is a kind of transfer.

2 In addition to work on "the cultural biography of objects" (Kopytoff 1986), see also scholarship on "the social life of things" (Appadurai 1986), and what has become known as "thing theory" (Brown 2001, 2003).

3 This is my own peculiar way of thinking of cups: I am aware they do not "really" have a hole as their heart. But I like to think of a cup this way, and I will turn to the significance of this description when discussing breaking cups.

4 Throughout this book, I reflect on the intimacy of use and necessity. See my discussion of Lamarck on need in chapter 2 and need as a politics in my conclusion.

5 Classical and early modern references are referred to using book number, chapter number (when relevant), and page number.

6 In chapter 2, I explore Darwin's model of use as hap-filled or happy (natural selection makes use of what *happens* to exist). In chapter 4, I show how hap is eliminated from use in the determination of a requirement. Please note as well that if *The Promise of Happiness* (2010) asked how happiness lost its hap, this book shows how the elimination of hap is a reproductive mechanism.

7 Throughout the course of the book, I complicate (but do not abandon) the implied distinction between designed objects and what we might call provisionally organic bodies, in particular by thinking about how environments can be built for some, so they can survive and thrive, without appearing to be built. I consider how living bodies and physical arrangements become entangled with each other but the entanglement is often only revealed when bodies do not fit, drawing on Rosemarie Garland-Thomson's (2011, 2014) work on misfitting.

8 Risatti does acknowledge that use, when separated from function, can teach us something. He just argues that such uses do not teach us very much: we do not learn much about things that are heavy enough to function as paperweights, as many different kinds of things are heavy enough to fulfill that function. Perhaps the more use strays from function, the more imprecise use becomes. Risatti offers a diagram to show the difference between use and intended function. On one side a cup is being used as a holder of a hot drink; on the other it is a paperweight. These sides are divided by a ≠ sign. Use could be placed on both sides of the equation: on the left, the cup is being used in a way that it was intended to be used; on the right, the cup is being used in a way that was not intended. So the picture might

be use + function ≠ use − function. My own argument will imply that the imprecision of use might have quite a lot to teach us.

9 The evolution of paper is a much longer, complex, and fascinating history than I can describe here. For a fuller discussion, see Kurlansky (2016).

10 In his classic work, *Notes on the Synthesis of Form*, Christopher Alexander expresses this argument in the following way: "We should always expect to see the process of achieving good fit between two entities as a negative process of neutralizing the incongruities, or irritants, or forces, which cause misfit" (1964, 24). I return to this description in the following chapters. Also note the term *misfit* is used by Rosemarie Garland-Thomson (2011) to discuss how some bodies do not fit the requirements of an environment.

11 Gayatri Chakravorty Spivak shows how Marx's idea of use value is "slippery" because use value is not simply and clearly opposed to exchange value (Spivak [1993] 2012, 117). This lack of a clear opposition between use value and exchange value is in part because of how use cannot simply be subtracted from a "thing in its nudity" but depends on laboring bodies (117). In this chapter, I connect Marx's discussions of "use value" in the first chapter of *Capital* with his discussion of "wear and tear" in relation to machines and labor power in chapter 15.

12 Heidegger suggests that usefulness does not reside in something; a thing is not simply a useful thing. He notes, "Strictly speaking, there 'is' no such thing as a useful thing. There always belongs of a useful thing a totality of useful things in which the useful thing can be what it is" ([1927] 1962, 100).

13 Kathryn Westcott, "Letter Boxes: The Red Heart of the British Streetscape," *BBC News Magazine*, January 18, 2013, http://www.bbc.co.uk/news/magazine-21057160.

14 Mark Nicholls, "Village Post Boxes at the Hearts of Communities Need Protection," *Eastern Daily Press*, February 26, 2016, http://www.edp24.co.uk/news/village-post-boxes-at-the-hearts-of-communities-need-protection-1-4435492.

15 Thank you to Amarpreet Kaur and Mark Curtis, who found this occupied toilet sign for me.

16 For a discussion of bathrooms as places of gender policing, see Halberstam (1998, 20–29), Cavanagh (2010), and Riggle (2018).

17 I am referring here to how words can fall out of use not simply as an organic process but as a result of policies, some of which are officially declared, others not. For example, some words can be discouraged by the introduction of alternative words that are deemed more appropriate or by the correction of words deemed inappropriate (a correction can take the form of a speaker simply using an alternative word, as if trying to put that word into someone else's mouth). Correction is a correction of use. Or we could consider how the imposition of the requirement to use the words and languages of the colonizer is central to the colonial project: being forced not to use words can

be how you are forced out of a culture and history. Radical traditions exist because of the failure of force.

18 Sacred human remains can also be preserved in museums, becoming objects, kept apart by artificial means or even by any means. Sometimes the value of something might require being degraded, becoming part of the soil.

19 You can find many examples of postboxes that have become nests in the UK: it is policy to take boxes out of use when birds enter. I have replicated an image that I originally found online, as we decided my use of this image was not covered by fair use. A Royal Mail spokesperson describes the policy in an article about a postbox that had become a nest: "Birds nest in our post boxes from time to time during the spring. In such circumstances, we would place a notice on the box requesting that customers do not use it so that the nesting birds are not disturbed. The box is then reopened once the birds have left the nest. In the meantime, we advise customers to use other postboxes nearby or they can drop mail off at any post office branch in the area." Angela Singer, "Royal Mail Post Box Is Out of Use while Birds Nest in It—A Tweet from Duton Hill near Dunmow," *Dunmow Broadcast*, April 27, 2016, http:// www.dunmowbroadcast.co.uk/news/royal-mail-post-box-is-out-of-use-while -birds-nest-in-it-a-tweet-from-duton-hill-near-dunmow-1-4511822.

20 In the UK, the Royal Mail claims that postboxes are not taken out of use because of underutilization. For an explanation, see Royal Mail, "Postbox Removal and Relocation," accessed August 8, 2018, https://personal.help .royalmail.com/app/answers/detail/a_id/132/~/postbox-removal-and -relocation. However, there have been controversies over postboxes that are not replaced when they are stolen. Residents have claimed that they are not replaced because of cost cutting while the Royal Mail claims that they are not replaced for other reasons (such as danger). See, for example, Andy Russell, "Village Unites to Save 80-Year-Old Postbox after Royal Mail Brands It 'Dangerous,'" *Daily Mail*, February 20, 2010, http://www.dailymail.co.uk /news/article-1252542/Village-unites-save-80-year-old-postbox-Royal-Mail -calls-dangerous.html. Even when underuse is not used as an official explanation for taking something out of use, it does not mean underuse is not used. In Australia, postboxes are often removed if they are not used enough. See Brendan Trembath, "Least Used Red Post Boxes under Review for Decommissioning," *AM*, March 19, 2016, http://www.abc.net.au/am/content /2016/s4428154.htm.

21 The provision or enabling is referred to as affordance, a term that was introduced by psychologist James J. Gibson (1979) in his work on the ecological nature of perception. That term has since migrated into design studies, as I discuss with reference to usability. My example of Poppy's puddle could be described as affordance: her drinking of water is enabled by the structure of the land. For further discussions of affordance, see also Ingold (1987) and Norman ([1988] 2013).

22 You might be able to hear an allusion here to a thesis that is typically offered in a field of philosophy known as object-oriented ontology (OOO). I would not argue that there is a real postbox that is withdrawn when the postbox is in use. To make such a claim would be to define what is real and withdrawn in terms that point back toward human usage (this is true with many objects, from hammers to tables: they are named by how they function for humans). Postbox does not capture all of what something can be; something can be different things, depending on how it is used. It is worth noting that Graham Harman's analysis of the significance of Heidegger reads as a treatise against utility; he treats utility as the reduction of being. In *Tool Being* (2002), Harman writes, "Being is being, not use" (117). He offers a critique of the pragmatist tradition, in particular the work of Mark Okrent, who, Harman suggests, "misses the point when he reads equipment in terms of human usefulness" (121). Harman suggests the pragmatic concern with usefulness as a form of humanism. While I understand the critique of usefulness as humanism, the phenomenological consideration of objects in use is not exhausted by such a critique. After all, for Heidegger, it is when things are in use that we learn about their being however withdrawn. We might reformulate Harman's proposition in the following way: "being is being, in use" (and the comma reminds us that being in use is not all that being is being).

23 I could have written this chapter by making tables my primary example, as I did in the first chapter of *Queer Phenomenology* (2006), but I sensed that I could rather exhaust tables by using them as my examples. I have too much affection for tables to wear them out!

24 Thank you to Barry Samuels for permission to use his photograph, which appears on his website, an "unofficial guide to Great Britain," under a section dedicated to public rights of way (footpaths and bridleways). This footpath is on St. Catherine's Hill, Hampshire. It is used as an example of a "well used and, therefore, well worn" path. See *BeenThere—DoneThat*, accessed November 12, 2018, http://www.beenthere-donethat.org.uk/.

25 In chapter 3, I explore how utilitarian policy took this exact formula: to make what is understood to deviate from the path of general happiness harder to follow.

26 See Aaron D. McClelland, "Demystifying Neuroplasticity," *Mental Health—Okanagan* (blog), March 21, 2013, http://admcclelland.blogspot.com/2013/03/demystifying-neuroplasticity.html.

27 In chapter 4, I consider how diversity work involves a consciousness of use.

28 For a discussion of the history of chairs as designed objects, see Cranz (1998). Also note that a chair can be a social position. In *Queer Phenomenology* (2006), I suggest, with reference to Edmund Husserl, that to describe the world from the point of view of the body that loses its chair is to offer a quite different view of the world. I think in that book, however, I was so

overwhelmed by the queerness of tables that I did not quite catch sight of the queerness of chairs.

29 This means, for instance, that you could use something in secret by trying not to leave traces, like how you might smooth out a pillow or a blanket to remove an impression left by someone having been there or to create an impression that nobody has been there.

30 Wittgenstein's argument here is often evoked through the saying: "ask for the use not the meaning" or "don't ask for the meaning, ask for the use" (for example, see Collins 2010, 20). This is another interesting demonstration of the queer history of use as Wittgenstein does not use such a saying. See also Gilbert Ryle and J. N. Findlay's important essay on use, usage, and meaning, which describes "don't ask for the meaning ask for the use" as "a famous saying" without attributing that saying to Wittgenstein (1961, 229). I want to acknowledge here that I am referring briefly to Wittgenstein, whose uses of use have more complexity and nuance than I can deal with in this section.

31 In earlier work, I understood this process as stickiness: how words tend to pick things up, which we can now understand as an argument about use (Ahmed 2004). An example is the expression "Islamic terrorist." That figure is a history of use; the words "Islamic" and "terrorist" are used as if one follows the other, such that to use one is to bring up the other.

32 In chapter 4, I discuss how a singular exclamation point is used as a warning sign. An exclamation point on a sign on the side of the road means Don't! Danger! Stop! We do not have to think about it when we see it; we might automatically slam on the brakes. By stopping, we are making use of the exclamation point; we are following the point.

33 One thinks, for instance, of dead metaphors, metaphors that become dead when they have been used too much. But this story of death by overuse is also a life story; if anything, it tells us how an expression comes to be used more by ceasing to operate as a metaphor. For example, the legs of a table are no longer a metaphor as the term *leg* has expanded to include any supporting pillar. When a metaphor has become dead, an expression has acquired a wider range of uses.

34 Marx begins his chapter on machinery and large-scale industry by quoting from John Stuart Mill: "It is questionable if all the mechanical inventions yet made have lightened the day's toil of any human being" ([1867] 1990, 492).

35 See also Anthony Dunne's work on "user unfriendliness." He suggests that "if user friendliness characterizes the relationship between the user and the optimal object, user-unfriendliness then, a form of gentle provocation, could characterize the post-optimal object" (2005, 35). He relates user unfriendliness to "functional estrangement" (41). While Dunne tends to approach user unfriendliness as an attitude that can be adopted toward designed objects (what he calls critical design), we could consider how use can be unfriendly and estranging for some users given how the world is built.

36 Rosemarie Garland-Thomson's work on misfitting helps expose the limits of what Leroi-Gourhan called functional plasticity. I have noted that most things are designed so that more than one person can use them. If small variations are permitted by loosening the relation of function to form, some variations remain nonfunctional; if it does not fit, you do not fit. If corporeal diversity loosens the relation of form and function, corporeal diversity can also become a container. For a discussion of misfits and creativity, see my conclusion.

37 Chapter 3 of the Fair Housing Act Design Manual, accessed March 6, 2019, is available: https://www.huduser.gov/portal/publications/pdf/fairhousing/fairch3.pdf.

38 This definition is from the website of the Center for Universal Design, accessed October 3, 2017, https://projects.ncsu.edu/ncsu/design/cud/about_ud/about_ud.htm.

39 Dolmage suggests that although Universal Design is sometimes understood as a series of specifications for what is needed to create an environment that is accessible to everyone, it can be treated as "a form of hope, a manner of trying" (2017, 116). However, Dolmage also suggests that Universal Design in the context of the neoliberal university may be "promising everything while not doing much of anything" (139). Such critiques of Universal Design are not necessarily calling for an abandonment of its promise but rather for an animation of disability justice to provoke concern for its limits.

40 In chapter 4, I explore how the well-used path can also work as a funnel: when more information, resources, and energy are funneled through fewer paths, they become narrower at the exit points.

41 We do not need to presume the human. Animal trails are also shaped by use and shape the environment. I turn to the question of environmental change in chapter 2.

42 When something becomes unusable, it is not simply that we gain "access to properties," as Heidegger suggested in his analysis of the broken hammer (see my introduction to this chapter). By drawing upon scholars in disability studies, we could put the lesson in somewhat different terms: the inaccessibility of things is how we learn about their properties.

43 In chapters 2 and 3 of this book, I explore how the uneven distribution of the effects of use has a history; and in chapter 4, I explore how this uneven distribution can be understood as structure.

2. The Biology of Use and Disuse

1 There has been a renewed interest in Lamarck because of how his arguments about the inheritance of acquired characteristics for which he tends to be known, which were understood to have been discredited by the development of modern genetics in the early twentieth century, have been revived by epigenetics.

2 For curious readers, the number is thirteen times.

3 This is important as Lamarck is often represented as assuming the direct effect of the environment. For a discussion, see Mayr (1972, 57–58).

4 Following Aristotle, to give emphasis to function or use is to consider the primacy of ends. As Aristotle writes in *Physics*, "It belongs to the same study to know the end or what something is for" (11.2, 27). As such, "what a thing is, and what it is for, are one and the same" (11.2, 29). Although Aristotle's model of nature is teleological, he does not assume conscious intent on the part of a creator or of design in the sense of a plan. André Ariew observes "teleology pertaining to natural organisms is distinct; *non*-purposive (though seemingly so); *non*-rational; *non*-intentional, and immanent; that is, an inner principle of change" (2002, 9). For Aristotle, Ariew observes, "Evidence that particular dental arrangements are *useful* to the organism comes from the fact that it is a *regular occurrence in living nature*" (9). I have decided to focus in this chapter on nineteenth-century biological writings. But my useful archive could be widened to include most writing on life, including from classical times.

5 One of the ways Lamarck was dismissed relates to how *besoin* was persistently translated as want/desire rather than need. For a discussion, see Mayr ([1976] 1997, 225).

6 So, for example, the word *necessary* when used as a noun is taken to refer to "needed, required, or useful things." *Online Etymology Dictionary*, accessed March 6, 2019, https://www.etymonline.com/.

7 It is quite clear what Lamarck is not saying: that the animal by will or effort simply modify itself in order to enable it to survive or flourish in an environment. But it is important to note that this was how Lamarck was often represented. In his spirited defense of Lamarck, Alpheus S. Packard notes how attempts to discredit Lamarck often implied his model of modification was volitional. We can see this implication in the following description of Lamarck's argument: "that progressive changes in species have been produced by the attempts of animals to increase the development of their own organs, and thus modify their structure and habits" (cited in Packard 1901, 352). Packard calls this description a "caricature of what Lamarck really taught" (352). As Packard himself explains, "Wants, needs (*besoin*), volitions, desires are not mentioned by Lamarck in his two fundamental laws, and when the word *besoin* is used it refers as much to the physiological needs as to the emotions of the animal resulting from some new environment which forces it to adopt new habits" (352). More recently, Sharon Kim also notes how "Lamarck has been caricatured as believing that organisms 'will' themselves to evolve" (2012, 91). Lamarck does in fact use the language of will but describes will not as a form of inner causality but as a physiological process, associated with irritability or responsiveness to the environment. In offering such a model of the will, Lamarck joins other writers on the will from the early nineteenth century such as Théodule

Ribot. For a discussion of Ribot, among other writers on the will, see Ahmed (2014).

8 Have you ever watched a nature program where a complex and fascinating scene of animal social interaction is flattened out by the voice-over that speaks only in tired tropes of hetero-gender? These tropes are what get in the way of an appreciation of complexity. See also Jack Halberstam, who reflects on "the long march of the penguins" as a "resolutely animal narrative about cooperation, affiliation, and the anachronism of the homo-hetero divide" (2011, 41), and Myra Hird for a discussion of nonlinear biology as providing a "wealth of evidence to confound static notions of sexual difference" (2004, 85; see also 2009).

9 In previous work, I have considered how being upright or straight is an achievement primarily with reference to the phenomenological tradition. In my book, *Queer Phenomenology*, I referred to Merleau-Ponty's discussion of experiments in perception in which queer moments happen: "If we so contrive it that a subject sees the room in which he is, only through a mirror which reflects it at an angle at 45 degrees to the vertical, the subject at first sees the room 'slantwise.' A man walking about in it seems to lean to one side as he goes. A piece of cardboard falling down the door-frame looks to be falling obliquely. The general effect is 'queer'" (Merleau-Ponty [1945] 2002, 289). Merleau-Ponty discusses how a "sudden change" occurs: "the walls, the man walking about the room, and the line in which the cardboard falls become vertical" (289). Merleau-Ponty argues that what is perceived becomes vertical not because of correspondence with objective space but in order to enable bodies to extend into space: "What counts for the orientation of the spectacle is not my body as it in fact is, as a thing in objective space, but as a system of possible actions, a virtual body with its phenomenal 'place' defined by its task and situation. My body is wherever there is something to be done" (291). In *Willful Subjects* (2014) I drew on Hegel's argument that being upright has become a habit that no longer needs to be willed. Hegel suggests that human beings "stand upright" as an act of will that has been converted into habit: "a human being stands upright has become a habit acquired through his own will" ([1827–28] 2007: 156–157). A habit is thus a "continuation" of willing: "it is a continuous will that I stand, but I no longer need to will standing as such" (157). It has been useful to think of "uprightness" as a biological as well as social achievement because it shows how queerness in the social world is continuous with queerness in the natural world; to show the connection between the upside-down, topsy-turvy, wonky, and weird as well as to show how not-fitting can be the site of creativity and invention.

10 At times Darwin was scathing and dismissive of Lamarck: for example, he describes *Zoological Philosophy* as "a wretched book" (cited in C. Johnson 2015, 184).

11 Did Darwin come to use Lamarck's laws of use and disuse more in each edition? Curtis Johnson argues that Lamarck's influence was there from the

first edition, and shows, for instance, that in the sixth edition of *The Origin of Species*, which introduces a new chapter referring to the example of giraffes, the argument was not in fact evidence of Darwin becoming more Lamarckian but written as a rebuttal to one of Darwin's most vehement critics (Johnson 2015, 166). I was reminded reading Johnson's account of how books themselves carry traces of their contexts of utterance: how debates and contestation shape the very form arguments take, the examples used, and words too. Books are sociable objects before they are read.

12 I return in chapter 3 to this definition of instrumentality in considering how use becomes a technique of instruction.

13 In *The Descent of Man*, Darwin suggests he "probably attributed too much to the action of natural selection or the survival of the fittest." He writes, "I have altered the fifth edition of the Origin so as to confine my remarks to adaptive changes of structure. I had not formerly sufficiently considered the existence of many structures which appear to be, as far as we can judge, neither beneficial nor injurious; and this I believe to be one of the greatest oversights as yet detected in my work. I may be permitted to say, as some excuse, that I had two distinct objects in view, firstly, to shew that species had not been separately created, and secondly, that natural selection had been the chief agent of change, though largely aided by the inherited effects of habit, and slightly by the direct action of the surrounding conditions. Nevertheless I was not able to annul the influence of my former belief, then widely prevalent, that each species had been purposely created; and this led to my tacitly assuming that every detail of structure, excepting rudiments, was of some special, though unrecognized, service" ([1871] 1992, 147). This qualification of the role of natural selection is also a qualification of the extent to which usefulness is a determining force.

14 See, for example, a description of a study into the usefulness of the appendix: Duke University Medical Center, "Appendix Isn't Useless at All: It's a Safe House for Good Bacteria," *ScienceDaily*, October 8, 2007, www.sciencedaily.com/releases/2007/10/071008102334.htm.

15 The implication here is that methodical selection while presuming biological plasticity as a capacity can also reduce that capacity: the selection of useful traits involves the stabilization of form in accordance with function.

16 See, for example, Bergson's ([1911] 1920) critique of finalism, which places a strong emphasis on the implications of his own critique for our understanding of the relation between form and function.

17 Gould and Lewontin explain their choice as follows: "We deliberately chose non-biological examples in a sequence running from remote to more familiar: architecture to anthropology" (1979, 584).

18 This is where Lamarck's approach has direct links to developments in epigenetics, given that epigenetics has placed a strong emphasis on the hereditary effects of diet.

19 As Curtis Johnson describes, "Ducks were not Darwin's only examples of Lamarckian 'use-inheritance.' Other favourites were the drooping ears of domesticated animals like dogs (disuse), the enlarged intestines of domesticated pigs (disuse) and perhaps even the enlarged arms of blacksmiths (use)" (2015, 71). Even if there is some qualification of the status of the arms of the blacksmiths ("perhaps even"), they often appear as one of Darwin's favored examples of Lamarckian principles. An example of Darwin's use of the blacksmith's arm as an example of Lamarckian use inheritance is in the following statement in his notebooks: "An habitual action must some way affect the brain in a manner which can be transmitted—this is analogous to a blacksmith having children with strong arms—The other principle of those children, which *chance*? produced with strong arms, outliving the weaker ones, may be applicable to the formation of instincts, independently of habits—the limits of these two actions either on form or brain very hard to define" (1838, note 42). Here we can see that natural selection and the law of use and disuse are both used to explain the sons of blacksmiths having strong arms. It might be that those strong arms are selected because they are useful (a selection that happens independently of habit) or that they are an effect of the habitual actions of previous generations.

20 With thanks to Sarah Franklin for this formulation.

21 In my book *The Cultural Politics of Emotion* (2004), I took up the idea of "impression" (via David Hume) to think through the sociality of emotion, noting how an impression can mean both the mark left behind on a surface and a vague idea of something. In *The Promise of Happiness* (2010) and *Willful Subjects* (2014), I then consider the figure of the child as impressionable (as capable of receiving an influence), discussing how power is manifest by directing the child in the right way (molding as shaping what is received).

22 I would argue that Judith Butler (1993) offers one of the most astute analyses of the *dynamic nature of matter*, despite how she is sometimes critiqued for assuming the passivity of matter. For an example of such a critique, see Karen Barad, who argues in a footnote that "Unfortunately, however, Butler's theory ultimately reinscribes matter as a passive product of discursive practices rather than as an active agent participating in the very process of materialization" (2003, 821).

23 We can note how the traffic between biological and social domains is brought out by following the uses of use. The idea that advancement requires the specialization of each part in accordance with function is shared across these domains. As Sarah Franklin shows in *Biological Relatives*, Darwin's approach to higher and lower levels of organization is also used by Marx in *Capital* to describe industrial organization: "By a low level of organization I mean a *low degree of differentiation of the organs* for different particular operations" (cited in Franklin 2013, 40). For a collection of essays on the traffic between the biological and social domains, see Maasen, Weingart, and Mendelsohn (1995).

24 In later editions, Spencer withdraws this confidence in adaption. This
note appears in a later edition of *Social Statics*: "With the exception
of small verbal improvements, I have let this chapter stand unaltered,
though it is now clear to me that the conclusions drawn in it should be
largely qualified" (1899, 32). The first important qualification relates to
race: "Various races of mankind, inhabiting bad habitats, and obliged to
lead miserable lives, cannot by any amount of adaptation be moulded
into satisfactory types" (32). This qualification is very important: racism
is exercised as a way of avoiding an implication that anyone can become
more perfect even according to the strictly limited sphere of their social
function.

25 "Handling Tons of Metal like a Toy," *Popular Science Monthly* 93, no. 3 (1918):
356, https://archive.org/stream/PopularScienceMonthlyVolume93Part1/The
_Popular_Science_Monthly_Volume_93_Part_1_djvu.txt.

26 I am developing my argument about the function of the laboring arm
from chapter 3 of *Willful Subjects* (2014). See also Henri Bergson's "Frenzy,
Mechanism and Mysticism," which reflects on the relationship between
bodily organs and technology: "If our organs are natural instruments, our
instruments must be artificial organs: the *workman's tool is a continuation
of his arm*, the tool-equipment of humanity is therefore a continuation
of its body" ([1932] 2002: 339, emphasis added). In political theory, the
term *living tool* would reference Aristotle's discussion of slavery in *Politics*.
Aristotle distinguishes production from activity as different uses of use:
a tool is used to create something else; property is useful in itself (so for
instance you use a shuttle "to produce something other than its own use"
in a way you do not use a bed other than to rest). He uses this distinction to suggest that the slave is in the sphere of action, not production.
Agamben has drawn on Aristotle's distinction to suggest that the slave is
an example of the noninstrumental nature of use (suggesting we are too
used to think of use in terms of production). My own view is that Aristotle's distinction needs to be understood as *convenient*. Aristotle is trying to
defend slavery as natural. The slave is a slave by nature, as property of and
part of the master. A person becomes an instrument *by being defined as
part of the body of another*. Instrumental use is ownership of the body and
its parts (the master owns the slave, which means the master also owns
whatever the slave produces; the point of a slave is to free the master from
doing certain kinds of work). Instrumental use can be understood not only
as how some beings become "for" by being rendered both utensil and part
but how in becoming for, they free up energy and time. This is more than
clear in Aristotle's own discussion: "The use, too, of slaves hardly differs
at all from that of domestic animals: from both we derive that which is essential for our bodily needs. It is then part of nature's intentions to make
the bodies of free men to differ from those of slaves, the latter strong
enough for the necessary menial tasks, the former erect and useless for

that kind of work, but well-suited for the life of a citizen of a state, a life divided between war and peace" (1.6.34). My own commitment is to think of affection and instrumentality together in rendering some bodies into parts and tools.

27 I am picking up on a point I made in chapter 1: that the category of the unused is a highly political category. There I pointed out how something is declared unused or made unusable to justify an appropriation. Here the unused is used as a threat. And the unused becomes a threat when being used is itself an appropriation; in other words, the unused arm becomes a threat directed toward those workers who lay down their arms, who are not willing to be appropriated by becoming the arms of industry.

28 I will return to this implied intimacy of queerness and uselessness in the conclusion of the book.

3. Use as Technique

1 In chapter 2 I explore Lamarck's argument that use can be an effect as much as a cause or an effect that becomes a cause: parts are used more because there is more of a need for them given the demands of an environment (even if being used more brings them, in a certain way, into existence). A technique can be how an effect becomes a cause in another sense: as a principle or a commitment of a movement. This chapter explores how use can be a technique for bringing a class of persons into existence. In chapter 4 I suggest that use can be a technique by stabilizing what is required or needed to survive or thrive within an environment.

2 Anne Brunon-Ernst (2012a) offers a useful discussion of the relationship between Foucault and Bentham with specific reference to Foucault's use of the Panopticon. She points out that Foucault develops his theory of power with reference to only one of Bentham's many uses of the Panopticon (including in "Chrestomathia"), thus producing a very narrow account of Bentham's work. In *Utilitarian Biopolitics*, Brunon-Ernst notes, "Foucault has been criticized for having portrayed Bentham as the inventor of disciplines, overshadowing Bentham's achievements in other fields of thought: he has been considered as *persona non grata* in the world of Bentham studies" (2012b, 2). I return in the third section of this chapter to Brunon-Ernst's important work in considering the role of indirect legislation.

3 See Hassard and Rowlinson (2002) for a discussion of Foucault's reference to the Lancaster Method and for a detailed analysis of how the monitorial system worked through the disciplinary logics identified by Foucault. My own argument is somewhat different: I think the full significance of the monitor in the school system (who is also a student) is not picked up by Foucault despite his reference to Lancaster.

4 As Alexander G. Weheliye notes in *Habeas Viscus* (2014), Foucault, despite his analysis of state racism, does not attend to the colonial project.

5 "Parochial Schools Bill," *Commons and Lords Hansard*, vol. 9, June 13, 1807, 788–806, http://hansard.millbanksystems.com/commons/1807/jun/13 /parochial-schools-bill.

6 In *Willful Subjects* (2014), I explored the following logic: if you are not willing you will be forced, such that willing becomes a way of avoiding being forced. Here the logic operates as a preventative one: do not educate the workers because they would become unwilling (to work) and would have to be forced (to work).

7 I return to the significance of paper to the colonial mission in my conclusion to this book.

8 For further discussion of the criminalization of vagrancy (drawing on Marx), see chapter 3 of *Willful Subjects* (2014). See also Nicolazzo (2014) for a discussion of the "vagrant figures" across the empire in the eighteenth century.

9 This definition is from *Online Etymology Dictionary*, accessed March 6, 2019, https://www.etymonlinc.com/word/vagrant.

10 For a useful history of the changing policies of the East India Company in relation to the Eurasian population, see V. Anderson (2011).

11 This connection between virtue and function is explicit in Aristotelian ethics. Virtue is a way of thinking about ends. As Christine Marion Korsgaard describes, "Both Plato and Aristotle recognize a conceptual connection between *ergon*, function, and *arete*, virtue. A virtue is not merely an admirable or socially useful quality: it is quite specifically a quality that makes you good at performing your function" (2008, 133). My analysis in this chapter is in effect an analysis of *the function of virtue*: how some individuals become reduced to a function as members of a subordinate class.

12 See also Sarah Jordan's (2003) important history of idleness. She explores how idleness was understood as a natural tendency (and thus a vice) of the laboring classes at home as well as of racial others in the colonies. She also shows how idleness was not defined as a vice for the British upper classes and how idleness for the elite was even identified as a sacrifice of the happiness that would have followed employment (48).

13 I have been showing throughout this book how histories of use meet in materials. It is worth noting the significance of sand here. Joseph Lancaster gave an account of his correspondence with Bell on the matter of sand. He asks Bell about the sand: should it be wet or dry? The sand should be dry, was Bell's answer ([1803] 1807, 43). The sand is useful because it is light and temporary; the letters can be imprinted only to be made to disappear. Perhaps the sand matters because the sand in being a lighter material can accommodate the lightness of the monitor; students, who have not been weighed down by accumulated knowledge, can use sand more safely to create impressions, because of how easily errors can be wiped away.

14 What Thorndike called the law of effect can also be used as the basis of more negative styles of teaching. For example, in *The Promise of Happiness* (2010),

I explored how in Jean-Jacques Rousseau's *Émile* ([1762] 1993) unhappiness is used to redirect children toward the right ends: a child is not prevented from going the way the tutor does not wish him to go, but the tutor arranges for the child to be teased so that the child comes to associate the wrong way with unhappiness. Something becomes "the wrong way" by being associated with unhappiness.

15 In the conclusion to *The Promise of Happiness*, I offered a critique of what has become known as "the affirmative turn" in part by questioning the association of positive affect with activity and negative affect with passivity (2010, 210–13). I noted how Deleuze follows Baruch Spinoza in suggesting that "despots and priests" might "need the sadness of their subjects" (1978, 4). Here my critique proceeds in a somewhat different direction. I would argue, as I did then, that the "despots and priests" (but also patriarchs, technocrats, and teachers) need the happiness of their subjects insofar as they need subjects that are more active as well as agreeable. So I am accepting the association between happiness and activity as an association with a history, even if that association does not always hold. For me, the point is not so much about the positive or negative value given to an affective encounter but about *direction*: increasing activity is often understood as an opening up of possibility, but I am showing how an increasing of activity can function as a narrowing of possibility.

16 Returning to the colonial context in which Bell was working as a schoolmaster, we might consider why the figure of the monitor-as-mediator matters; the colonized subject who identifies with the colonizer's culture is not only active and useful but can take on the role of the colonizers in surveying and disciplining other members of the subordinate class.

17 In Neighborhood Watch, which we can think of as a monitorial system that ties improvement with surveillance, the citizen is asked to become "the eyes and ears of the police." The citizen thus takes on the gaze of the police not simply by looking at themselves but by looking out for strangers, as "bodies out of place." In earlier work, I have argued that injunction to look out for strangers has been generalized as a form of national citizenship: to become citizen is to align one's own self with the police by the act of looking out for signs of suspicion (Ahmed 2000, 2004). I am now showing how this injunction has a longer history.

18 The monitor as method thus depends on an architectural principle of design: the panoptical principle. Lancaster suggests the best form for a schoolroom is a long square, or parallelogram. Within that room he offers some precise instructions on how desks should be arranged as well as on the kinds of desks that should be used. "All the desks should front the head of the school, that the master may have a good view of each boy at once; the desks should all be single desks, and every boy sit with his face towards the head of the school. Room should be left between each desk for a passage for the boys that the scholars in one desk may go out without disturbing those

in another. It is desirable the desks and forms should be substantial, and firmly fixed in the ground, or to the floor. The ends or corners of the desks and forms should be rounded off, as boys, when running quickly in and out, are apt to hurt themselves by running against them. At the head of the school there should be an elevated platform for the master's desk, as a convenient place to overlook the school; passages should be left at the bottom and on one side of the school, or on both sides when space allows. Children confined in a small school-room, can no more be expected to be in order, than soldiers can perform their exercise without a parade. No half desks should be placed against the walls, nor should any double desks be admitted into the school-room. Desks so placed and constructed, merely afford pretence for idleness and play, the scholars being wholly, or partly, out of the master's sight. A very important maxim for school furniture, as books, 8cc. and which must never be departed from, is, a place for every THING, AND EVERY THING IN ITS PLACE" (1812, 4).

19 I visited the British School Museum in Hitchin in 2016, which is the last remaining monitorial schoolroom in the world. I was invited to join a tour with the tour guide acting as the master, and we his students. He began by asking us how many students we thought would be taught here. All the guesses were much lower than the three hundred boys the school was designed to accommodate. He spoke of the building, of the windows above; of the materials used on the floor, as well as the curtains; how they mattered as a way of muffling the noise that would have been made by having so many boys in such a small space. The room is light and breezy. "The building was built with this attitude," he said with reference to light.

20 In more recent work, Anne Brunon-Ernst (2017) has related Bentham's indirect legislation, as well as John Stuart Mill's harm principle, to the "nudge phenomenon." The nudge phenomenon refers to a body of work in behavioral and political science that advocates for the use of positive enforcements to influence behavior of individuals and groups. The relevance of Bentham's work to our contemporary political landscape could not be clearer.

21 This phrase has itself an interesting biography of use, given that it is often used to exemplify Bentham's utilitarianism but is used only once in writing published by Bentham himself. See Burns (2005) for a helpful discussion of Bentham's use and nonuse of this phrase and its implication for an understanding of Bentham's approach to happiness and government.

22 This slide is of course central to Bentham's own rather tautological definitions: utility tends to be defined in terms of what is the most beneficial or happiest, while happiness tends to be defined in terms of what is the most useful or beneficial. We learn about both words from how they can be used *almost* interchangeably. But there are moments when Bentham offers more precision. In a note added to the opening chapter, "The Principle of Utility," of *An Introduction to the Principles of Morals and Legislation* in 1822, Bentham

describes the difference between happiness and utility in affective terms: "The word *utility* does not so clearly point to the ideas of *pleasure* and *pain* as the words happiness and felicity do" ([1789] 2007, 1). The principle of utility is also described as a "property in any objects," which "tends to produce benefit, advantage, pleasure, good or happiness" (2), suggesting that the distinction between utility and happiness corresponds to a distinction between object and subject.

23 In *The Promise of Happiness*, I connected Bentham's approach to happiness as the end of government to Aristotle's idea of happiness as the moral end without realizing that Bentham had already made that connection in his writings on education. Also note that given the focus on conduct, Bentham's utilitarianism is closer to virtue-based ethics than we might have assumed.

24 All the quotations here are drawn from the obituary, as quoted by Bentham.

25 See also Laura Peters's (2000) important study of the role and function of the figure of the orphan as the one "bereft of protection, advantages, benefits, or happiness, previously enjoyed (OED)" (2000, 1).

26 This story of a fallen hero is itself a classed story—of someone who is deemed fallen because he elevated himself above himself: "His father's pension as an old soldier added to his earning as a sieve-maker gave the family a position 'decent and comfortable but still not raised so far above the poor as to open the prospects of ambition'" (Salmon 1932, vii). Lancaster attended meetings with gentlemen but was not himself a gentleman; he even met the king at the height of his fame. His own biographer says it was a shame he did not die earlier so he could have avoided his disgrace. This history of the monitorial schools that is told happily in the official publications left by Bell and Lancaster (as well as Bentham) can be told quite differently; happy and official versions can miss out on who (and what) does not correspond to that happiness.

4. Use and the University

1 "The Four Founders of UCL," accessed April 14, 2019, https://www.ucl.ac.uk /culture/ucl-art-museum/four-founders-ucl.

2 "Who Was Jeremy Bentham?," accessed April 14, 2019, https://www.ucl.ac .uk/bentham-project/who-was-jeremy-bentham.

3 Please see Ahmed (2012) for a detailed discussion of how I collected the data for the first project. I will be writing a monograph drawing on my data on complaint, which has primarily been generated by interviews (I have conducted 40 interviews). For posts drawing on this project, which provide more details on my methodology, please see my blog, www.feministkilljoys .com.

4 Anna Holmes, "Has 'Diversity' Lost Its Meaning?," *New York Times*, October 27, 2015.

5　Thank you to Suzie Hefford, who took the photo of a school wall from Frisby on the Wreake Old School, Leicestershire, UK.

6　You can watch this brilliant panel discussion online. "Why Isn't My Professor Black? UCL Panel Discussion," YouTube, uploaded March 21, 2014, https://www.youtube.com/watch?v=mBqgLK9dTk4.

7　I think it is interesting that I could perceive the form because I encountered it in a historical document: distance from the present can allow us to encounter the present in a different way.

8　That the suspension of the usual procedures becomes usual has specific implications in cases where students make complaints about abuses of power. Rules, policies, and procedures are supposed to be in operation to safeguard the interests of parties, including students, a population that is precarious by virtue of its position (needing to pass examinations in order to pass through the organization). In universities, such procedures would include record keeping of meetings and systems for monitoring student progression. I have learned that when sexual harassment is institutionalized, record keeping is also often suspended, sometimes by being identified as mere bureaucracy. The suspension of regulations is a method for ensuring there is no record, no public memory, of what has gone on. For example, a student might complain at a yearly panel, but if there is no record of the panel, there is no record of the complaint.

9　An exception is the work of Helen Small in *The Value of Humanities*, which discusses how debates about use and usefulness (among other key terms) have a much longer genealogy within the academy. Interestingly, in her discussion of Matthew Arnold's work, she notes how he "wrestles with the remit" of use, with the word *use* crossed out a number of times in his book (2013, 79). I think we can learn from how use, so often in the background, becomes the site of anxiety when it comes to the front. What is also of interest is Small's suggestion, which she characterizes as a "moderate claim," that usefulness or practical utility "diminishes in importance" for the humanities the higher you go up the educational ladder (5). My work offers a different kind of critical lens with which to investigate the uses of use: how utility becomes social hierarchy.

10　Writing about the history of the idea of useful knowledge has also led me to realize that some critiques of the requirement to be useful under neoliberalism take a similar form to some of the arguments against the expansion of education (whether through schools or universities) in the nineteenth century. We can learn from this similarity without assuming that is all there is to say about these critiques. Take, for example, Claire Fox, "Academy Strikes Back: The Fight for 'Useless' Knowledge Starts Here," *Times Higher Education*, October 1, 2009, https://www.timeshighereducation.com/news/academy-strikes-back-the-fight-for-useless-knowledge-starts-here/408474.article. Fox refers to a document produced by the Higher Education Funding Council "announcing that academics wishing to secure the biggest grants will need to prove the 'relevance' of their research to the real world and evaluate its impact on the economy, public policy or society." She refers also to the outcry that follows, the outcry that comes from academics not liking being treated as "instruments for business." What I want to note here is how the expectation that you should be able to demonstrate how knowledge would have use beyond the academy is reduced to a market-driven logic. Fox argues that academics have been too willing to participate in this neoliberal agenda not only in terms of using the terms (such as "evidence-based research") but also in modeling courses available to students/consumers: "We are told that 'Mickey Mouse' degrees will be culled. In truth, these courses exist only because of academia's collusion in making studies 'relevant' for ever-expanding numbers of students and to fit the 'knowledge society' model, regardless of intellectual merit." I should note here that Mickey Mouse degrees can be used to refer not only to courses that are vocational but also courses such as cultural studies and women's studies— which then become dismissible as derivable from academia's complicity with market-based logic. The conclusion of this critique is a turn from usefulness to uselessness: Fox calls for academics to refuse complicity with this regime and engage in "an intellectual fight for speculative research, experimentation, serendipitous discovery and 'useless' knowledge." From the history of the emergence of the idea of useful knowledge we have learned how usefulness comes up at the moment of widening access to education, including schools as well as universities. And from critiques of the requirement for useful knowledge, such as those offered by Fox, we can learn how defenses against the requirement of knowledge to be useful can also function as a defense of elites against the widening of accessibility ("ever-expanding numbers of students").

11 What I am implying here is that management has the right to make a decision about who or what to fund, and that the criteria for the decision are unstable. Take the example of the cutting of philosophy from Middlesex University. This decision was presented to the media as being predicated on finances. So a spokesman for the university said, "Over recent years there has been insufficient demand from students to study philosophy at Middlesex" and "Middlesex does not receive any funding from external research bodies and earns only 5% of the university's total HEFCE quality-related grant, which does not cover the research costs incurred by philosophy staff." So philosophy was closed because of the financial cost, with this cost to the university a drain on its resources. Peter Osbourne, the head of the Department of Philosophy, responded, "The management are saying that this is a financial decision and that there is insufficient demand, but this is not true." If the closure of a program can be justified on financial grounds, without

it being justifiable on these terms, then "financial" can be used to conceal what else is going on. Finances might even become a placeholder for ideology. Frederika Whitehead, "International Academics Protest at Middlesex Philosophy Closure," *The Guardian*, May 7, 2010.

12 Michael Power (1994) has described what he calls "an audit explosion." The arrival of systems of audit into higher education involves the adoption of a set of self-regulatory mechanisms from the private sector (in particular from finance) to the public sector. A performance culture is at once "a disciplinary system of judgments, classifications and targets" (Ball 1998, 190). Jill Blackmore and Judyth Sachs suggest to perform is "being seen to perform" (2007, 108). As I noted in *On Being Included* (2012), audit culture is generative: documents are created that are auditable; a paper trail becomes what you have to leave to show where you have been. If we think of Bentham's description, noticing and marking then become ways of producing a public rather than simply evidence of a public.

13 See, for example, George Bowden, "Oxford University Chancellor Lord Patten Believes Diversity Quotas Will Lower Standards," *Huffington Post*, May 16, 2016, http://www.huffingtonpost.co.uk/entry/lord-patten-ethnic -diversity-quota-will-mean-lower-standards_uk_57398f80e4b0f0f53e36664e. We can hear how uses of meritocracy within and by universities draw on the same terms as eugenics, described in the concluding section of chapter 2, when equality is understood as the artificial reproduction of the weak. Exposing the artifice of advantage would be one way of describing my project in this book. For a recent exploration of meritocracy that attends to the genealogy of the term, see Jo Littler (2017). For a discussion of diversity and meritocracy in elite institutions, see Natasha K. Warikoo (2016), who shows how diversity can become acceptable within elite institutions, often by being packaged as a commodity that enhances the experience for students. See also Bill Readings (1996) on the problem of how "excellence" is used by universities. In *On Being Included* (2012), I described how some elite institutions often say they "do diversity" because they "care about excellence." One practitioner working at an elite institution described how "people really care about excellence," which meant "they really get hacked off when somebody second rate is appointed to anything and they don't care what they look like." Here best or excellent are used as if they can be stripped of a history of past use. Once these categories have been treated as empty, as unoccupied, those who appear different can be selected, a selection that is usable as evidence that structure has been overcome. Brown, black, and working-class individuals who are selected have to be the best, a "having to be" that involves labor—you have to demonstrate you are the best when you are not how the best usually appears.

Conclusion

1 "Queer Use for Cloisters," *Los Angeles Herald*, August 28, 1899, available at California Digital Newspaper Collection, https://cdnc.ucr.edu/cgi-bin/cdnc ?a=d&d=LAH18990828.2.165.

2 It is beyond the scope of this conclusion to offer a full elaboration of queer architecture. For a recent essay that understands queer and trans* architecture as a project of "unbuilding," see Halberstam (2018).

3 To talk about the "uses of biology" is to imply a reversal of the usual sequence: rather than the sequence of sex *then* gender, the sequence would be gender *then* sex; in other words, biological sex can be understood as an effect of gender. This reversal was performed by Judith Butler in her classic *Gender Trouble: Feminism and the Subversion of Identity* (1990), which drew on many other feminist theorists to show how physical and sexed bodies are shaped right from the very beginning (or even before a beginning) by social norms and values. We can return to my discussion of the blacksmith's arm: it is the very references to that arm (which is not originary but is assumed to be originary) that become substantial. *The substantiality of what follows an assumption about something is mistaken as evidence of something.* Following the "uses of use" has deepened my understanding of the complexity of chains of cause and effect. When effects are treated as causes there are further effects (including on causes). If sex is an effect of gender, *the assumption that sex is a cause is what gender effects.* The very assumption of causality brings worlds as well as bodies into existence. I think doors are especially useful to think through *the materializing effects of assumptions.*

4 While Sarah Franklin does not explicitly relate her conception of transbiology to transfeminist or transgender politics, she uses some of the same references used by transgender theorists such as Susan Stryker (1994) and Sandy Stone (2006). All writers place the potential of trans in relation to Donna Haraway's figure of the cyborg, who combines the technological and the natural in surprising and strange ways.

5 In chapter 3, I show how happiness becomes tied to the full employment of the worker's limbs. An arm is supposed to labor; a worker is supposed to work. The strong arm of the blacksmith is overused as evidence of this principle.

6 This definition is adapted from the *Online Etymology Dictionary* entry on vandals; accessed March 18, 2019, https://www.etymonline.com/word /vandal#etymonline_v_4628.

7 See "Press Release: Feminists Occupy Holloway Prison to Demand More Domestic Violence Services," *Sisters Uncut*, May 27, 2017, http://www .sistersuncut.org/2017/05/27/press-release-feminists-occupy-holloway -prison-to-demand-more-domestic-violence-services/.

8 We could think of whose deaths matter, whose deaths leave traces. In chapter 3, I discussed how Bentham's dead body is preserved and displayed. We

can also recall the tablet in Westminster Abbey that preserves the memory
of Andrew Bell, even though Bell has become a relatively obscure footnote in
educational history. Lancaster did not get a tablet at Westminster, perhaps
because by the time of his death, he was in debt and disgrace. His name does
appear on the Reformers Monument at Kensal Green Cemetery, one name
among many. What about the children who passed through the schools? Did
they leave traces in places? If we return to the weighty volumes of Andrew
Bell's biography, which he commissioned before he died, we can hear from
some of the children, such as William Smith (in fact later described as "the
first boy"), Samuel Sawyer, and Mark Dunhill (C. C. Southey 1844, 191–96).
It is the monitors whose letters appear; these letters are thank-you notes,
and the stories they tell are happy stories: education as progression, as
redemption. We might speculate that if other letters had been received by
Bell, less happy accounts, or unhappy accounts, they would not have been
included. It is the willful children who are missing: those who did not send
letters, those who might have refused an instruction, those who do not
become monitors. What about the children who passed through Lancaster's
schools? The references are to the children who had been monitors: you can
read about Robert Ould, an apprentice who then went to head up teaching
at Swansea; he and his brother went to America and taught there, including setting up a school for Indian children. In Ould's case, you can even find
online a picture of his gravestone; it is crumbling, a ruin, but you can find
it. To become a monitor is to leave more behind, however much what is left
has not been maintained, however much what is left is left to crumble and
decay. Or you could find out about John Lovell, "the extremely popular Lancastrian school master at New Haven," also described as "a monitor under
Lancaster." Becoming a monitor is to become part of the archive; you have
to look for them, but you can find them. I have suggested that the monitor
as method works as a commitment to memory. An archive is a holder of
memories, a way names are preserved. *To become a monitor is to be more likely
to be committed to memory.* Those children who did not become monitors,
who never left that "we" of the many in a classroom: we do not know how
many of you are missing—unmarked graves, unmourned deaths, lives not
remembered.

9   Camilla Turner, "Students Accused of 'Cultural Vandalism' over Calls to
    Remove the Legacy of Victorian Polymath They Claim 'Invented Racism,'"
    The Telegraph, February 21, 2017, https://www.telegraph.co.uk/education
    /2017/02/21/students-accused-cultural-vandalism-campaign-remove-legacy
    -victorian/.
10 Edward Said, "Reith Lectures 1993: Representations of an Intellectual,"
    lecture 4, "Professionals and Amateurs," BBC Radio 4, August 2, 1993, http://
    downloads.bbc.co.uk/rmhttp/radio4/transcripts/1993_reith4.pdf.
11 In *Willful Subjects* (2014), I described this task as a "philosophy of the not" or
    "not philosophy."

12 See Alexis Pauline Gumbs, "Outlasting Everything: Breathing Affirmation in the Wake of Hurricane Harvey," *Eternal Summer of the Black Feminist Mind*, August 30, 2017, https://blackfeministmind.wordpress.com/2017/08 /30/outlasting-everything-breathing-affirmation-in-the-wake-of-hurricane -harvey/. See also Alexis Pauline Gumbs (2016) for a poetic and theoretical black feminist text on the creativity of survival.

13 Thank you to Marilyn Strathern for sharing this important paper with me and for the example of her work.

14 Liz Jackson, "We Are the Original Life Hackers," *New York Times*, May 30, 2018. Jackson founded the Disabled List, a disability self-advocacy organization creating pathways into design for disabled people. Accessed August 8, 2018, https://www.disabledlist.org/.

15 Alison Piepmeier, "What a Shattered Coffee Mug Says about Life," *Charleston City Paper*, June 2, 2016, https://www.charlestoncitypaper.com/charleston /what-a-shattered-coffee-mug-says-about-life/Content?oid=5953698. Alison Piepmeier left behind a beautiful and fragile archive of work.

16 In this book, I have further developed my argument in *Living a Feminist Life* (2017) about how we can revalue fragility as a source of ethical and social connection.

17 Eric Marcus, "Making Gay History: The Podcast," episode 1, "Sylvia Rivera," October 13, 2016, http://makinggayhistory.com/podcast/episode-1-1/. Thank you to Sylvia Rivera for her wisdom and inspiration as well as to Eric Marcus for the release of this important interview.

18 See Marlon Riggs, "Tongues Untied," clip uploaded by California Newsreel, YouTube, March 4, 2013, accessed September 27, 2017, https://www.youtube .com/watch?v=tWuPLxMBjM8. For further discussion, see Riggs ([1991] 1999) and P. E. Johnson (1995).

19 I first discussed the queerness of desire lines in *Queer Phenomenology* (2006) and referred to them again in the introduction of *Willful Subjects* (2014).

20 There are clear resonances between my own approach to "queer use" and Giorgio Agamben's discussion of profanation and play. He argues that play can liberate us from an old use: "The creation of a new use is possible only by deactivating an old use, rendering it inoperative" (2007, 86). In this book I have tried to describe how old uses are built into the system. It thus requires political work to render an old use (and users) inoperative. This is why I describe queer use as the work you have to do to queer use. Given that occupation is often concealed by the use of vacancy signs creating the impression of an opening, much of the work you have to do to queer use is not visible as work.

References

Adelman, Richard. 2011. *Idleness, Contemplation and the Aesthetic, 1750–1830*. Cambridge: Cambridge University Press.

Agamben, Giorgio. 2007. *Profanations*. Translated by Jeff Fort. New York: Zone Books.

Agamben, Giorgio. 2013. *The Highest Poverty: Monastic Rules and Form-of-Life*. Translated by Adam Kotsko. Stanford, CA: Stanford University Press.

Agamben, Giorgio. 2015. *The Use of Bodies*. Translated by Adam Kotsko. Stanford, CA: Stanford University Press.

Ahmed, Sara. 2000. *Strange Encounters: Embodied Others in Post-Coloniality*. London: Routledge.

Ahmed, Sara. 2004. *The Cultural Politics of Emotion*. Edinburgh: Edinburgh University Press.

Ahmed, Sara. 2006. *Queer Phenomenology: Orientations, Objects, Others*. Durham, NC: Duke University Press.

Ahmed, Sara. 2010. *The Promise of Happiness*. Durham, NC: Duke University Press.

Ahmed, Sara. 2012. *On Being Included: Racism and Diversity in Institutional Life*. Durham, NC: Duke University Press.

Ahmed, Sara. 2014. *Willful Subjects*. Durham, NC: Duke University Press.

Ahmed, Sara. 2017. *Living a Feminist Life*. Durham, NC: Duke University Press.

Aldrich, Richard. 2013. "The British and Foreign School Society, Past and Present," *History of Education Researcher*, no. 91 (May): 5–12.

Alexander, Christopher. 1964. *Notes on the Synthesis of Form*. Cambridge, MA: Harvard University Press.

Anderson, Kent. 2002. "The Useful Archive." *Learned Publishing* 15, no. 2: 85–89.

Anderson, Valerie E. R. 2011. "The Eurasian Problem in Nineteenth-Century India." PhD diss., School of Oriental and African Studies (SOAS), University of London. http://eprints.soas.ac.uk/13525.

Appadurai, Arjun. 1986. "Introduction: Commodities and the Politics of Value." *The Social Life of Things: Commodities in Cultural Perspective*, edited by Arjun Appadurai, 3–63. Cambridge: Cambridge University Press.

Ariew, André. 2002. "Platonic and Aristotelian Roots of Teleological Arguments." In *Function: New Essays in the Philosophy of Psychology and Biology*, edited by André Ariew, Robert Cummins, and Mark Perlman, 7–32. Oxford: Oxford University Press.

Aristotle. 1992. *Physics*. Translated and edited by William Charlton. Oxford: Clarendon Press.

Arneil, Barbara. 1996. *John Locke and America: The Defence of English Colonialism*. Oxford: Oxford University Press.

Austin, J. L. 1975. *How to Do Things with Words*. Edited by J. O. Urmson and M. Sbisà. Oxford: Oxford University Press.

Bagemihl, Bruce. 1999. *Biological Exuberance: Animal Heterosexuality and Natural Diversity*. New York: St. Martin's.

Ball, Stephen J. 1998. "Performativity and Fragmentation in 'Postmodern Schooling.'" In *Postmodernity and the Fragmentation of Welfare*, edited by John Carter, 187–203. London: Routledge.

Barad, Karen. 2003. "Posthumanist Performativity: Toward an Understanding of How Matter Comes to Matter." *Signs* 28, no. 3: 801–31.

Beauvoir, Simone de. [1945] 2011. *The Useless Mouths and Other Literary Writings*. Urbana: University of Illinois Press.

Beckert, Sven. 2014. *Empire of Cotton: A Global History*. New York: Vintage Books.

Bell, Andrew. 1797. *An Experiment in Education, Made at the Male Asylum in Madras*. London: Cadell and Davies.

Bell, Andrew. 1808. *The Madras School*. London: John Murray.

Bell, Quentin. 1972. *Virginia Woolf: A Biography*. London: Hogarth Press.

Bentham, Jeremy. [1789] 2007. *An Introduction to the Principles of Morals and Legislation*. Mineola, NY: Dover.

Bentham, Jeremy. [1802] 1914. *Bentham's Theory of Legislation*. Translated and edited from the French of Étienne Dumont by Charles Milner Atkinson. London: Humphrey Milford, Oxford University Press.

Bentham, Jeremy. 1834. *Deontology, Or the Science of Morality*. Vol. 1. Edited by John Bowring. London: Longman.

Bentham, Jeremy. 1843a. "The Rationale for Reward." In *The Works of Jeremy Bentham*. Vol. 2. Edited by John Bowring, 189–266. Edinburgh: William Tate.

Bentham, Jeremy. 1843b. "Panopticon: Or the Inspection House." In *The Works of Jeremy Bentham*. Vol. 4. Edited by John Bowring, 37–172. Edinburgh: William Tate.

Bentham, Jeremy. 1843c. "Chrestomathia." In *The Works of Jeremy Bentham*. Vol. 8. Edited by John Bowring, 1–192. Edinburgh: William Tate.

Bentham, Jeremy. 1843d. "Tracts on Poor Laws and Pauper Management." In *The Works of Jeremy Bentham*. Vol. 8. Edited by John Bowring, 359–439. Edinburgh: William Tate.

Bergson, Henri. [1911] 1920. *Creative Evolution*. Translated by Arthur Mitchell. New York: Henry Holt.

Bergson, Henri. [1932] 2002. "Frenzy, Mechanism and Mysticism." In *Bergson's Key Writings*, edited by Keith Ansell Pearson and John Mullarkey, 329–42. London: Continuum.

Bhabha, Homi K. 1985. "Signs Taken for Wonders: Questions of Ambivalence and Authority under a Tree outside Delhi, May 1817." *Critical Inquiry* 12, no. 1: 144–65.

Bhabha, Homi K. 1994. *The Location of Culture*. London: Routledge.

Bhandar, Brenna. 2018. *Colonial Lives of Property: Law, Land, and Racial Regimes of Ownership*. Durham, NC: Duke University Press.

Blackmore, Jill, and Judyth Sachs. 2007. *Performing and Reforming Leaders: Gender, Educational Restructuring, and Organizational Change*. Albany: State University of New York Press.

Bourdieu, Pierre. 1986. *Distinction: A Social Critique of the Judgment of Taste*. Translated by Richard Nice. New York: Routledge.

Brown, Bill. 2001. "Thing Theory." *Critical Inquiry* 21, no. 1: 1–22.

Brown, Bill. 2003. *A Sense of Things*. Chicago: University of Chicago Press.

Brown, Wendy. 2015. *Undoing the Demos: Neoliberalism's Stealth Revolution*. New York: Zone Books.

Brunon-Ernst, Anne. 2012a. "Deconstructing the Panopticon into the Plural Panopticons." In *Beyond Foucault: New Perspectives on Bentham's Panopticon*, edited by Anne Brunon-Ernst, 17–42. New York: Routledge.

Brunon-Ernst, Anne. 2012b. *Utilitarian Biopolitics: Bentham, Foucault and Modern Power*. London: Routledge.

Brunon-Ernst, Anne. 2017. "Nudges and the Limits of Appropriate Interference: Reading Backwards from J. S. Mill's Harm Principle to Jeremy Bentham's Indirect Legislation." *History of European Ideas* 43, no. 1: 53–69.

Bryan, Beverley, Stella Dadzie, and Suzanne Scafe. [1985] 2018. *Heart of the Race: Black Women's Lives in Britain*. 2nd ed. London: Verso.

Burkhardt, Richard W. [1977] 1995. *The Spirit of System: Lamarck and Evolutionary Biology*. Cambridge, MA: Harvard University Press.

Burns, James. 1986. "From 'Polite Learning' to 'Useful Knowledge.'" *History Today* 36, no. 4. https://www.historytoday.com/james-burns/polite-learning -useful-knowledge.

Burns, J. H. 2005. "Happiness and Utility: Jeremy Bentham's Equation." *Utilitas* 17, no. 1: 46–61.

Butler, Judith. 1990. *Gender Trouble: Feminism and the Subversion of Identity*. London: Routledge.

Butler, Judith. 1993. *Bodies That Matter: On the Discursive Limits of "Sex."* London: Routledge.

Butler, Judith. 1997. *Excitable Speech: On the Politics of the Performative.* London: Routledge.

Butler, Judith. 2004. *Precarious Life: The Powers of Mourning and Violence.* London: Verso.

Campbell, Thomas. 1825. *Reprint of Mr. Campbell's Letter to Mr. Brougham on the Subject of a London University . . . Together with Suggestions Which Appeared in the April Number of the New Monthly Magazine.* London: Longman.

Capra, Fritjof, and Pier Luigi Luisi. 2014. *The Systems View of Life: A Unifying Vision.* Cambridge: Cambridge University Press.

Carlson, Licia. 2010. *The Face of Intellectual Disability: Philosophical Reflections.* Bloomington: Indiana University Press.

Cavanagh, Sheila L. 2010. *Queering Bathrooms: Gender, Sexuality, and the Hygienic Imagination.* Toronto: University of Toronto Press.

Chauncey, George. 1996. "Privacy Could Only Be Had in Public: Gay Uses of the Streets." In *Stud: Architectures of Masculinity*, edited by Joel Sanders, 224–61. New York: Princeton Architectural Press.

Church Missionary Society. 1817. *Missionary Register.* London: L. B. Seeley.

Collins, Henry. 2010. *Tactic and Explicit Knowledge.* Chicago: University of Chicago Press.

Crampton, Henry Edward. 1912. *The Doctrine of Evolution: Its Basis and Its Scope.* New York: Columbia University Press.

Cranz, Galen. 1998. *The Chair: Rethinking Culture, Body, and Design.* New York: W. W. Norton.

Darwin, Charles. 1838. *Notebook N: Metaphysics and Expression.* Transcribed by Kees Rookmaaker. Edited by Paul Barrett. *Darwin Online.* Accessed March 18, 2019. http://darwin-online.org.uk/content/frameset?itemID=CUL-DAR126.-&viewtype=text&pageseq=1.

Darwin, Charles. [1859] 2009. *The Origin of Species.* 6th ed. Cambridge: Cambridge University Press.

Darwin, Charles. 1868. *The Variation of Animals and Plants under Domestication.* Vols. 1 and 2. London: John Murray.

Darwin, Charles. [1871] 1992. *The Works of Charles Darwin.* Vol. 21, *The Descent of Man and the Selection of Sex.* London: Routledge.

Deleuze, Gilles. 1978. "Lecture Transcripts on Spinoza's Concept of Affect." Edited by Emilie Deleuze and Julien Deleuze. https://www.gold.ac.uk/media/images-by-section/departments/research-centres-and-units/research-centres/centre-for-invention-and-social-process/deleuze_spinoza_affect.pdf.

Derrida, Jacques. 1994. *Specters of Marx: The States of Debt, the Work of Mourning, and the New International.* Translated by Peggy Kamuf. New York: Routledge.

Dever, Maryanne. 2015. "Papered Over, or Some Observations on Materiality and Archival Method." In *Out of the Closet, into the Archives: Researching Sexual Histories*, edited by Amy L. Stone and Jamie Cantrell, 65–98. Albany: State University of New York Press.

Dolmage, Jay Timothy. 2017. *Academic Ableism: Disability and Higher Education.* Ann Arbor: University of Michigan Press.

Doucette, Erika, and Marty Huber. 2008. "Queer-Feminist Occupations." eiPCP 6. Accessed March 18, 2019. https://transversal.at.

Douglas, Mary. [1966] 1994. *Purity and Danger: An Analysis of the Concepts of Pollution and Taboo.* London: Routledge.

Dunne, Anthony. 2005. *Hertzian Tales: Electronic Products, Aesthetic Experience, and Critical Design.* Cambridge, MA: MIT Press.

Eggleston, Ben, and Dale E. Miller, eds. 2014. *The Cambridge Companion to Utilitarianism.* Cambridge: Cambridge University Press.

Eliot, George. [1861] 1994. *Silas Marner.* Hertfordshire, UK: Wordsworth Classics.

Eliot, George. 1884. *Essays and Leaves from a Notebook.* Edinburgh: Blackwood.

Eliot, George. [1895] 1961. *Adam Bede.* New York: Signet Classics.

Ellis, Havelock. 1932. *Views and Reviews.* London: Desmond Harmsworth.

Ellis, Havelock. 1940. *Psychology of Sex.* London: William Heinemann.

Felski, Rita. 2013. "Introduction." In "Use," special issue, *New Literary History* 44, no. 4: v–xii.

Firestone, Shulamith. 1970. *The Dialectic of Sex: The Case for Feminist Revolution.* New York. Bantam Books.

Fiske, John. [1884] 2009. *The Destiny of Man.* Cambridge: Cambridge University Press.

Flexner, Abraham. [1939] 2007. *The Usefulness of Useless Knowledge.* Princeton, NJ: Princeton University Press.

Foucault, Michel. [1976] 1990. *The History of Sexuality: Volume 1.* Translated by Robert Hurley. Harmondsworth, UK: Penguin Books.

Foucault, Michel. 1977. *Discipline and Punish: The Birth of the Prison.* Translated by Alan Sheridan. New York: Vintage Books.

Foucault, Michel. 1997. *The Politics of Truth.* Edited by Sylvère Lotringer and Lysa Hochroth. New York: Semiotext(e).

Foucault, Michel. 2008. *The Birth of Biopolitics.* London: Macmillan.

Fowler, O. S. 1847. *American Phrenological Journal and Miscellany.* Vol. 9. New York: Fowler and Wells.

Franklin, Sarah. 2001. "Biologization Revisited: Kinship Theory in the Context of the New Biologies." In *Relative Values: Reconfiguring Kinship Studies*, edited by Sarah Franklin and Susan McKinnon, 302–38. Durham, NC: Duke University Press.

Franklin, Sarah. 2006. "The Cyborg Embryo: Our Path to Transbiology." *Theory, Culture and Society.* 23, no. 7–8: 167–87.

Franklin, Sarah. 2007. *Dolly Mixtures: The Remaking of Genealogy*. Durham, NC: Duke University Press.

Franklin, Sarah. 2013. *Biological Relatives: IVF, Stem Cells, and the Future of Kinship*. Durham, NC: Duke University Press.

Franklin, Sarah. 2015. "Sexism as a Means of Reproduction." *New Formations* 86: 14–33.

Freeman, Elizabeth. 2010. *Time Binds: Queer Temporalities, Queer Histories*. Durham, NC: Duke University Press.

Freud, Sigmund. 1977. *On Sexuality: Three Essays on the Theory of Sexuality*. Translated by James Strachey. Harmondsworth, UK: Penguin Books.

Friedan, Betty. 1965. *The Feminine Mystique*. Harmondsworth, UK: Penguin Books.

Gagnier, Reginia. 2000. *The Insatiability of Human Wants: Economics and Aesthetics in Market Society*. Chicago: University of Chicago Press.

Galton, Francis. 1904. "Eugenics: Its Definition, Scope and Aims." *American Journal of Sociology* 10, no. 1: 1–25.

Garland-Thomson, Rosemarie. 2011. "Misfits: A Feminist Materialist Disability Concept." *Hypatia: A Journal of Feminist Philosophy* 26, no. 3: 591–609.

Garland-Thomson, Rosemarie. 2014. "The Story of My Work: How I Became Disabled." *Disability Studies Quarterly* 34, no. 2. http://dx.doi.org/10.18061/dsq.v34i2.4254.

Gibson, James J. 1979. *The Ecological Approach to Visual Perception*. Boston: Houghton Mifflin Harcourt.

Gossett, Reina, Eric A. Stanley, and Johanna Burton. 2017. "Known Unknowns: An Introduction to Trap Door." In *Trap Door: Trans Cultural Production and the Politics of Visibility*, edited by Reina Gossett, Eric A. Stanley, and Johanna Burton, xv–xxvi. Cambridge, MA: MIT Press.

Gould, Stephen Jay. 1985. *The Flamingo's Smile: Reflections in Natural History*. New York: W. W. Norton.

Gould, Stephen Jay. 1993. *Eight Little Piggies: Reflections in Natural History*. New York: W. W. Norton.

Gould, Stephen Jay. 1999. *Leonardo's Mountain of Clams and Diet of Worms: Essays on Natural History*. New York: Three Rivers Press.

Gould, Stephen Jay. 2002. *The Structure of Evolutionary Theory*. Cambridge, MA: Belknap Press of Harvard University Press.

Gould, Stephen J., and R. C. Lewontin. 1979. "The Spandrels of San Marco and the Panglossian Paradigm: A Critique of the Adaptationist Programme." *Proceedings of the Royal Society of London: Series B, Biological Sciences* 205, no. 1161: 581–98.

Graber, Robert Bates. 1995. *Valuing Useless Knowledge: An Anthropological Inquiry into the Meaning of Liberal Education*. Kirksville, MO: Thomas Jefferson University Press.

Grabow, Stephen, and Kent Spreckelmeyer. 2015. *The Architecture of Use: Aesthetics and Function in Architectural Design*. New York: Routledge.

Gumbs, Alexis Pauline. 2016. *Spill: Scenes of Black Feminist Fugitivity*. Durham, NC: Duke University Press.

Halberstam, Jack. 1998. *Female Masculinity*. Durham, NC: Duke University Press.

Halberstam, Jack. 2006. *In a Queer Time and Place: Transgender Bodies, Subcultural Lives*. New York: New York University Press.

Halberstam, Jack. 2011. *The Queer Art of Failure*. Durham, NC: Duke University Press.

Halberstam, Jack. 2018. "Unbuilding Gender," *Places Journal*, October. Accessed March 19, 2019. https://doi.org/10.22269/18100.

Hall, William Whitty. 1869. *The Guide-Board to Health, Peace and Competence: Or, The Road to Happy Old Age*. Springfield, MA: Fisk.

Hamraie, Aimi. 2017. *Building Access: Universal Design and the Politics of Disability*. Minneapolis: University of Minnesota Press.

Haraway, Donna. 1991. "The Cyborg Manifesto," *Simians, Cyborgs and Women: The Reinvention of Nature*, 149–82. New York: Routledge.

Haraway, Donna. 1997. *Modest_Witness@Second_Millenium.FemaleMan Meets_OncoMouse*. New York: Routledge.

Harman, Graham. 2002. *Tool Being: Heidegger and the Metaphysics of Objects*. Chicago: Open Court.

Hartman, Saidiya V. 1997. *Scenes of Subjection: Terror, Slavery and Self-Making in Nineteenth-Century America*. New York: Oxford University Press.

Hassard, John, and Michael Rowlinson. 2002. "Researching Foucault's Research: Organisation and Control in Joseph Lancaster's Monitorial Schools." *Organization* 9, no. 4: 615–39.

Hawes, Christopher J. 1996. *Poor Relations: The Making of a Eurasian Community in India 1773–1833*. London: Routledge.

Hegel, G. W. F. [1827–28] 2007. *Lectures on the Philosophy of Spirit*. Translated by Robert R. Williams. Oxford: Oxford University Press.

Heidegger, Martin. [1927] 1962. *Being and Time*. Translated by John Macquarrie and Edward Robinson. Oxford: Blackwell.

Hill, Jonathan. 2003. *Actions of Architecture: Architects and Creative Users*. London: Routledge.

Hird, Myra J. 2004. "Naturally Queer." *Feminist Theory* 5, no. 1: 85–89.

Hird, Myra J. 2009. *The Origins of Sociable Life: Evolution after Science Studies*. Houndmills, UK: Palgrave Macmillan.

Hochschild, Arlie Russell. [1983] 2003. *The Managed Heart: Commercialization of Human Feeling*. Berkeley: University of California Press.

Hogan, David. 1989. "The Market Revolution and Disciplinary Power: Joseph Lancaster and the Psychology of the Early Classroom System." *History of Education Quarterly* 29, no. 3: 381–417.

Honig, Bonnie. 2017. *Public Things: Democracy in Disrepair*. New York: Fordham University Press.

hooks, bell. 1994. *Teaching to Transgress: Education as the Practice of Freedom*. New York: Routledge.

hooks, bell. 2000. *Feminist Theory: From Margin to Centre*. London: Pluto Press.

Houkes, Wybo, and Pieter E. Vermaas. 2010. *Technical Functions: On the Use and Design of Artefacts*. Dordrecht: Springer.

Husserl, Edmund. 1969. *Ideas: General Introduction to Pure Phenomenology*. Translated by W. R. Boyce Gibson. London: George Allen and Unwin.

Ingold, Tim. 1987. *The Appropriation of Nature: Essays on Human Ecology and Social Relations*. Manchester, UK: Manchester University Press.

James, William. [1890] 1950. *The Principles of Psychology*. Vol. 1. New York: Dover.

Johnson, Curtis. 2015. *Darwin's Dice: The Idea of Chance in the Thought of Charles Darwin*. Oxford: Oxford University Press.

Johnson, Edward. 1842. *Nuces philosophicæ: Or, The Philosophy of Things as Developed from the Philosophy of Words*. London: Simpkin Marshall.

Johnson, Patrick E. 1995. "Snap! Culture: A Different Kind of 'Reading.'" *Text and Performance Quarterly* 15, no. 2: 21–42.

Jordan, Sarah. 2003. *The Anxieties of Idleness: Idleness in Eighteenth-Century British Literature and Culture*. Lewisburg, PA: Bucknell University Press.

Kafer, Alison. 2013. *Feminist, Queer, Crip*. Bloomington: Indiana University Press.

Kim, Sharon. 2012. *Literary Epiphany in the Novel: Constellations of the Soul*. London: Palgrave Macmillan.

Kopytoff, Igor. 1986. "The Cultural Biography of Things." In *The Social Life of Things*, edited by Arjun Appadurai, 64–91. Cambridge: Cambridge University Press.

Korsgaard, Christine Marion. 2008. *The Constitution of Agency: Practical Reason and Moral Psychology*. Oxford: Oxford University Press.

Koyama, Emi. 2003. "Transfeminist Manifesto." In *Catching a Wave: Reclaiming Feminism for the Twenty First Century*, edited by Rory Dicker and Alison Piepmeier, 244–62. Boston: Northeastern University Press.

Kuhn, Annette. [1995] 2002. *Family Secrets: Acts of Memory and Imagination*. London: Verso.

Kurlansky, Mark. 2016. *Paper: Paging through History*. New York: W. W. Norton.

Lamarck, Jean-Baptiste. [1809] 1914. *Zoological Philosophy*. Translated by Hugh Elliot. Cambridge: Cambridge University Press.

Lancaster, Joseph. 1803. *Improvements in Education*. 2nd ed. London: Darton and Harvey.

Lancaster, Joseph. [1803] 1807. *Improvements in Education*. New York: Collins and Perkins.

Lancaster, Joseph. 1812. *British System of Education*. Georgetown, DC: Joseph Milligan.

Lancaster, Joseph. 1824. "The Psychology of Monitorial Instruction." *Westminster Review* 1 (January): 53–55. http://constitution.org/lanc/psychmon.htm.

Leroi-Gourhan, André. [1964] 1993. *Gesture and Speech*. Translated by Anna Bostock Berger. Cambridge, MA: MIT Press.

Littler, Jo. 2017. *Against Meritocracy: Culture, Power and Myths of Mobility*. London: Routledge.

Locke, John. [1689] 1824. *Two Treatises of Government*. London: C. and J. Rivington.

Locke, John. [1690] 1997. *An Essay Concerning Human Understanding*. London: Penguin Books.

Lorde, Audre. 1978. *Black Unicorn*. New York: W. W. Norton.

Lorde, Audre. 1984. *Sister Outsider: Essays and Speeches*. Trumansburg, NY: Crossing.

Lorde, Audre. 1988. *A Burst of Light: Essays*. Ithaca, NY: Firebrand Books.

Love, Henry Davison. 1913. *Vestiges of the Old Madras, 1640–1800*. London: John Murray.

Lowe, Lisa. 2015. *The Intimacies of Four Continents*. Durham, NC: Duke University Press.

Lucretius. 2007. *The Nature of Things*. Translated by A. E. Stallings. Harmondsworth, UK: Penguin Books.

Maasen, Sabine, Peter Weingart, and Everett Mendelsohn, eds. 1995. *Biology as Society, Society as Biology: Metaphors*. Dordrecht: Kluwer Academic Publishers.

Macaulay, Thomas Babington. [1832] 2003. "Minute on Indian Education." In *Archives of Empire: From the East India Company to the Suez Canal*, edited by Barbara Harlow and Mia Carter, 227–38. Durham, NC: Duke University Press.

MacLaren, Archibald. 1861. "Systematized Exercise: Expansion and Development of the Chest." In *MacMillan's Magazine*, vol. 3, edited by David Masson, 35–40. London: Macmillan.

Malabou, Catherine. 2012. *The Ontology of the Accident: An Essay on Destructive Plasticity*. Cambridge, MA: Polity.

Manning, Erin. 2017. "For a Pragmatics of the Useless, or the Value of the Infrathin." *Political Theory* 45, no. 1: 97–115.

Marx, Karl. [1867] 1990. *Capital: Volume 1*. Translated by Ben Fowkes. London: Penguin Classics.

Mayr, Ernst. [1976] 1997. *Evolution and the Diversity of Life: Selected Essays*. Cambridge, MA: Harvard University Press.

Mayr, Ernst. 1972. "Lamarck Revisited." *Journal of the History of Biology* 5, no. 1: 55–94.

Mbembe, Achille. 2003. "Necropolitics." *Public Culture* 15, no. 1: 11–40.

Meisel, Joseph S. 2008. "The Magnificent Fungus on the Political Tree: The Growth of University Representation in the United Kingdom, 1832–1950." In *History of Universities*, Vol. 23, nb 1. Edited by Mordechai Feingold, 109–86. Oxford: Oxford University Press.

Merleau-Ponty, Maurice. [1945] 2002. *Phenomenology of Perception*. Translated by Colin Smith. London: Routledge.

Mill, James. 1812. *Schools for All, in Preference to Schools for Churchmen Only*. London: Richard Taylor.

Mill, James. [1818] 1997. *History of British India*. London: Routledge.

Mill, John Stuart. [1863] 2001. *Utilitarianism*. Indianapolis: Hackett.

Miller, Alice. 1987. *For Your Own Good: The Roots of Violence in Child-Rearing*. London: Virago.

Mirza, Heidi. 2017. "'One in a Million': A Journey of a Post-Colonial Woman of Colour in the White Academy." In *Inside the Ivory Tower: Narratives of Women of Colour Surviving and Thriving in British Academia*, edited by Deborah Gabriel and Shirley Anne Tate, 39–53. London: UCL Press.

Mirza, Heidi. 2018. Afterword to *Heart of the Race: Black Women's Lives in Britain*, 2nd ed., by Beverley Bryan, Stella Dadzie, and Suzanne Scafe, 241–73. London: Verso.

Moreton-Robinson, Aileen. 2005. "The House That Jack Built: Britishness and White Possession." *Australian Critical Race and Whiteness Studies Association* 1: 21–29.

Muñoz, José Esteban. 1996. "Ephemera as Evidence: Introductory Notes to Queer Acts." In "Queer Acts," edited by José Esteban Muñoz and Amanda Barrett, special issue, *Women and Performance: A Journal of Feminist Theory* 8, no. 2: 5–16.

Nearing, Scott, and Nellie M. S. Nearing. 1912. *Woman and Social Progress: A Discussion of the Biologic, Domestic, Industrial and Social Possibilities of American Women*. New York: Macmillan.

Nicolazzo, Sarah. 2014. "Vagrant Figures: Law, Labor, and Refusal in the Eighteenth-Century Atlantic World." Publicly Accessible Penn Dissertations. 1386. http://repository.upenn.edu/edissertations/1386.

Norman, Donald A. [1988] 2013. *The Design of Everyday Things*. Cambridge, MA: MIT Press.

Ordine, Nuccio. 2017. *The Usefulness of the Useless*. Translated by Alistair McEwen. Philadelphia: Paul Dry Books.

Packard, Alpheus S. 1901. *Lamarck: The Founder of Evolution; His Life and Work*. London: Longmans.

Pascal, Blaise. [1669] 2003. *Pensées*. Translated by W. F. Trotter. New York: Dover.

Peters, Laura. 2000. *Orphan Texts: Victorian Orphans, Culture and Empire*. Manchester, UK: Manchester University Press.

Petroski, Henry. 1994. *The Evolution of Useful Things*. New York: Vintage.

Power, Michael. 1994. *The Audit Explosion*. London: Demos.

Price, Margaret. 2016. "Unshared Space: The Dilemma of Inclusive Architecture." In *Disability, Space, Architecture: A Reader*, edited by Jos Boys, 149–72. London: Routledge.

Puwar, Nirmal. 2004. *Space Invaders: Race, Gender and Bodies Out of Place*. Oxford: Berg.

Readings, Bill. 1996. *The University in Ruins*. Cambridge, MA: Harvard University Press.

Richards, Robert J. 1989. *Darwin and the Emergence of Evolutionary Theories of Mind and Behavior*. Chicago: University of Chicago Press.

Richardson, Alan. 1994. *Literature, Education, and Romanticism: Reading as Social Practice, 1780–1832*. Cambridge: Cambridge University Press.

Riggle, Ellen D. B. 2018. "Experiences of a Gender Non-Conforming Lesbian in the "Ladies (Rest)Room." *Journal of Lesbian Studies* 22, no. 4: 1–14.

Riggs, Marlon T. [1991] 1999. "Black Macho Revisited: Reflections of a Snap! Queen." In *Black Men on Race, Gender, and Sexuality: A Critical Reader*, edited by Devon W. Carbado, 306–11. New York: New York University Press.

Risatti, Howard. 2007. *A Theory of Craft: Function and Aesthetic Expression*. Chapel Hill: University of North Carolina Press.

Robinson, Cedric J. [1984] 2000. *Black Marxism: The Making of a Radical Black Tradition*. Chapel Hill: University of North Carolina Press.

Roughgarden, Joan. 2004. *Evolution's Rainbow: Diversity, Gender, and Sexuality in Nature and People*. Berkeley: University of California Press.

Rousseau, Jean-Jacques. [1762] 1993. *Émile, or, On Education*, translated by Barbara Foxley. London: Everyman.

Rowlinson, Matthew. 2010. *Real Money and Romanticism*. Cambridge: Cambridge University Press.

Russell, Bertrand. [1935] 2004. *In Praise of Idleness and Other Essays*. London: Routledge.

Ryle, Gilbert, and J. N. Findlay. 1961. "Use, Usage and Meaning. "*Proceedings of the Aristotelian Society*, vol. 35: 223–42.

Said, Edward. 1978. *Orientalism*. London: Routledge.

Said, Edward. 1979. "Zionism from the Standpoint of Its Victims." *Social Text*, no. 1 (winter): 7–58.

Salmon, David. 1932. *The Practical Parts of Lancaster's Improvements and Bell's Experiments*. Cambridge: Cambridge University Press.

Sarkar, Benoy Kumar. 1918. "The Futurism of Young Asia," *Ethics* 28, no. 4: 521–41.

Seddon, Tony. 2016. *Essential Type: An Illustrated Guide to Understanding and Using Fonts*. New Haven, CT: Yale University Press.

Sedgwick, Eve Kosofsky. 1993. "Queer Performativity: Henry James's *The Art of the Novel*." *GLQ* 1, no. 1: 1–14.

Sedgwick, Eve Kosofsky. 2003. *Touching Feeling: Affect, Pedagogy, Performativity*. Durham, NC: Duke University Press.

Sen, Satadru. 2012. *Disciplined Natives: Race, Freedom and Confinement in Colonial India*. Delhi: Primus Books.

Shulman, George. 2016. "White Supremacy and Black Insurgency as Political Theology." In *Race and Secularism in America*, edited by Jonathon S. Kahn and Vincent W. Lloyd, 23–42. New York: Columbia University Press.

Simpson, Audra. 2014. *Mohawk Interruptus: Political Life across the Borders of Settler States*. Durham, NC: Duke University Press.

Small, Helen. 2013. *The Value of the Humanities*. Oxford: Oxford University Press.

Smith, Barbara. 1989. "A Press of Our Own: Kitchen Table Women of Colour Press." *Frontiers: A Journal of Women Studies* 10, no. 3: 11–13.

Smith, Southwood. 1828. *Use of the Dead to the Living*. London: Baldwin and Cradock.

Smith, Southwood. 1832. *A Lecture Delivered over the Remains of Jeremy Bentham*. London: Effingham Wilson.

Smith, Southwood. 1843. "Introduction to *Chrestomathia*." In *The Works of Jeremy Bentham*, vol. 8, edited by John Bowring, i–iii. Edinburgh: William Tate.

Sofia, Zoë. 2000. "Container Technologies." *Hypatia* 15, no. 2: 181–201.

Southey, Charles Cuthburt. 1844. *The Life of the Rev. Andrew Bell*. Vol. 2. London: John Murray.

Southey, Robert. 1844. *The Life of the Rev. Andrew Bell*. Vol. 1. London: John Murray.

Spencer, Herbert. 1851. *Social Statics: Or, The Conditions Essential to Human Happiness*. London: John Chapman.

Spencer, Herbert. [1860] 1981. "The Social Organism." In *The Man versus the State*, 383–434. Caldwell, ID: Liberty Classics.

Spencer, Herbert. 1873. "The Study of Sociology." *Popular Science Monthly* 3 (September): 594–614.

Spencer, Herbert. 1899. *Social Statics, Together with Man versus the State*. New York: D. Appleton.

Spivak, Gayatri Chakravorty. [1993] 2012. *Outside in the Teaching Machine*. 2nd ed. London: Routledge.

Stallybrass, Peter. 1998. "Marx's Coat." In *Border Fetishisms*, edited by Patricia Spyer, 183–207. London: Routledge.

Stanley, Liz, and Catherine Naji. 2011. "*The Useless Mouths* (a Play): Introduction." In *"The Useless Mouths," and Other Literary Writings*, by Simone de Beauvoir, edited by Margaret A. Simons and Marybeth Timmermann, 9–88. Urbana: University of Illinois Press.

Starck, Nigel. 2006. *Life after Death: The Art of the Obituary*. Melbourne: Melbourne University Press.

Steedman, Carolyn. 2001. *Dust*. Manchester, UK: Manchester University Press.

Stone, Sandy. 2006. "The Empire Strikes Back: A PostTransexual Manifesto." In *The Transgender Studies Reader*, edited by Susan Stryker and Stephen Whittle, 21–53. London: Routledge.

Strathern, Marilyn. 2005. "Useful Knowledge." Isaiah Berlin Lecture. In *Proceedings of the British Academy*, vol. 139, 73–109. Oxford: Oxford University Press.

Stryker, Susan. 1994. "My Words to Victor Frankenstein above the Village of Chamounix: Performing Transgender Rage." *GLQ* 1, no. 3: 237–54.

Sullivan, Louis. 1896. "The Tall Office Building Artistically Reconsidered." *Lippincott's Magazine*, March, 403–9.

Tate, Shirley Anne. 2017. "How Do You Feel? 'Well-Being' as a Deracinated Strategic Goal in UK Universities." In *Inside the Ivory Tower: Narratives of Women of Colour Surviving and Thriving in British Academia*, edited by Deborah Gabriel and Shirley Anne Tate, 54–66. London: UCL Press.

Taylor, Joyce. [1996] 2012. *Joseph Lancaster, The Poor Child's Friend: Educating the Poor in the Early Nineteenth Century*. Hitchin, UK: British Schools Museum Publication.

Thorndike, Edward L. 1911. *Animal Intelligence: Experimental Psychology*. New York: Macmillan.

Titchkosky, Tanya. 2011. *The Question of Access: Disability, Space, Meaning*. Toronto: University of Toronto Press.

Todd, Zoe. 2016. "An Indigenous Feminist's Take on the Ontological Turn: 'Ontology' Is Just Another Word for Colonialism." *Journal of Historical Sociology* 29, no. 1: 4–22. https://onlinelibrary.wiley.com/doi/abs/10.1111/johs.12124.

Tschurenev, Jana. 2008. "Diffusing Useful Knowledge: The Monitorial System of Education in Madras, London and Bengal, 1789–1840." *Paedagogica Historica*, 44, no. 3: 245–64.

Tschurenev, Jana. 2014. "A Colonial Experiment in Education: Madras 1789–1796." In *Connecting Histories of Education*, edited by Barnita Bagchi, Eckhardt Fuchs, and Kate Rousmaniere, 105–20. New York: Berghahn Books.

Tuck, Eve. 2018. "Losing Patience for the Task of Convincing Settlers to Pay Attention to Indigenous Ideas." In *Indigenous and Decolonizing Studies in Education*, edited by Linda Tuhiwai Smith, Eve Tuck, and K. Wayne Yang, 13–16. New York: Routledge.

Turkle, Sherry. 2007. "Introduction: The Things That Matter." In *Evocative Objects: Things We Think With*, edited by Sherry Turkle, 1–10. Cambridge, MA: MIT Press.

Vickery, Donald, Larry Matson, and Carol Vickery. 2012. *Live Young, Think Young, Be Young . . . at Any Age*. Boulder, CO: Bull.

Vogler, Pen. 2015. "The Poor Child's Friend." *History Today*, February 10. https://www.historytoday.com/poor-child%E2%80%99s-friend.

Wall, Thomas Carl. 1999. *Radical Passivity: Levinas, Blanchot, and Agamben*. Albany: State University of New York Press.

Ward, Steven C. 2012. *Neoliberalism and the Global Restructuring of Knowledge and Education*. New York: Routledge.

Warikoo, Natasha K. 2016. *The Diversity Bargain: And Other Dilemmas of Race, Admissions, and Meritocracy at Elite Universities*. Chicago: University of Chicago Press.

Weheliye, Alexander G. 2014. *Habeas Viscus: Racializing Assemblages, Biopolitics, and Black Feminist Theories of the Human*. Durham, NC: Duke University Press.

Wekker, Gloria. 2016. *White Innocence: Paradoxes of Colonialism and Race*. Durham, NC: Duke University Press.

Wells, H. G. 1901. *Anticipations of the Reaction of Mechanical and Scientific Progress upon Human Life and Thought*. New York: Harper and Brothers.

Wendling, Amy E. 2009. *Karl Marx on Technology and Alienation*. London: Palgrave Macmillan.

Whitehead, Judy. 2010. "John Locke and the Governance of India's Landscape: The Category of Wasteland in Colonial Revenue and Forest Legislation." *Economic and Political Weekly* 45, no. 50: 83–93.

Whitley, Leila, and Tiffany Page. 2015. "Sexism at the Centre: Locating the Problem of Sexual Harassment." *New Formations* 86: 34–53.

Williams, Raymond. 1983. *Culture and Society*. New York: Columbia University Press.

Wittgenstein, L. [1953] 1958. *Philosophical Investigations*. Translated by G. E. M. Anscombe. Malden, MA: Wiley Blackwell.

Woolf, Virginia. [1915] 2001. *The Voyage Out*. Oxford: Oxford World Classics.

Woolf, Virginia [1925] 1953. *Mrs Dalloway*. New York: Harvest Books.

Woolf, Virginia. [1937] 2012. *The Years and Between the Acts*. Ware, Hertfordshire, UK: Wordsworth Classics.

Yocum, W. F. 1876. "The Reflex Influence of Teaching." *Indiana School Journal* 21, no. 12: 543–53.

Young, Robert J. C. 1992. "The Idea of a Chrestomathic University." In *Logomachia: The Conflict of the Faculties*, edited by Richard Rand, 97–126. Lincoln: University of Nebraska Press.

Zandy, Janet. 2004. *Hands: Physical Labor, Class, and Cultural Work*. New Brunswick, NJ: Rutgers University Press.

Index

epigenetics, 239n1, 242n18

equality, 55, 100–101, 145–49, 169, 223, 252n13

eugenics, 98–102, 144, 166, 213, 252n13

The Evolution of Useful Things (Petroski), 25

Excitable Speech (Butler), 198

exclamation points, 49–53, 76, 158–59, 173, 221, 238n32. *See also* emphasis

exhaustion, 56–57, 94, 162, 219. *See also* overuse

An Experiment in Education, Made at the Male Asylum in Madras (Bell), 109

Fair House Design Act Manual, 60–61

family, queerness and, 200–201, 208–12. *See also* queerness

fatalism, 90, 133, 222

Felski, Rita, 5–6

feminism: killjoys and, 1–2, 12, 185–86, 212, 233n14; queerness and, 209–11, 215–17, 220, 223; universities and, 165–66, 169, 174–75, 185–86, 190, 193–96; use expressions and, 1–3, 12. *See also* gender; queerness

Ferguson, Adam, 113

files, 162–63, 172

Findlay, J. N., 238n30

Firestone, Shulamith, 209

Fisher, Carrie, 226

form and function: biology and, 68–98, 242n15; queerness and, 204–6, 239n36; using things and, 24–25, 34, 44, 234n8. *See also* biology

Forty, Adrian, 200

Foucault, Michel, 11, 104–5, 112, 116–18, 122, 125–27, 132, 245nn2–4

The Four Founders (Tonks), 141–42

Fox, Claire, 250n10

frames of use, 46–48, 238n29. *See also* use

Franklin, Sarah, 69, 80, 83, 93, 203, 212, 234n1, 243n20, 243n23, 253n4

Freeman, Elizabeth, 75, 218

"Frenzy, Mechanism and Mysticism" (Bergson), 244n26

Freud, Sigmund, 206

friction, 39–41, 224–26

functionalism, 70, 133, 222

functional plasticity, 44, 239n36

Futurism of Asia (Sarkar), 110

Gabriel, Deborah, 166

Gagnier, Reginia, 92

Galton, Francis, 98–99, 166–67, 213

Galton Must Fall Campaign, 213

Garland-Thompson, Rosemarie, 19, 60, 171, 223–24, 235n10, 239n36

garments. *See* clothing

gender: biology and, 88–90, 99, 253n3; fatalism and, 90, 133; queerness and, 200–202, 209; universities and, 145, 150, 160–69, 172–84, 189–90, 193, 196; use and objects and, 30–31. *See also* class; disability; feminism; queerness; race

Gender Trouble (Butler), 253n3

Gentleman's Magazine, 135

Gibson, James J., 236n21

Giddy, Davies, 106

giraffes, 73, 86–87

Gossett, Reina, 225

Gould, Stephen Jay, 74–75, 84–87, 199, 242n17

Gumbs, Alexis Pauline, 19, 213, 221

Habeas Viscus (Weheliye), 245n4

Habermas, Jürgen, 192

habitats, 71–72, 244n24

habits, 42–43, 71–75, 91, 111–12, 124, 240n7, 241n9, 243n19

Halberstam, Jack, 241n8, 253n2

hammers, 21, 24, 89, 93, 237n22, 239n42

Hamraie, Aimi, 19, 59, 62, 225

happiness: about the exploration of, 3–5, 232n10, 232n12, 233n15, 246n14; class and, 107, 119, 126–30, 137–38,

negative value, 65–66

neoliberalism, 191, 239n39, 250n10. *See also* capitalism

nests, 33–35, 178, 200, 203, 228–29, 236n19

neuroscience, 4, 41–42

New Literary History (Felski), 5

nonperformativity, 153, 160, 178

Norman, Donald, 57–59

Notes on the Synthesis of Form (Alexander), 235n10

occupation: colonialism and, 47–48, 95; queerness and, 200, 209–13, 229, 255n20; of spaces, 26–33; of universities, 164–70, 175–76, 179, 184–85, 189; useful knowledge and, 129, 133. *See also* employment

Okrent, Mark, 237n22

On Being Included (Ahmed), 233n14, 252nn12–13

On Our Knowledge of the Causes of the Phenomena of Organic Nature (Huxley), 87

Ordine, Nuccio, 10

Organization of Women of Asian and African Descent (OWAAD), 220

orientalism. *See* race

The Origin of Species (Darwin), 69, 78–81, 219, 240n2, 241n11

orphans, 139–40, 249n25

Osbourne, Peter, 251n11

othering, 101, 109–14, 168, 189, 207, 246n12. *See also* race

Ouls, Robert, 253n8

overuse, 48–53, 76, 87, 94–95, 146–49, 172, 221, 238n33, 253n5. *See also* exhaustion; use

Oxford University, 141, 145

Packard, Alpheus S., 240n7

Page, Tiffany, 172

Palestine, 47–48

Palmer, Lisa Amanda, 166

Panopticon, 104, 122, 127, 245n2, 247n18. *See also* surveillance

paper, 15, 24–26, 45–46, 108–9, 178–79, 195, 206–8, 214, 217, 252n12

paperweights, 24–26, 234n8

Parochial Schools Bill, 106

Pascal, Blaise, 11, 101, 134

paths: queerness and, 20, 201–5, 208, 212–18, 221, 228; universities and, 152–53, 167–68, 171, 184–86, 193, 196; use and biology and, 73–74, 86, 98; use and objects and, 40–45, 48–49, 63–64, 237n24, 239n41

Pearson, Karl, 98

Pensées (Pascal), 11, 233n15

perversion, 201–7, 227. *See also* queerness

Peters, Laura, 249n25

Petroski, Henry, 25

phantom limbs, 88–90, 93, 113, 143, 208. *See also* blacksmith's arm

Physics (Aristotle), 240n4

Piepmeier, Alison, 226–27

plasticity, 4, 42–44, 80–82, 103, 239n36, 242n15

Plato, 246n11

policy: institutions and, 150–58, 169, 176, 191–96, 214, 250n8; monitorial schools and, 105, 111; queer use and, 202, 208, 222; use as technique and, 127, 139; using things and, 235n17, 236nn19–20

Politics (Aristotle), 244n26

poor laws, 100, 106, 126, 129. *See also* class

Poor Relations (Hawes), 139

positive pedagogy, 118–24, 127, 232n12, 247n15, 248n20. *See also* negative teaching

positive value, 7, 65, 127, 247n15

postboxes, 13, 27, 33–35, 144, 154, 178–79, 200–203, 228–29, 236nn19–20, 237n22

universities, 141–96, 239n39, 250n8, 250–52nn10–13. *See also* institutions

University College London (UCL), 14–15, 98, 141–46, 166, 213

University of London. *See* University College London (UCL)

unused things, 8, 21, 45–48, 96–99, 139, 216, 245n27

usability: institutions and, 155, 171, 193, 252n13; queerness and, 206, 212, 225; science and, 98, 137; use and things and, 14, 31, 45, 49, 57–65, 236n21, 239n42, 245n27

use: about the exploration of, 3–20, 231–32nn6–8, 232n10, 232–33nn12–16, 250n9; archives and, 10–20, 81, 135–36; biology and, 68–102, 240nn3–7, 242n15, 243n19, 243n23, 244n26; common, 29–31, 61–62, 231n7; expressions, 1–4, 12, 45–46, 53, 135, 233n14; frames of, 46–48, 238n29; history of the idea of, 8–12; instructions, 28–30, 151, 176, 204, 208, 211; queer, 20, 26, 197–229, 255n20; status, 7, 22; as a technique, 11–12, 103–40, 245n1, 246–47nn11–18; temporalities of, 9, 22–24, 27, 52, 55–57, 81, 85, 164, 219; and things, 21–67, 234n8, 235n12, 236–37nn18–22, 237n24, 237–38nn28–29, 238–39nn33–36, 239n42; universities and, 141–96, 250–52nn10–13; up, 53–57, 64, 94–95, 155–56, 226; value, 25–26, 235n11

used objects, 13–14, 35–41, 45

"The Useful Archive" (Anderson), 14

useful knowledge, 9–10, 16, 19, 106–32, 136, 144, 192, 222, 250n10

useless knowledge, 10, 222, 232n13, 250n10

The Useless Mouths (Beauvoir), 101

uselessness: biology and, 65–67, 81–83, 96–102; exasperation and,

1–3; queerness and, 218–19; things and, 38, 48, 55–56, 195; utilitarianism and, 104–5, 116–18, 134

The Use of Bodies (Agamben), 231n7

Use of the Dead to the Living (Smith), 136

use relations, 6–7, 11, 21–23

Utilitarian Biopolitics (Brunon-Ernst), 245n2

utilitarianism, 9–12, 19, 80–81, 97–101, 104–44, 189–92, 213, 237n22, 246nn11–12, 248–49nn21–23. *See also* happiness; use

vacancy, 31, 129–30, 170–71, 176–77, 211–12, 255n20

The Value of Humanities (Small), 250n9

vandalism, queer, 208–17

The Variation of Animals and Plants under Domestication (Darwin), 83

vestigial structures, 81, 219. *See also* biology

violence: class and, 101, 115, 140; queer use and, 204, 207, 210–11, 215, 227–29; universities and, 175, 183, 196; using things and, 33, 47

The Voyage Out (Woolf), 2

walls, 60, 151–57, 166, 178, 188, 191, 212–13, 217–20

Ward, Steven C., 191

Warikoo, Natasha, 252n13

warnings, 134, 158–60, 172, 186, 238n32

waste, 47, 54–55, 93, 98, 139–40, 155

watches, 66

Weheliye, Alexander G., 245n4

Wekker, Gloria, 19

Wells, H. G., 100–101

Wendling, Amy E., 56

"What a Shattered Coffee Mug Says about Life" (Piepmeier), 226

Whitebread, Samuel, 106

Whitehead, Judy, 139

Whitley, Leila, 172
"Why Isn't My Professor Black" panel, 166–67, 213
Wilkins, William, 141
will, 3–5, 10–11, 67, 97, 246n6
Willful Subjects (Ahmed), 3–4, 10–13, 96, 124, 186, 232n12, 233n15, 243n21, 246n6, 254n11
Wilson, Richard, 110
Winnicott, Donald, 41
Wittgenstein, Ludwig, 49–50, 238n29

Woman and Progress (Nearing and Nearing), 97
Woolf, Virginia, 1–3, 223, 233n14

The Years (Woolf), 1–2, 233n14
Young, Robert, 143

"Zionism from the Standpoint of Its Victims" (Said), 47–48
Zoological Philosophy (Lamarck), 70, 85, 241n10